THE INTEGRATIVE ART OF MODERN THAILAND

HERBERT P. PHILLIPS

Lowie Museum of Anthropology

University of California at Berkeley

Participating Museums

LOWIE MUSEUM OF ANTHROPOLOGY
University of California at Berkeley
October 19 – December 15, 1991

ELVEHJEM MUSEUM OF ART
University of Wisconsin, Madison
February 8 – April 12, 1992

THE ART MUSEUM
Arizona State University, Tempe
May 24 – August 2, 1992

THE BURKE MUSEUM
University of Washington, Seattle
September 16 – December 15, 1992

THE BOWERS MUSEUM
Santa Ana, California
January 15 – March 15, 1993

Cover:
THREE CONCENTRATIONS, 1986, by Panya Vijinthanasarn
Acrylic, gold leaf, and silver paper, 4.5" x 7.63"

Designed by:
Gordon Chun Design
[Gordon Chun, Dana Nakagawa, Suzanne Chun, Mary Jo Sutton]
Berkeley, California

Printed and bound in Thailand by
the Amarin Printing Group Company Limited

Distributed by the University of Washington Press,
PO Box 50096, Seattle, WA 98145

Library of Congress Catalog Card Number: 92-081701
ISBN Number 0-936127-02-3

Library of Congress Cataloging-in-Publication Data

Phillips, Herbert P.
The integrative art of modern Thailand / Herbert P. Phillips.
p. cm.
Exhibition catalog.
Includes bibliographical references.
ISBN 0-936127-02-3 (alk. paper)
1. Art, Thai—Exhibitions. 2. Art, Modern—20th century—Thailand—Exhibitions. I. Title.
N7321.P437 1992
709'.593'07479—dc20 92-81701
CIP

C O N T E N T S

The Essence of Contemporary Thai Art iv

Funding Sponsors vi

Acknowledgments vii

HISTORICAL AND CULTURAL CONTEXT

CHAPTER ONE: *The Emergence of Contemporary Thai Art* 3

CHAPTER TWO: *Other Artistic Genres* 17

CHAPTER THREE: *The Art Community* 31

CHAPTER FOUR: *International Influences* 51

EXHIBITION ARTWORK

Celebrations of Buddhism 63

Impressions of Daily Life 79

At One with Nature 95

In Search of Identity 111

Artists' Profiles 129

Bibliography 136

The essence of contemporary Thai art is that it be both uniquely Thai and characteristically innovative. These two recent art works (opposite page) are examples of such a synthesis. They are contemporary representations of the footprint of the Lord Buddha—which is one of the oldest and most ubiquitous icons of Thai culture and of Thai Buddhist belief.

Whatever their design or material, all Buddha Footprints share certain iconographic elements: a circle in the center and circles in the toes or heels representing the Buddhist law that all things are in perpetual change; one hundred and eight icons, often bound by grids, symbolizing one hundred features of the Lord Buddha's character and teachings, and the eight directions in which these teachings are disseminated. The grid design is itself iconic and appears repeatedly in Thai art to convey a spirit of order, constraint, and clarity of thought. The footprint is a symbol of the Lord Buddha as a wandering preacher.

Figure 2.
A detail of one of the icons from the Wat Pho Buddha Footprints. The icons are made of lacquer and mother of pearl.

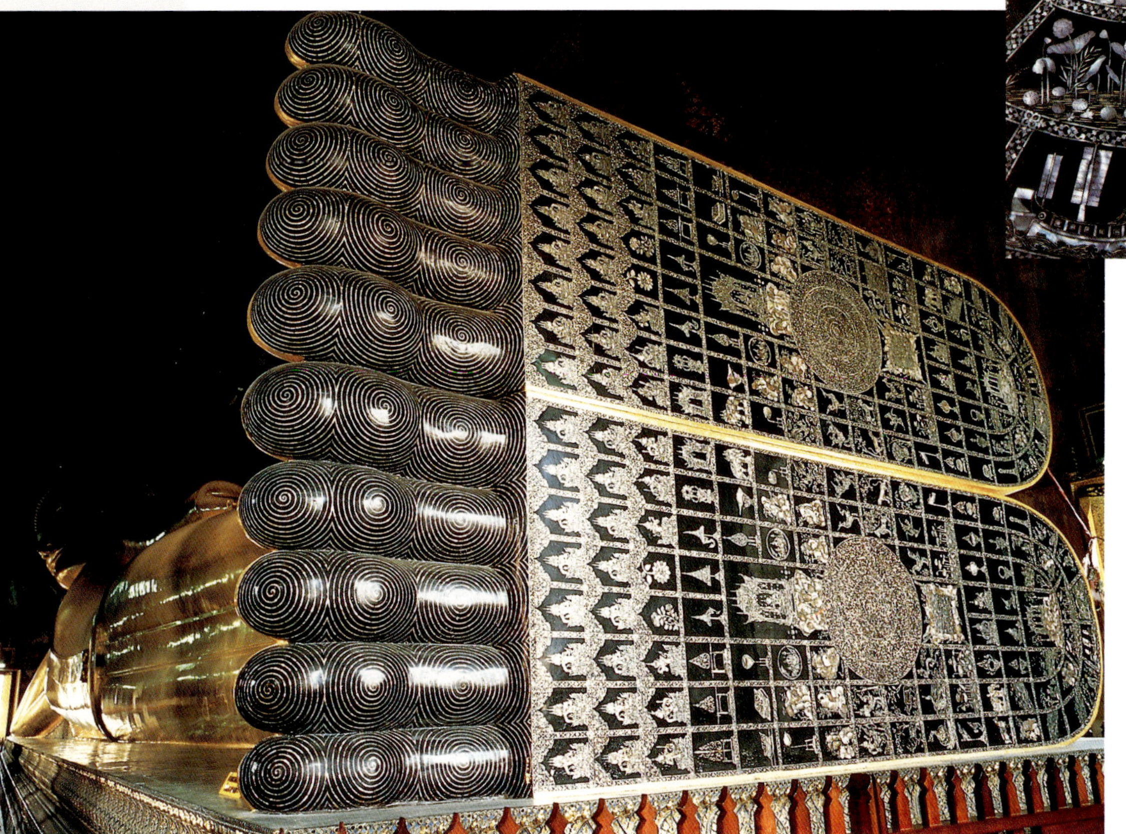

Figure 1.
The footprints from the "Reclining Buddha" at Wat Pho in the Grand Palace area of Bangkok, dated 1835. Because of its craftsmanship, grand proportions (49 x 148 feet), and the fact that it is housed in Bangkok's oldest and largest temple, the statue and its footprints are among the most revered religious objects in Thailand.

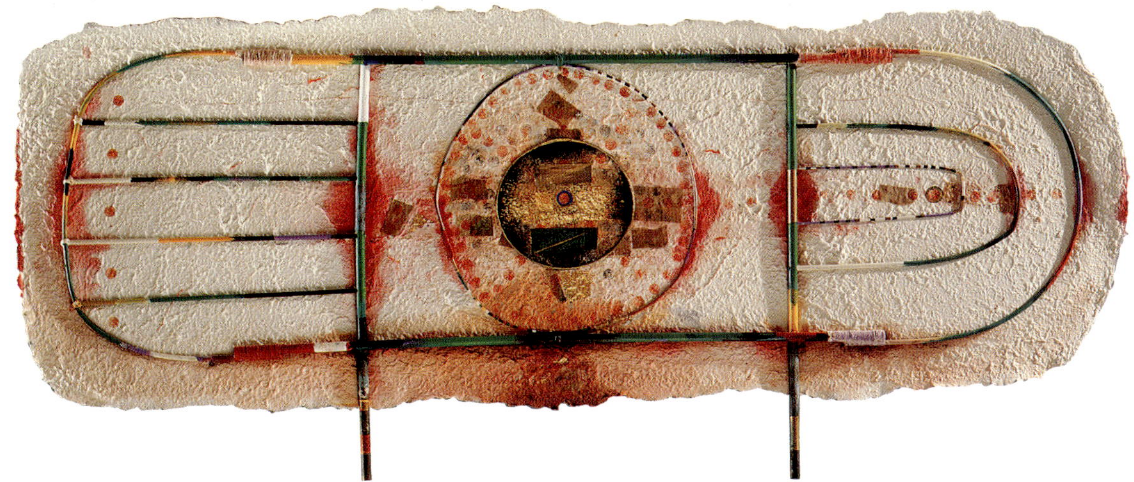

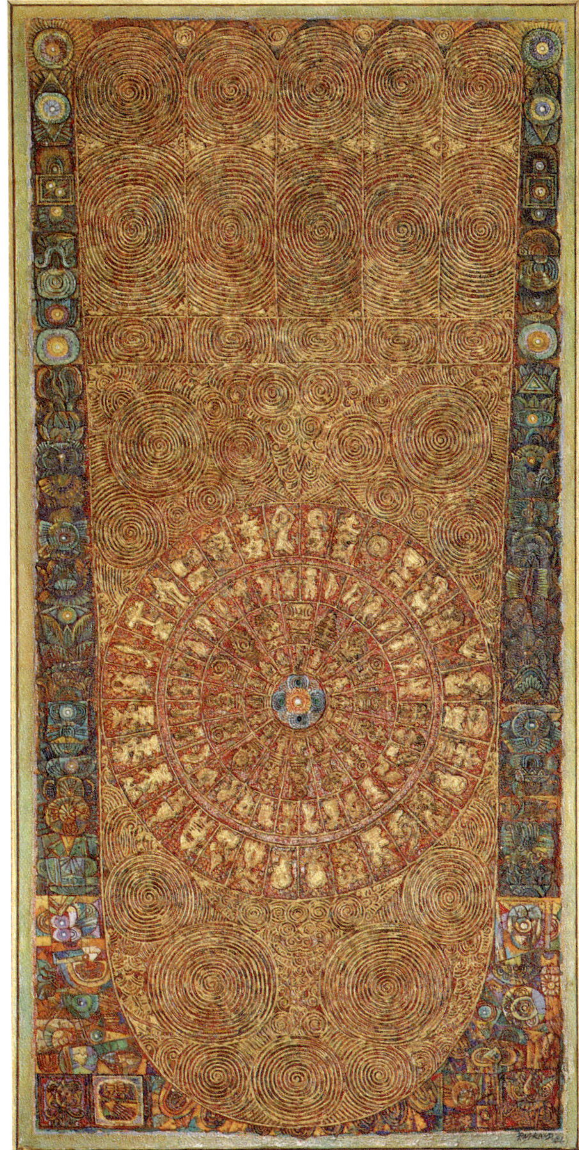

PLATE 1

KAMOL TASSANANCHALEE

BUDDHA FOOTPRINT, *NANGYAI* (2ND SERIES), 1982
Handmade paper, acrylic, gold leaf, ink, thread, wood dowels

This vision of Buddha's footprint is by a Thai artist who has lived and worked in California for more than two decades. While the form and basic components of the footprint conform to the classical Thai model, its design, materials, and colors are products of the artist's imagination. In fashioning this work, Kamol was inspired as much by the folk as by the classical traditions of Thai culture, using handmade paper from Northern Thailand and the same style of wood frame that has been used for centuries in Central Plain *nangyai,* or "large puppet" shadow-play theatre. *Nangyai* is the term for the puppet, its structure, and the theatrical performance.

Loaned by the artist

PLATE 2

PICHAI NIRAND

BUDDHA FOOTPRINT, 1968
Oil paint, glue, and sand on canvas

While this Buddha footprint emulates classical models, the artist's use of oil paints, glue, and sand gives the work a distinctive texture and, for Thai viewers, an innovative aesthetic quality. The use of polychrome designs on the periphery—many of which suggest shells, clams, and other marine creatures—represents a new way of expressing familiar Buddhist notions about the timelessness of the universe: a universe of infinite colors and infinite living forms.

Loaned by Visual Dhamma Gallery

This exhibition has been made possible by generous grants from

NATIONAL ENDOWMENT FOR THE HUMANITIES

AMERICAN PRESIDENT COMPANIES FOUNDATION

NORTHWEST AIRLINES

ESSO STANDARD OF THAILAND

MR. WILLIAM ALEXANDER

This catalogue is meant as a permanent record of the "Integrative Art of Modern Thailand" exhibition and a discussion of some of the major social and cultural factors that affect the production of contemporary Thai art. Both the mounting of the exhibition and the writing of the catalogue have been informed by my general knowledge of Thailand, derived from several field studies I have conducted in the kingdom over the past thirty years. However, the venture into examining the work and lives of contemporary artists, and the effort to organize an international exhibition, were totally novel professional experiences. I justified the research portion of the project on the grounds that it would provide a rich comparison with my recent work on contemporary Thai literature and writers (Phillips 1987). The art show was justified on the more compelling grounds that there never before had been in the United States a travelling exhibition of contemporary Thai works, nor had there been many exhibitions presenting contemporary non-Western art in terms of its indigenous cultural meanings and aesthetic values.

For a person who had spent much of his scholarly life working one-on-one with individual informants or by himself in the privacy of his study, the implementation of this enterprise came as something of a shock. In particular, the orchestration of the exhibition became an adventure in an extraordinarily complex managerial process. Funds had to be raised; museums and art owners contacted and contracts signed; the advice of museum exhibition professionals sought out; appraisals and insurance costs calculated; shipping crates and exhibit furniture fabricated; museum floor plans, brochures, an exhibit poster and catalogue designed; fine arts shipping, customs clearances, and museum registration procedures arranged for; videotapes shot, edited, and the accompanying narration written; programs accompanying the exhibit—lectures, Thai dance troupes, educational materials for children, and films with English subtitles—negotiated; catalogue-quality photographs shot and processed; and publicity materials written and distributed.

Such an enterprise obviously could not have been undertaken without the help and commitment of a great many people, both in Thailand and the United States. I cite them here not only out of professional courtesy, but because the project would never have happened without each of their unique contributions.

Foremost among all these persons is my collaborator and spouse, Barbara H. Phillips, who has participated in the project since its inception. She shared in its earliest formulation, and in Thailand shared all interviewing responsibilities, the translation and recording of field data, the examination and selection of the art works, and the considerable in-country travel involved in locating artists and other members of the art community. She was also a crucial member of the exhibition planning team, helped write a portion of our principal funding grant application, returned to Thailand to obtain the artworks from their owners, and shared in the editing of this catalogue.

Special thanks are owed to the following persons and institutions in Thailand: Weena Sunthongjhin and Sucharat Rojanaphiraphajon were our two research assistants without whose skill and loyalty the project would never have gotten off the ground. Silpakorn University was especially critical in making the enterprise possible. My old friend, Professor Damrong Wong-Uparaj, was our official host and sponsor with the Thai government, and gave us scores of hours of his precious time, particularly as an informant on the history and social organization of contemporary art. My recent Berkeley colleague, Dr. Chetana Nagavajara, expedited virtually every one of my requests with Silpakorn officials, and in his serendipitous style, stimulated me to follow a number of fruitful research leads. M.C. Subhadradis Diskul, recent president of Silpakorn, welcomed us to the Thai art scene, and his successor, Prof. Kaisri Sri-aroon, provided us with both the sponsorship to send the exhibition to the United States and the space to receive and pack the art for international shipment. Khun Somporn Rodboon, Director of the Silpakorn Art Gallery, and Mrs. Jutamat and Khun Veradej of her staff, were all especially helpful in this regard. In addition to being one of her nation's finest artists, Kanya Charonesupkul also played a critical role in overseeing the Bangkok printing of this catalogue.

Several persons played key advisory roles in the research. Domnern and Ti Garden, Piriya Krairiksh, Chartvichai Promadhattavedi, Marc Bogerd, Sivaporn Dardarananda, Alfred Pawlin, Sooklek Chanyawongse, and Pisanu Supanimit were critical informants on the state of contemporary art, criticism, collection, and dealership. Wattana Wattanapun and Thongchai Rakpathum were superb sources of information on the nature of Thai art education and the social structure of the art community.

Dow Wasiksiri and Kitti Amornpatanakul photographed almost all of the art work and contextual photos appearing in this catalogue, and Luca Tettoni and the National Identity Board of Thailand, through Khunying Temsiri Punyasingh, provided certain key photos in their possession. Very special thanks are due Chumpol Donsakul of the Bank of Thailand, Earth Saiswag of the Holiday Inn Crowne Plaza, Tchaisiri Samudavanija of Thai Airways, Vicharat Vichit-Vadakan of Capital Securities and Finance Company, and Tom Seale of the American Chamber of Commerce of Thailand for their psychological support at critical turning points in the project.

I am also indebted to Dean Juree Vichit-Vadakan of the National Institute of Development Administration for obtaining the films that were used in the special Thai movie program that accompanied the exhibit. Special thanks are also due to Revat Krabuanrat of ESSO Standard of Thailand for expediting the funds which helped us produce the in-house videotape, "Five Perspectives on Thai Art," and to the Centre Foundation of Thailand for providing support funds at critical points in the enterprise. Varvavuth Tulyayon of the Bangkok Bank Public Relations Department also provided material for use in the videotape. I am also grateful to Chukiat Utakapan of Amarin Publishing for his excellent cooperation in printing this catalogue.

On the American side, I am indebted to James Deetz, former director of the Lowie Museum, for his strong advocacy of the concept that an anthropological museum should sponsor an exhibition on contemporary non-Western art, and to his successor, Burton Benedict, for providing the support system of personnel and facilities to see the project through.

Certain individuals at the organizations that provided financial support for the project require special acknowledgment. The exhibition would not have happened without the patient advice and cooperation of Dr. Suzi Jones and her predecessor, Dr. Tom Wilson, at the National Endowment for the Humanities. Ted Hemmert of Northwest Airlines and his colleagues in Bangkok were wonderful in expediting the transportation of project personnel and the posters and catalogue from Bangkok. We are also deeply indebted to Joel Greenberg, Deborah Soso, Christina del Villar, and Tom Olsen (Bangkok Office) of American President Lines for supporting and expediting the shipment of the art throughout its tour. William Alexander of Los Angeles is due very special thanks for his unsolicited support of the project, as is the Committee on Research of the University of California at Berkeley whose small annual research grants made my professional life run more smoothly.

There are five members of the exhibition planning team who crafted our inchoate ideas about the nature of the project into a professional art exhibition, and to whom we will forever be in debt. Marilyn Salvador, Chief Curator at the Maxwell Museum at the University of New Mexico, guided us in the development of the exhibit's principal themes and in the general process of transforming our scholarly pretensions into a format that would be enjoyed and understood by museum viewers. Judith Bettelheim of San Francisco State University assisted us in the excruciating process of selecting the final 57 works included in the exhibit (from a candidate list of 110 works) and in editing the phrasing of our interpretive labels; much of the coherence and clarity of the exhibit is a result of her professionalism. Hiram Woodward Jr. of the Walters Gallery of Baltimore was a significant source of information on the early history of contemporary Thai art, and Kamol Tassananchalee, the Thai-American artist, helped confirm our interpretations of the meanings and symbolism of the art works. Gordon Chun of Berkeley designed the exhibit, catalogue, poster, and brochure, and educated all of us in the elements of proper museum and art catalogue design.

Several members of the Lowie Museum staff worked long and hard on the project. Thanks are extended particularly to Louise Braunschweiger for her splendid ideas and her undeviating, if always unique, encouragement; Susan Booth for her help in editing our NEH proposal; Therese Babineau and Al Brown for tolerantly handling our aggravating requests; Paula Floro without whose managerial brilliance things could have easily fallen apart; Madeleine Fang whose professional dedication to the conservation of the art works was equalled only by her good will; Joan Knudsen, Lisa Plato, Kathleen Butler, and Lisa Dahlquist for their extraordinary care in examining and registering the art works; Frank Norick and Dave Herod for overseeing the Lowie segment of the project; Frank Pinto for his multiple contributions in receiving and shipping the art, designing and fabricating the exhibit furniture and shipping crates, and for preparing the exhibit hall; Eugene Prince for his efficient and professional response to all of my photographic requests; and Martha Muhs for preparing the project's educational materials for children.

Four of my own graduate students were directly involved in the project. Dawn Cunningham's enthusiasm launched "Five Perspectives on Thai Art," the videotape that accompanies the exhibition, and she also worked on its formulation, narration, and interviews. Jill Forshee coordinated the project during the planning period, worked with the planning team, and handled the voluminous correspondence with artists, museums, lenders, sponsors, appraisers, shippers, and other parties involved with the project. Her advice, professionalism, and delightful disposition will be long remembered. Sarah Murray coordinated the exhibition during the crucial first six months of its implementation phase, and without her professional sense of priorities, her writing and interpersonal skills, and her decision-making talents, the mounting of the exhibit and its coordinate programs would have been seriously impaired. Pamela Myers Moro, now a faculty member at Illinois Wesleyan University, selected and prepared the materials for the music tape that accompanies the exhibit and that has helped create its Siamese ambience.

Two members of the Department of Anthropology will always be remembered for the role they played in the enterprise. My colleague, Nelson Graburn, goaded, teased, criticized, and constantly encouraged me in every part of the project. His associate, Molly Lee, played a parallel role, although she was even tougher than he was. I will forever be in their debt for their professional honesty and warm support.

Tom Hutcheson and John Quick of the University of California Office of Media Services respectively directed and wrote the videotape, "Five Perspectives on Thai Art." Footage for the tape was shot over an eighteen month period by Quick, Tassananchalee, Barbara Phillips, and Joseph Scannella. The narrator of the tape is Pakvilai Sudhaswin, and Peter Kenevan and Susan Fulop Kepner helped translate much of the original Thai language footage. Nancy Chen also played a critical advisory role in the shooting of the videotape.

I am also indebted to Ruth Charloff who helped copy edit this catalogue, Karen Zukor and Carrie Ann Calay for their contributions in conserving several of the artworks, and Lynne Kimura for preparing the publicity materials. Sutham Songsiri and Plearn Kundhikanjana of the Thai Association of Northern California helped distribute these materials to the Thai community of California and helped bring the exhibit to the attention of the Thai media in both the United States and Thailand. Through them we also wish to express our appreciation to the abbot and monks of Wat Mongkolratanarm of Berkeley for blessing the exhibition at the beginning of its national tour.

My wife Barbara and I owe a special debt to our daughters, Heather and Claire, for their very real help and for their extraordinary tolerance, for five years, of their parents' intense preoccupation with "the project." It is our hope that they will someday come to see the value of "the project"—the year in Thailand, their own exploration of art, and their encounters with the people who live in the art and museum worlds—as just compensation for being deprived of their parents' time and attention.

Finally, my gratitude is greatest to the contemporary artists of Thailand and to the individuals and organizations who have loaned us their works during the tenure of the exhibit. The knowledge and friendship that they shared with us will be remembered as the single most enriching part of our experience.

Herbert P. Phillips
Berkeley, California

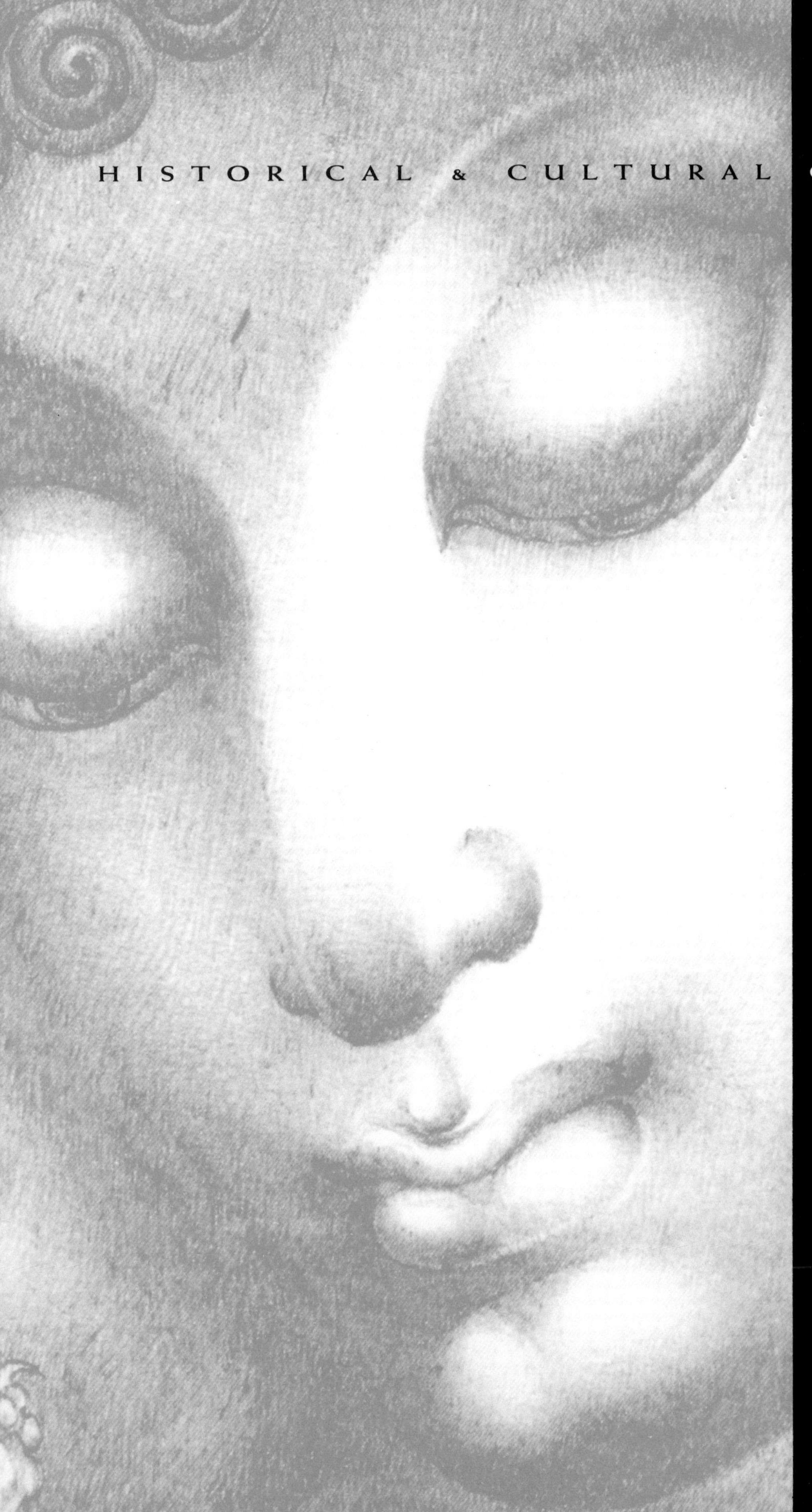

HISTORICAL & CULTURAL CONTEXT

ONE:
The Emergence of Contemporary Thai Art

TWO:
Other Artistic Genres

THREE:
The Art Community

FOUR:
International Influences

ONE:

THE EMERGENCE OF CONTEMPORARY THAI ART

This catalogue and its associated exhibition derive from a lengthy field study of the contemporary Thai art world. From its inception, the study was designed to be an ethnoaesthetic exploration of contemporary Thai art, not an attempt to analyze this art in terms of the history or aesthetic values of Euroamerican art. Our intent was to convey to Western viewers the ways modern Thai think about their art and, in so doing, to provide an account of the cultural meaning of contemporary Thai aesthetic activity. The project focussed on how indigenous Thai judge the merit of their art; their views on how contemporary art expresses Thai experience, perception, and emotion; and what artists, owners, and other members of the art community gain from their artistic encounters. From our point of view, it was much more important to find out what an artist was trying to communicate through his work or why Thai viewers appreciated it than to know whether or not he was influenced by Matisse or Modigliani—although if he was influenced, we certainly wanted to know why and in what manner.

The twenty-eight artists whose works are represented here were all selected by their peers as among Thailand's most accomplished or provocative creative artists. In conducting the research for the exhibit, the investigators examined approximately 8,000 works created during the past three decades; interviewed most of the kingdom's major institutional and private collectors, patrons, critics, museum directors, and gallery owners; discussed art with scores of artists and art students; and through intensive interviews, collected the life histories of all the artists whose works are shown here, including the detailed examination of virtually their entire portfolios. The choice of specific works included in the exhibit was based on native judgments of their artistic excellence and cultural significance, with a view as well toward demonstrating to American viewers the richness and diversity of contemporary artistic expressions. Our concern with diversity and richness as determined by native judges—as contrasted to limiting ourselves to only a few artists who might appeal to Western viewers—was in keeping with the ethnoaesthetic purposes of the enterprise.

Throughout the preparation of these materials, there has been constant tension between using informant-centered explanation on the one hand (what artists, collectors, and others actively involved in the art world think, fantasize, and try to justify about their art), and art historical explanation (the positing of historical relationships between different styles and works and the role of unconscious learning) on the other. To the extent that the two explanatory modes address different kinds of questions—the former issues of cultural meaning and value, the latter the genealogy of aesthetic forms—this tension has been largely reconcilable. However, since the art presented here was created by and for Thai, not Westerners, and since our purpose is to explain to Euroamerican viewers what the significance of this art is to those who are most directly associated with it, on balance we have given greater weight to ethnographic than to art historical formalist explanation.

Indigenous and International Influences

While the project was meant to be an exploration of contemporary Thai art, it was also meant to be a case study of one of the most widely occurring artistic phenomena of the 20th century—that of non-Western artists trying to contend with the conflicting standards of their indigenous aesthetic traditions and those of an encroaching international culture. The resolution of this conflict has taken a variety of routes, sometimes resulting in the enlargement or reinvention of the artist's own cultural traditions, sometimes in the straightforward copying of foreign models, and sometimes in an ongoing process of innovative accommodation among competing forces.

The evidence from Asia suggests that the choices made to deal with this historical tension are in part a function of the larger political forces impinging upon the societies in which artists and their patrons live. Thus, the sending of Japanese artists to France during the last two decades of the 19th century and the subsequent impact of European realism and French impressionism on the development of Japanese art was clearly a result of the policies of the Japanese government to avail itself of all things Western in the years following the Meiji restoration. (See particularly Miyagawa 1967, Shively 1971, Sullivan 1989, Takashima, et al. 1987, and Yamada 1976.)

In contrast to Japan is the Indonesian situation where, despite almost three hundred years of Dutch colonialism, Western art was largely ignored and untaught until the 1920's and 1930's. (See Holt 1967 and the essays by Kusnadi, Spanjaard, and Soedarso SP in Fischer 1990.) Dutch colonials clearly respected the beauty and integrity of Indonesian classical and folk traditions, but in accord with the Western orientalist vision (Said 1978), they maintained a system of aesthetic apartheid, defining the indigenous arts as the products of an idealized, but essentially static, Indonesian past. It was not until after independence in 1949 that a modern Indonesian art, utilizing indigenous and Western elements, began to bloom. However, in concordance with the numerous cross-currents of Indonesian society, this modern art has since its inception been marked by vigorous debate on whether it should be distinctively indigenous or directed toward the international world; should be tied to Indonesia's past or be radically innovative; should serve to define an "Indonesian identity" or should only serve aesthetic purposes; and whether, in this most ethnically diverse nation on earth, a "national" art could actually be fashioned from regional and local differences.

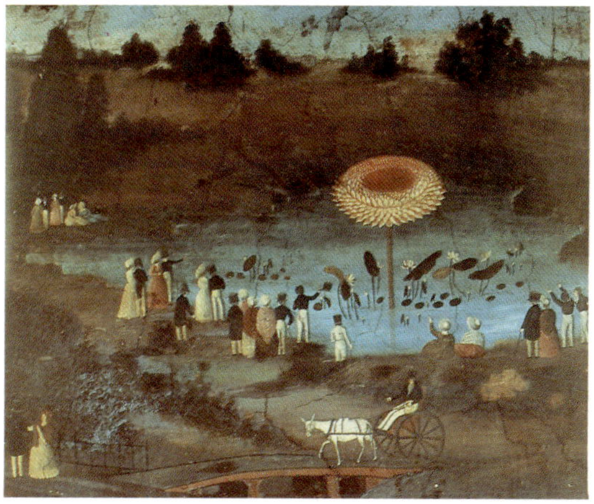

The Thai Encounter with Western Art

The Thai experience lies somewhere between these two extremes. Like Japan and unlike Indonesia, Thailand has been both a politically independent kingdom for all of its history and one of the most ethnically unfied nations in Asia. Its initial, mid-19th century encounter with Western art came at a time when European domination was a real, if uncertain, possibility, but one to which the Thai political leadership had responded with diplomatic skill and self-confidence. While there is never a one-to-one relationship between politics and art, it is not surprising that the Thai reaction to European art was congruent with this political response—rushing neither to copy nor reject European models, but using Western elements to enhance and illuminate their own vision of the world.

Figure 3.
Krua In Khong's mid-19th century conception of the Lord Buddha reincarnated as a lotus blossom, preaching to a Thai congregation.

Thus, the first evidence of Western influence on Thai art are the wall murals at Bangkok's Temple Bovornives, dating from the late 1850's. Painted by Khrua In Khong, they portray Thai in a most unlikely manner—wearing Western garments, living in an antebellum environment, and bidding farewell to persons sailing off in what seem to be European men-of-war (see figures 3 and 4). Despite their anomalous qualities, the murals are an expression of the traditional didactic purpose of all temple art—to glorify Buddhism—with the artist using Euroamerican references to convey the universality of Buddhism and the modernity of the Thai of his period. Thus, what appear to be men-of-war are in fact contemporary versions of the ships that can take Buddhists to *nirvana,* and what seems like a gigantic lotus blossom is a reincarnation of the Lord Buddha preaching to a congregation of the faithful. The artist's knowledge of Euroamerican models derived from two sources: the drawings he had seen on foreign postal cards and on the walls of the homes of American medical missionaries who had come to Thailand in the late 1820's (drawings which also may have helped to introduce three dimensionality to Thai painting), and European vessels that often docked in Bangkok, the most recent of which had carried British officials to negotiate a treaty with Thailand.

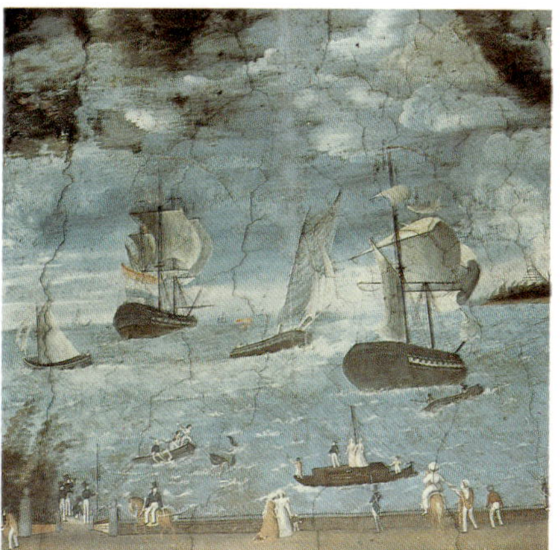

Figure 4.
Krua In Khong's portrayal of Thai bidding farewell to those who are sailing to nirvana.

In the years that followed, the Thai interest in European art became increasingly complex. Toward the end of the century, members of the royal family who had visited or studied in England became familiar with European cultural tastes, and returned to Thailand with the notion of art as collectible and as a form of interior decoration, thus enlarging the traditional Thai conception of art as a form of moral education. These aesthetic values quickly diffused to other members of the Thai elite.

In 1923, King Vajaravudh, who had been educated in England, invited an Italian sculptor to Bangkok to design and construct public monuments to glorify Thai history, its monarchs, and other heroes and heroines of the realm. The sculptor, Corrado Feroci, did create numerous patriotic structures—some of which were done in early Italian fascist style. But Feroci also fell in love with Thailand, changed his name to "Silpa Bhirasri," and during the next four decades introduced European artistic techniques, historical sources, and aesthetic values to thousands of Thai. With the help of others, he also induced the government to create a university of fine arts, sent scores of his own best students to Europe and America for further study, and established a national art competition. Bhirasri died in 1962, but three decades after his death he is still lionized by many Thai artists—principally for the spirit of artistic adventure and discovery he instilled in them. Too, more than anyone else, he helped elevate them from being unknown craftsmen *(naaj chaang)* in the service of others, repetitively copying conventional Thai designs, to artists *(silpakam)*—persons who were capable of perceiving and rendering new versions of the Thai world. His accounts of the mystique of European artists and their creative role in society were particularly inspiring to his Siamese students.

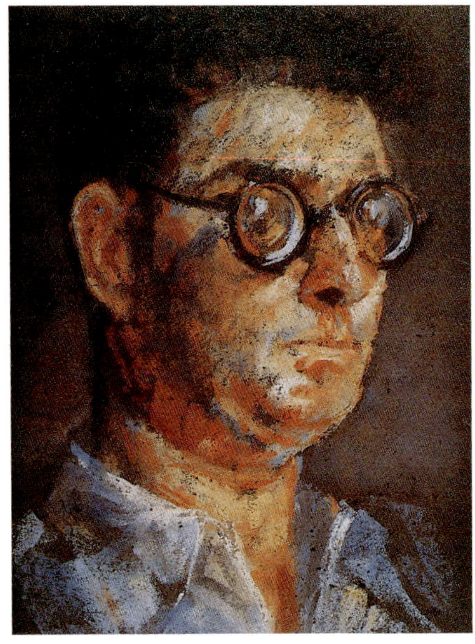

Figure 5.
A 1935 portrait of Corado Feroci, the Italian-born sculptor who directed the contemporary Thai art movement from the early 1920's until his death in 1962. This work is by Fua Harpitak, one of his earliest students.

Bhirasri's empowerment of Thai artists coincided with and was reinforced by the 1932 revolution that changed Thailand from an absolute to a constitutional monarchy, opened up the Thai social order, and greatly accelerated the modernization of the kingdom—which at the time was synonomous with "Westernization." Although Bhirasri urged his students to look to their own roots for inspiration and instituted programs in the history of Thai art and the restoration of temple paintings, most of his own energies went into teaching Western aesthetics, art history, and theories of art. This was very much in accord with the pro-Western interests of the various Thai military and civilian governments he served. In fact, Bhirasri's students were so captivated by the foreign aesthetic forms he taught them that for a period of twenty-five years before and after World War II, "contemporary Thai art" seemed almost indistinguishable from Euroamerican art—although in an oblique kind of way it also seemed ten to twenty years behind its Euroamerican prototypes. Many of his students later pointed out that Bhirasri's teaching of Western art usually stopped with post-impressionism, mainly because he believed (Silpa 1961:81) that abstract expressionism and subsequent 20th century movements were too alien to the Thai aesthetic spirit.

The Integrative Art of Modern Thailand

Contemporary Thai art changed dramatically after Bhirasri's passing from the scene. Whether as a result of the freedom afforded by the death of any powerful teacher or the dramatic changes that occurred in Thailand's historical circumstances, the past three decades have been marked by an outburst of artistic experimentation and ferment. The most significant of these experiments was the rediscovery and reworking of Thailand's classical and folk artistic traditions by many of the same artists who had earlier been trained by Bhirasri in Western art. A department of "Traditional Thai Art" was established at Silpakorn University, the fine arts institution that Bhirasri had helped to establish. But instead of retreating to the replication of classical Thai styles and motifs, the artists working in this program began to use traditional models as sources of inspiration and as elements for exploring newer contemporary forms. Simultaneously, many artists—particularly those who had studied in the West and returned home with an enhanced confidence in their own talent—greatly expanded the use of Euroamerican techniques, materials, and styles. Equally important, there was a revival of interest in classical Thai art which had been largely dormant during the Bhirasri years. While most of the persons working in this tradition were considered to be copyists, a few—Tarn Kudt, Somnuk Permthongkum—achieved considerable distinction for their extraordinary craftsmanship, use of modern materials, and their willingness sometimes to make fun of contemporary Thai life through their classical media.

The result of these events has been the development of a contemporary artistic genre that in its most essential features aims at integrating Thailand's thousand year old classical tradition, an even older folk tradition, and the Euroamerican tradition that has been known for 150 years. Although it was completely a local event, the eclectic, freely borrowing qualities of this genre are strikingly similar to what in the Euroamerican context is now called "postmodernism." It is our view that this particular form of "postmodernism," although always local, is also a world-wide phenomenon, and wherever it occurs, contains some elements that derive from indigenous, pre-modern aesthetic traditions.

It must be emphasized that, like postmodernism in the West, this synthesizing art of modern Thailand is very much an open-ended enterprise. It has no recognized artistic leaders, no canons of priority or choice, and lacks precise criteria of how it differs from other established genres. It also occurs across an extremely broad front that includes the expropriation and merging of techniques, materials, colors, conceptions, styles, inspirations, and subject matter. Its essence, however, is that it always utilizes artistic elements drawn from one or more of the three prior aesthetic traditions and amends these elements in a manner that resonates with contemporary Thai perception and experience. Some of the aesthetic forms presented in this catalogue may seem familiar to Western viewers, but, if our Thai informants are correct, they have been defined in the contemporary Thai context so that their meaning is significantly different from what Western viewers might surmise (see plate 37 by Somsak Chowtadapong and plate

55 by Thavorn Ko-udomvit). Conversely, there are other forms that reach back to Thai classical or folk sources that, if initially unintelligible to foreigners, are immediately meaningful to indigenous viewers for their fit with contemporary experience (see plate 1 by Kamol Tassananchalee and plate 49 by Panya Vijinthanasarn).

The attempt by Thai artists to synthesize the indigenous and the Euroamerican would probably not have occurred without the support and reinforcement of certain historical circumstances. The most important of these was the increasing realization on the part of the majority of reflective Thai that in their headlong pursuit of modernization—with its skyscrapers, choking traffic, integrated circuit factories, tourist resort towns, and the other excrescences of 20th century existence—they were losing touch with their culture's distinctiveness and with the sense of self-worth that it provides. There was, and continues to be, a great deal of controversy over what the constituent elements of "a modern Thai culture" might be, but there was broad consensus that these elements must bring together the past and the present, the traditional and the innovative, the indigenous and the international.

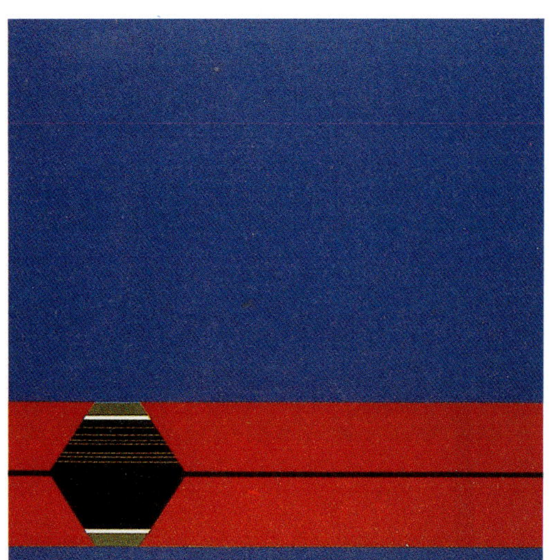

Figure 6. Itthi Kongkhakul, the creator of this hard-edge abstract work, is an articulate representative of the concept that contemporary art should be independent of indigenous traditions and national boundaries.

Other factors fed into this ethos of eclecticism. The dramatic increase in the number of foreigners in Thailand—initially, semi-permanent diplomats and businessmen, but more recently, hordes of foreign tourists—was central to the process. While the presence of these foreigners obviously contributed new, international standards and tastes to Thailand, the foreigners' own pursuit of mementos of their Thai experience—particularly those highlighting the authenticity and attractiveness of Thailand's aesthetic differences—stimulated among their hosts a heightened sense of pride about the inherent value of Thailand's indigenous traditions. (See Graburn 1976: 31–32 for a more general statement of this phenomenon.) Perhaps even more important than the foreigners were the large numbers of sophisticated Thai who returned home from study and work abroad, who, on the one hand, saw themselves as the vanguard of international standards and tastes, and, on the other hand, were themselves in search of symbols of the distinctiveness of the modern Thailand that they were helping to create. For many of these people the ownership of art works that were simultaneously Thai and modern became markers of their very special status in society. Perhaps the best evidence of the influence of these persons is the fact that as the years have passed and the prices of Thai art have moved steadily upward, the proportion of domestic to foreign collectors has changed significantly. Although there is considerable variation from artist to artist, the artists involved in this exhibition estimate that 65–70% of their work is currently being purchased by native Thai collectors.

Other Contemporary Genres

Although the integrative genre represents the thrust of contemporary Thai art, it is not the only modern art being done in Thailand—if only because the nation is too dynamic a place to be constrained by any notion of aesthetic correctness. There are at least two other contemporary genres that have significant followings. One is being pursued by those artists who see themselves as members of the Bangkok branch of the modern, international art community—creating analogues of the art they believe is still being done in New York, London, Paris, and Tokyo. Artists working in this tradition are particularly devoted to producing abstract color fields, hard-edge abstracts, and, more recently, conceptual works (see figure 6). The patrons of these artists are the architects and decorators who seek to project a modern international ambience in the designs of clients' homes and offices. Some of these artists take the position that in the contemporary world, art is the product of a creative individual who knows no cultural boundaries, and that international aesthetic traditions have greater value to the artist than those derived from the parochial features of his native culture. One of Thailand's six major art schools is predisposed to this view, requiring all of its faculty to have advanced degrees from foreign universities and to teach international art movements and techniques.

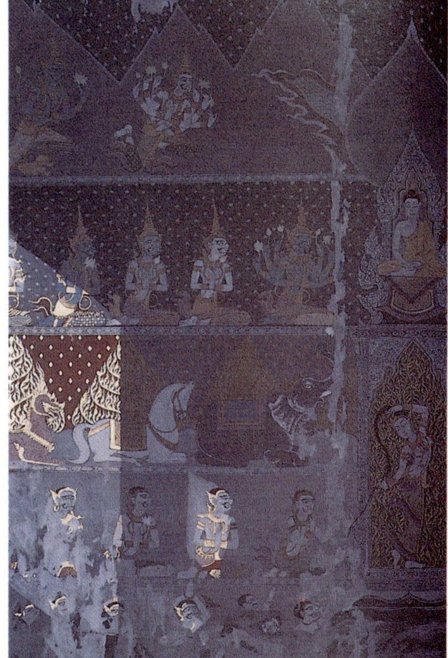

*Figure 7.
A detail from "The Temptation of Mara" (1981), showing Preecha Thaothong's vision of light and shade on a Thai temple mural.*

The other principal contemporary genre is made up of those artists who are experimenting with Thailand's classical tradition. Two very different directions are especially clear. One is exemplified by the work of Preecha Thaothong, who for more than twenty years has been working with the optics of light and shade as it plays upon and transforms the surfaces of Buddhist temples, particularly temple wall murals (see figure 7). Although the subject matter of Preecha's surfaces is artistically conventional, his complex contrasts between what is obvious and hidden, clear and opaque, known and unknown, are for many Thai powerful visual metaphors of the way most human beings actually understand the Buddhist teachings that his works are meant to convey. This merging of a novel technique with a traditional didactic purpose has brought Preecha a broad audience of patrons.

The other experiment with the Thai classical tradition is found in the work of Chakrabhand Posayakrit and his numerous followers. Chakrabhand portrays the heroes and heroines of Thai classical

Figure 8.
A portrait of a Thai feminine ideal by Chakrabhand Posayakrit.

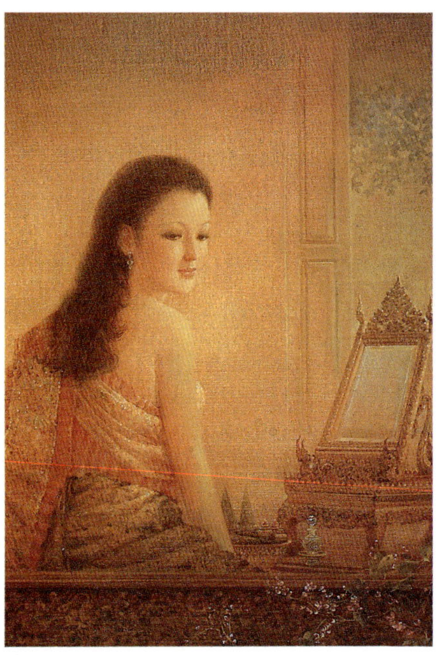

literature and myth in subdued, gossamer-infused settings, and in so doing he has helped transform the forms of Thai classical art into a decorative art for the home (see figures 8 and 9). Because he is particularly skilled at portraying idealized women and the symbols of romantic femininity, his work has special appeal to genteel, upper-class ladies and others with similar tastes. Thus, reproductions of some of his paintings have been widely distributed as greeting cards. Chakrabhand is one of Thailand's most heavily patronized artists, and for all the romantic excesses of his work, his paintings have profound appeal to viewers who expect artists to fashion a world that is more beautiful and perfect than real life.

Some Curatorial Reflections

It is impossible to predict the long-term life, stability, or primacy of the integrative art that currently represents the mainstream of contemporary Thai artistic activity. As a historical movement it holds what is essentially a compromise position between the achievements of Thailand's artistic past and the nation's participation in an international community that, notwithstanding the recent experiments of postmodernism, has become increasingly standardized in its aesthetic expressions. Despite the integrative movement's viability, and the fact that it parallels similar movements in Thai music and literature (see Myers-Moro 1990 and Phillips 1987), it is easy to imagine Thailand's integrative art eventually being dominated by the nation's classical and folk art traditions—if only because the latter are more authoritative symbols of the continuity and conservatism of Thai culture. Much depends, of course, on the extent to which Thai power brokers and opinion makers continue to be oriented to the realities of their ongoing and emerging culture rather than to the reconstructions and myths of their Thai past.

Given the extraordinary skill of Thai craftspersons and the fact that the kingdom does not have a powerful ethic of originality, it is also easy to imagine integrative art eventually giving way to the hegemonic nature of Euroamerican aesthetic forms—with more and more artists willingly producing variations on the cosmopolitan art of the international world. Always admitting to the possibility of the emergence of a Thai artist—genius or otherwise—who might have a major innovative impact on Euroamerican art, it is hard to imagine significant numbers of Thai artists who have been reared and educated in the Thai environment besting Euroamerican artists at the Euroamerican game.

If that scenario is unlikely, it is nonetheless true that some Thai artists are already actively participating in the Euroamerican game. One of the most obvious features of the current art scene is that artists working in different media have differential access to the international art community, and the nature of this access conditions their conception of what their art is about and who it is for. Thus, there are a number of Thai printmakers who, working with materials that are easily packaged and that can be readily airmailed throughout the world, are beginning to exhibit their work in international competitions and to show their portfolios to clients in numerous countries in Europe and Asia. At the same time, they are developing international liaisons and networks of critics and admirers whom they feel are just as significant to their artistic development as are their teachers, colleagues, or patrons back home. Frequently these foreign contacts turn up as visitors to Thailand, and stay on to advise or work with their Thai hosts. Most important, the printmakers acknowledge that they are working in a decorative medium where formal design elements and technical skill are artistically more significant than matters of cultural meaning, and that their work has to stand on its own—with no intercultural translations to make it more "understandable."

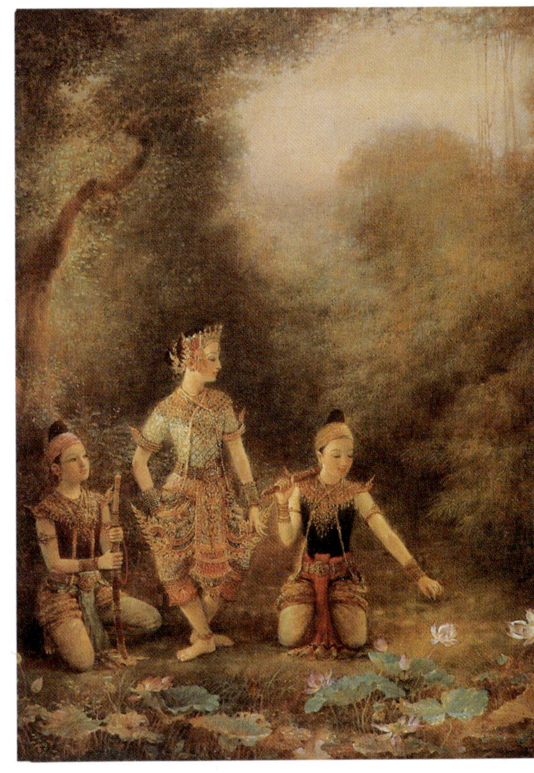

Figure 9.
A portrait of Phra Law and his courtiers by Chakrabhand Posayakrit. Phra Law displays the virtues of the prototypic hero of classical Thai literature—a person of delicacy, bravery and refinement.

It is our view that this international option makes sense for artists whose works are mainly decorative, but that it cannot, and does not, apply to the much larger group of artists whose works are representational, symbolic, or conceptual—if only because what they are representing, symbolizing, and conceptualizing almost always refers to the shared, implicit, and often intimate understandings of modern Thai culture. It is, of course, precisely because the integrative art movement focusses on these latter kinds of interests that it has become the dominant force of contemporary Thai art.

There is a peculiar irony in all of this—because if judged solely from a formalist, Euroamerican art historical point of view, it could be argued that the features that comprise Thailand's "integrative art" have produced a genre that is just as much an adulteration as it is a synthesis of the three prior artistic traditions. Such a view would be based upon the prejudice, widely shared in the West, that artistic forms are inherently more important than artistic content, and that there is greater aesthetic merit in creating novel forms—irrespective of their artistic value—than in elaborating established ones whose merit has already been demonstrated. However, if examined from the point of view of its cultural import and indigenous uses, it is equally clear that Thailand's integrative art is superbly suited to the social and psychological realities of contemporary Thai society.

The historical appropriateness of the genre derives from its inherently open-ended, assimilative nature. It is a genre that can move deep into the subtleties of the Thai imagination (see, for example, "Entry Into the Eternal," plate 36, by Prateung Emjaroen) but also outward into the world of international experimentation (see "Water," plate 42, by Kamol Tassananchalee). It honors and savors the past (see "Serenity," plate 11, by Chamreung Vichienket) but deals directly with the environmental realities of the contemporary Thai milieu (see "Cityscape," plate 22, by Jirapat Pitpreecha). In general, most of its attention is given to presenting traditional Thai issues in modern forms or to demonstrating the relevance of traditional concerns, and their symbols, to contemporary life. However, some works go beyond this and amplify issues that, while immanent to Thai thought, were traditionally avoided or muted, but that at the hands of the integrative artist are being reconfigured into central concerns of the contemporary Thai experience.

The most dramatic example of this creative reconfiguration can be found in the works of Thawan Duchanee, which are populated with drawings of wild animals, symbolic representations of humans as animals, and humans and animals intertwined within each other so that it is difficult to tell where either begins or ends (see particularly plate 33, "Earth"). While the formal elements of Thawan's art involve a melding of influences from classical Greece, Hieronymous Bosch, Nepalese tantric art, and Thai folk beliefs, the subjects of these works relate to Thai Buddhist notions about the moral and biological unity of man and animals, and man's inherent capacity for primitive, beastlike behavior. While traditional Thai Buddhist art acknowledged the significance of these notions in the struggle between the Lord Buddha and the evil forces of Mara's Army, the theme itself has always been secondary to the much greater emphasis the Thai have given to the beatific and didactic features of Buddhist ethical thought. Thawan's view, powerfully reinforced by his familiarity with pre-Buddhist folk conceptions, is that beasts and their aggressions are everywhere, and that in the modern world man can deal with them honestly only by acknowledging their presence on a higher level of consciousness and specificity. The bestial side of man is neither pleasant nor attractive, but because it is inherent to the human condition—and is one of man's principal links to other animals—it must be artistically acknowledged. As might be expected, Thawan's aesthetic vision is not without controversy in Thailand. While many viewers appreciate his perception into the character of animals and into the underside of the human psyche, many cannot abide his preoccupation with the more repugnant features of animal existence. However, his flourish, precision, and skill are admired by virtually everyone interested in art, and his works are increasingly sought out by native connoisseurs as well as by wealthy Europeans.

Thawan's attempt to reconfigure Thai cultural and aesthetic interests is by no means unique. One of the greatest strengths of the integrative art movement—as contrasted to both the classical and folk traditions—is its support for artists' experimenting with things that have never before been done. Thus, Montien Boonma has begun to use the natural materials of the Thai environment—soil, charcoal, mashed paper—to create forms that are ecologically sound representations of Buddhist symbols (see plate15). The Buddhist qualities of his work are found both in his symbolism and in the ecological soundness of his materials—the latter representing a recycling of what already exists in nature and thus a conscious fulfillment of the Buddhist premise that everything is inherently reusable and mutable. A very different form of experimentation can be found in the work of one of our youngest artists, Kamin Lertchaiprasert, who takes one of the most familiar items of Thai culture—the names of the letters of the Thai alphabet—and completely reconfigures them into a dazzling abstract commentary on the nature of modern Thai experience (see plate 56). Thus, the "k" for "kaw"—meaning "chicken"—is turned into a brutal cockfight; the "taa" for "taahaan"—meaning "soldier"—becomes a color field of brooding, ambiguous darkness; and the "ph" for "phyng"—meaning "bee"—is transformed into a color field almost alive with the texture of golden honey. And still different from Kamin is Angkarn Kalayaanapongse, one of the kingdom's most senior and honored artists. Angkarn's standing derives in part from his craftsmanship, but mostly from his capacity to express in culturally unprecedented—but visually arresting—ways some of the oldest and most cherished beliefs of Thai culture. Thus, in the drawing, "Moon Over Rice Fields," plate 30, Angkarn portrays the vitality of rice by drawing the rice seedlings in the conventional design of *khanok* or flames—which for the Thai viewer makes rice the equivalent of the sun or fire, and thus the source of power that fires human existence and accomplishment. A somewhat parallel use of the rice symbol can be found in the painting, "Crisis of Civilization, II" by Panya Vijinthanasarn, plate 49.

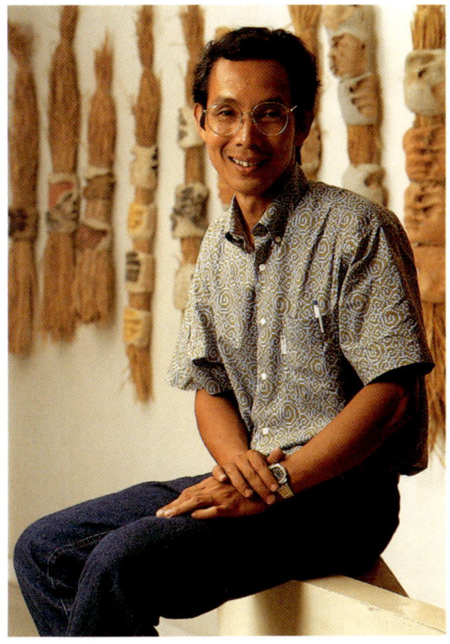

Figure 10. Montien Boonma

We have detailed a few of these cultural meanings—and will do so more completely below—because these are precisely the kinds of matters that Thai viewers attend to when they perceive and judge their contemporary works of art. Since most of these meanings are not apparent to Western viewers, we have given over a large part of this catalogue, and the exhibition itself, to their elucidation. However, we would emphasize that although these meanings are understood by most Thai, it is the originality of their artistic usage, or the domains of contemporary experience that they illuminate, that makes the works in which they appear so compelling to indigenous viewers. This is perhaps the single, greatest strength of the contemporary integrative genre.

Finally, we must note that the phrase "the integrative art of modern Thailand" that is used throughout this catalogue is not a natural native category. In accord with the simplifying tendencies of most natural lexicons, virtually all the art shown here is the work of artists who define themselves as "contemporary artists"—as contrasted with "classical artists" and "craftspersons" who fashion the numerous objects comprising "Thai folk art." However, the semantic distinction between "contemporary artists" and "classical artists" is also not very precise in the Thai language, if only because almost all "contemporary artists" have been trained in and are minimally competent in "classical art," even when the majority of them choose not to practice it. Some collectors of the works of Pichai Nirand, Panya Vijinthanasarn, Chalermchai Kositpipat, Thawan Duchanee, Sompop Budtarad, and Angkarn Kalayaanapongse (see particularly plates 3–5, 7, 8, 10, 13, 14, 21, and 30) have tried to apply the term "modern spiritual art" to the collective efforts of these particular artists, but the label has not caught on. Some artists and collectors have also used the terms "innovative" *(kaanmaj)* or "creative" *(kaanpradid)* art to describe the types of works presented here, but these terms also lack consensual usage.

However, if what we are calling "contemporary integrative art" lacks a single, simple native term, it does not lack native conceptualization and often heated debate among members of the art community. Every Thai artist and collector with whom we spoke during the research resulting in this exhibit was keenly aware, and often articulate, about the highly electic nature of his or her own work. While the artists each preferred to emphasize the distinctiveness of their own efforts, they also knew where they as individuals were coming from historically—the multiple influences that impinged upon them and how these influences were utilized, departed from, or added to at various points in their own careers. Artists were also articulate—although at times also evasive—about the contributions of teachers, fellow artists, patrons, friends and enemies.

The single, most salient fact about their self-reflections was their awareness of their having melded together, each in his or her own distinctive manner, the influences of Thailand's artistic past with the international influences of their current historical situation. This sense of awareness took many forms. For some—especially among the almost 65% of our group who had studied abroad—it often took the simple form of acknowledging that they had become thoroughly accustomed to the expensive materials and techniques they had learned to use overseas, and that they never could go back to using native Thai materials. (On the other hand, there were some who revived the use of long-obsolescent Thai materials, e.g., handmade Thai paper, in order to enhance the ethnic authenticity of their own work. And one artist intentionally used the cheapest, least stable imported materials as a way of subverting the Euroamerican belief in "the permanence of art" and demonstrating the proof of the *dharmic* premise that "everything changes.") Others, particularly those who had not gone abroad, referred to the liberating spirit of international art that Bhirasri had earlier introduced to Thailand and that in their view had since become the hallmark of all contemporary Thai art. Thus, even Angkarn Kalayaanapongse, the most traditionally oriented of all modern artists, spoke of the joy of breaking through the constraints of traditional Thai artistic conventions, and bringing to some of the most familiar icons of Thai art a vitality and animation that was never before allowed (see particularly plates 30 and 32). Others developed explicit philosophies of artistic integration. Thus, Chalermchai Kositpipat has been clear and consistent in his assertions that the only way Thai artists can be aesthetically "distinctive" is by creating an art that joins the didactic purposes of traditional Thai temple art with the forms, techniques, and materials of the late 20th century. He also argues that in the modern world the didactic themes of temple art should not be confined to sacred environments, but should also be displayed in the secular surroundings of home and workplace.

Our own view is related to, but somewhat broader, than Chalermchai's position. That is, solely on an empirical basis (rather than on any kind of programmatic grounds) it is clear to us that although the process of artistic integration is occurring along a broad front—involving styles, materials, techniques, colors, and even inspirations—in its artistic conceptions and in its subject matter it is heavily biased toward indigenous, if not traditional, Thai concerns. But, unlike Chalermchai, we do not see how in the complex environment of the late 20th century a viable artistic genre can limit itself solely to didactic or ethical interests. Having said this, we would also assert that contemporary Thai art—like art everywhere—is overwhelmingly self-referring or self-refractive in nature. (We say "self-refractive" rather than "self-reflective" to underscore the interpretive, as contrasted to the factual, nature of art.) Thus, we would argue that, despite the seeming familiarity to Western viewers of many of the images in this exhibition, there is virtually no image that addresses either a universal or Euroamerican issue in terms that are aesthetically or culturally self-evident. Clearly many of the works in the exhibit can be appreciated for their formal artistic features, and their meanings can be decoded to some level of personally satisfying intelligibility. But if the works are to be understood in the sense that their creators intended—with some sense of the subtlety, irony, innovation, humor, respect, and complexity that the artists gave to fashioning them—they require some type of explanatory scaffolding.

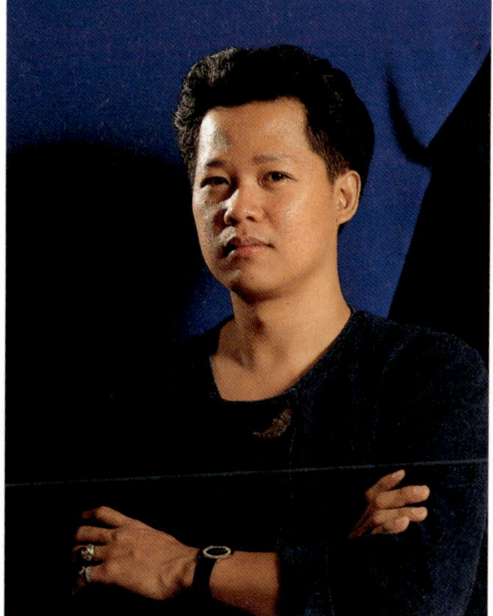

Figure 11.
Chalermchai Kositpipat

If this view is correct, it has significant implications to the nature of visual art as a universal, panhuman communicative phenomenon. In essence it means that contemporary integrative Thai art—or the art of any other culturally foreign tradition—should never be considered to speak for itself or be presented without some kind of meaningful intellectual intervention. This view demands sensitivity to the fact that visual art—like literature, humor, dance, or any other institutionalized expressive act—does not exist in a social vacuum, as something complete unto itself. It is always embedded in the meanings and intentions of its creators—sometimes very complex ones designed to stimulate the attention and pleasure of viewers, and perhaps even to provide them with some enhanced understanding of the world. It is our hope that the intercultural translations of this catalogue can clarify some of these meanings and intentions, and thus contribute to that understanding.

TWO:

OTHER ARTISTIC GENRES

As indicated earlier, contemporary Thai art contrasts with—but in several critical ways refers to, interacts with, and is perhaps even dependent upon—some of the other artistic genres that exist in late 20th century Thailand. Certainly the ideas that most Thai have of contemporary art—in terms of both its aesthetic nature and its value as a cultural phenomenon—are as much a function of its relationships to these other genres as they are a function of contemporary art's own defining qualities.

Most Thai interested in art recognize at least four artistic genres in addition to contemporary art: classical Thai art, folk art, tourist art, and commercial art. While the artists who work in these genres compete with one another for public attention, acclaim, and financial support, the genres are in no sense mutually exclusive. Many artists move back and forth between several genres, and virtually every artist (excepting perhaps the self-taught) has been trained in and has some skill in classical art. Too, there is constant feedback among the genres: classical art has in recent decades been directly influenced by modern conventions of three-dimensionality, perspective, and shading, and all the genres have in one way or another felt the impact of tourism. Also, a few artists work at the margins of two or more genres and happily blend these multiple influences. And beyond these genres themselves, there is an extremely active world of art-related professionals pursuing careers in photography, television, cinema, architecture, advertising, graphic design, interior decoration, fabric design, publishing, movie poster work, and billboard and sign design, all of whom influence the visual ambience of Thai culture. Members of this latter group, which involves the largest proportion of people in Thailand who have actually been trained in art, are crucial not only for the role they play as art collectors, but as people who help both to set and to alter the volatile tastes of the art-buying public.

Classical Thai Art

Classical Thai art is the most culturally familiar and widely respected—if for some Thai, also somewhat well-worn—of all of Thailand's artistic genres. Based in part on Sinhalese and Khmer prototypes, it has been practiced for more than a millennium on the walls and architectural elements of temples and palaces, on the surfaces of cabinets, screens, and manuscripts of both royal and village Thailand, and in individual Buddha images representing as many as nine historically different styles. Too, it has been executed in virtually every medium—painting, sculpture, stone and wood bas-relief, stucco, lacquerware, woodcarving, neilloware, and leather. Unlike all other genres, it also has a literary and theatrical counterpart. The essence of classical art is its religious content, didactic purpose, and highly decorative designs, although this last attribute has its roots in Thailand's folk tradition. Like its medieval European counterpart, Thai classical art has always been in the service of the kingdom's religious and political institutions, and has had as its principal purpose the legitimization and glorification of these institutions, as well as the human values associated with them. In seemingly unending repetition (but with subtle stylistic variations through the centuries), it has portrayed scenes from the *Jataka* tales (depicting events from the last ten lives of the Lord Buddha), the Ramakien (the Thai version of the *Ramayana*), and such Thai literary classics as *Inao, Phra Lauau,* and *Phra Aphajmanii*—all but the last having been commissioned or rewritten by Thai monarchs. Classical art conveys a poignant vision of traditional Thai values and social structure with celestial and royal figures shown to be larger than life and in states of stoical serenity, while villagers (typically in smaller scale) are shown as happy jokesters or suffering sinners.

Because of its historical depth, relative[1] distinctiveness, and associations with the court and the temple, classical art has become virtually a logo for Thailand. It represents simultaneously the kingdom's continuity, its high culture, and its preoccupation with Buddhist teachings and other "classical" issues depicted in the art itself—the ideals of heroism, loyalty, morality, beauty, and the like. These expressions of the "civilized" nature of Thai life have been sufficiently important to the Thai establishment that classical artists (and folk artists in royal service) have had for almost a century the support of a Department of Fine Arts within the Thai government. The sheer magnitude of the monumental art of the Ayuthia and Sukothai kingdoms suggests that such governmental patronage goes back to the 13th century origins of the Thai state, and perhaps even earlier to the Dvaravati art of the first millennium A.D. Today classical art comprises the principal holdings of the kingdom's National Museum, a significant part of the permanent collection of the National Gallery, and, in more modernized versions, represents the principal decorative elements of such public buildings as the National Cultural Centre and the Queen Sirikit Exposition and Convention complex.

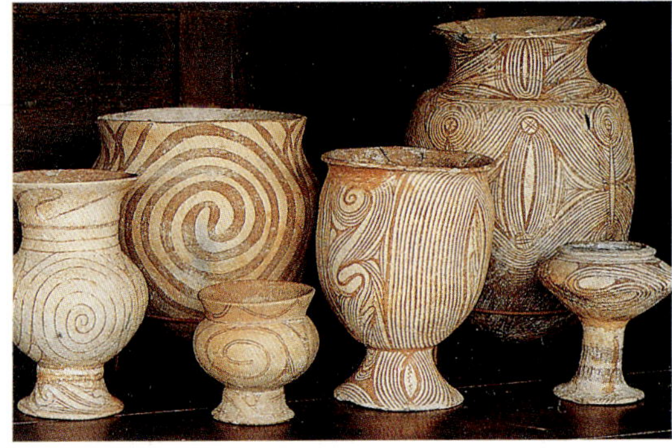

Figure 12.
Clay pottery with the characteristic whorl design from Ban Chiang, Thailand, approximately 5th century B.C. While Thai recognize that the date is too early to indicate the presence of Buddhism in Thailand, some believe that the circular design might be an earlier incarnation of the symbol representing the Law of Perpetual Change.

1. We say "relative" because classical Thai art is obviously related to classical Khmer (from which it in part derives), Lao, and Burmese art. However, the modern versions of classical Thai art are more complex and experimental, and also have a more broadly based patronage, than those of their mainland Southeast Asian counterparts—largely, we suspect, because of Thailand's more salubrious political and economic situation.

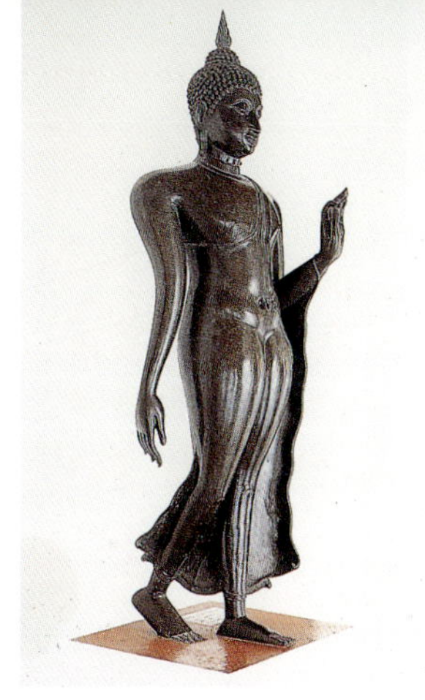

Figure 13. Buddha images have over the centuries been the single most important focus of Thai artistic energy. Thai art historians recognize as many as nine different styles of these images. The most "classical" of the schools—in the simplicity and elegance of its imagery—is the 13th–15th century Sukothai style. Because of its antiquity and its similarity to modern aesthetic forms, it is the most emulated of all classical Buddha figural styles.

The viability of classical art is maintained in the contemporary world by being part of the required curriculum at the kingdom's six major art schools and the largest segment of the art education programs provided at the nation's teacher training colleges. Some of the graduates of these schools later apply their training to painting or restoring temple murals, to sculpting Buddha images, or more prosaically to decorating hotels and restaurants, greeting cards, shopping bags, T-shirts, and other tourist mementos. A few artists specializing in classical work have developed their own distinctive styles, and responding to the wave of nostalgia and nationalism that has swept through Thailand in recent years, have cultivated large clienteles of socially prominent collectors (see particularly figures 8 and 9). Some of these painters are in fact among the most renowned and financially successful artists in the kingdom.

However, for all its beauty, grace, and popularity, classical art is an inherently uncreative enterprise. As practiced over the centuries, it has been essentially a craft tradition with unknown artists copying from other unknown artists or from their own teachers. (The practice of signing art work with one's name or logo is a mid-twentieth century invention.) Teachers always kept close control of their apprentices' innovative impulses, and even today most classical works, particularly temple murals, are copies of other works, in part so sponsors will know precisely what they are getting. In fact, during most of Thailand's history, valued art works—valued primarily for their sacred, not aesthetic, qualities—were always viewed as the product of their sponsor's religious and financial commitment rather than of their artists' imagination or skill. It was not until the 19th century that a few extraordinary artists (and poets as well) began to be singled out and rewarded with public recognition of their attainments.

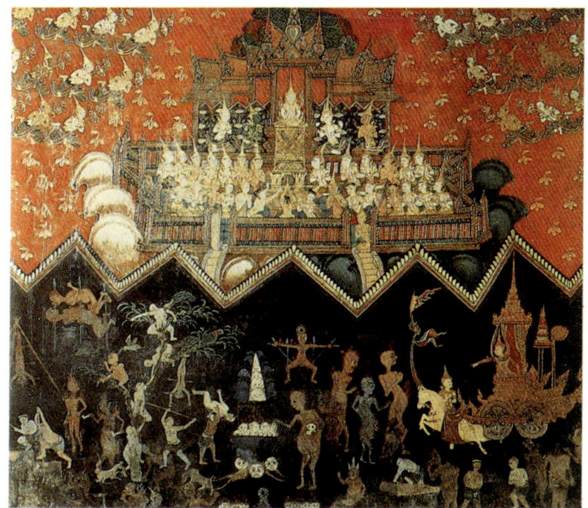

Figure 14. The practice of painting murals on the walls of temples reached its florescence in the murals of the early and mid-19th century. This painting from a temple in Cholburi Province, a scene from one of the Lord Buddha's last ten lives, provides a 19th century vision of heaven and hell. The zig-zag line in the center of the work was the conventional way of dividing the scenes of the narrative.

Many artists assert that although it is currently easier to make a living doing classical rather than contemporary art, it is tedious, unchallenging work which any trained artisan can do. Some members of the art community even argue that its continuing popularity is holding back the development of new Thai artistic forms. A few perceive the situation as part of a capitalist plot, claiming that it is Westerners who have fallen in love with classical art, defined its value, and created a market for it, which has then induced members of the Thai elite to enter the market as a way to affirm both their own status and the glory of the traditional Thai social order.

Our own materials overwhelmingly demonstrate that the majority of contemporary artists—at least innovative, self-confident ones—perceive classical art much more as a source of stimulation and inspiration than as an obstacle to the pursuit of their own work. For these artists such dour interpretations of

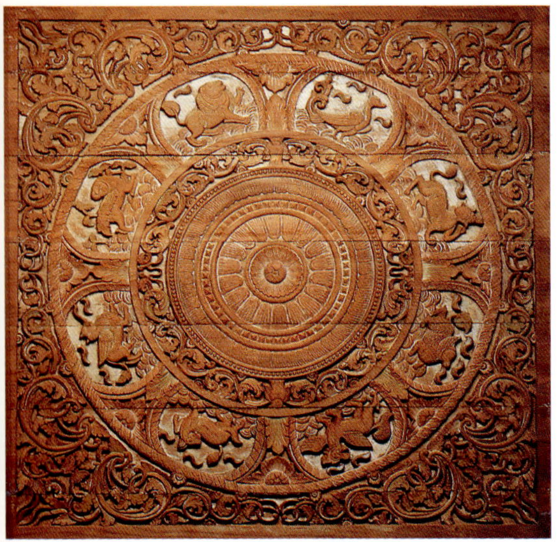

Figure 15. Together with the Buddha Footprint, the lotus blossom and the bho tree, the Wheel of the Law, or thammachak, *is one of the principal symbols of Buddhism. However, like many icons of the classical tradition, this thammachak is embedded in and surrounded by symbolic elements—the animal figures and filigree designs—that come primarily from Thai folk tradition.*

the classical influence represent a misreading of the nature of art, if only because they see the history of Thai art as a natural process of accretion and change rather than as a competition between fixed, unrelated genres. Thus, rather than perceiving classical art in adversarial terms, some of these artists—Angkarn, Panya, Chalermchai, and Pichai to cite but a few—see their classical tradition as something that they are refiguring to fit with the realities and opportunities of their own lives and interests. They—and their viewers—are keenly aware that their work is neither a replication nor a continuation of the classical tradition. However, they are also aware that the meaning and power of their own art is profoundly dependent on classical Thai precedents. Some artists—Thawan (plate 33), Kamol (plate 2)—are uninhibited in their mixture of historically and geographically discrete genres, and produce an art that, if seemingly culture-free in its aesthetic power, nevertheless has explicit reference to the conceptions and icons of their classical and folk traditions. Others—Chamreung the sculptor (plate 11) and Wattana the painter (plates 43 and 45)—seem to be "contemporary artists" in an Euroamerican sense, but both use forms that derive directly from some of the most revered models of the Thai classical tradition, thus demonstrating simultaneously both the timelessness and modernity of these forms.

However, it must be emphasized that these views exist in a subtle balance. Thus, if most contemporary Thai artists are deeply indebted to some of the precedents of classical Thai art—especially its symbols, didactic purposes, and aesthetic forms—they also turn their back on some of its other features. Many say that classical art is marked by artistic conventions (e.g., its lack of visual perspective and its stereotyped rendition of mythological figures) that, although historically charming, are not to be taken seriously in the late 20th century. Others point to classical art's inattention to the personal identities of artists and its indifference to the exploratory nature of the artistic spirit. And still others point to its portrayal of matters that, although morally relevant to contemporary life, are not presented in a manner that addresses the real moral issues of contemporary experience. Such reservations are perhaps inherent to the very process of trying to maintain a classical tradition in the multivalent milieu of the modern world.

Thai Folk Art

Thai folk art encompasses the production of the many different forms and qualities of weaving, ceramics, jewelry, silver and gold work, wood carvings, stucco work, lacquerware, vegetable and fruit carvings, lathe turnings, paper maché fabrication, flower decorations, leatherwork, and neilloware and mother of pearl mosaics. In terms of the numbers of practioners and the development of regional and local traditions, it is the most widespread, highly ramified, deeply rooted, and heavily patronized of Thailand's artistic genres. In recent years, several folk art activities—particularly weaving, wood carving, and jewelry and lacquerware crafting—have become increasingly mechanized and aesthetically conventionalized as they have been expropriated by elements of the Thai tourist industry. Conversely some folk artists have been stimulated by this same tourist market into creating more carefully crafted and innovatively designed folk products.

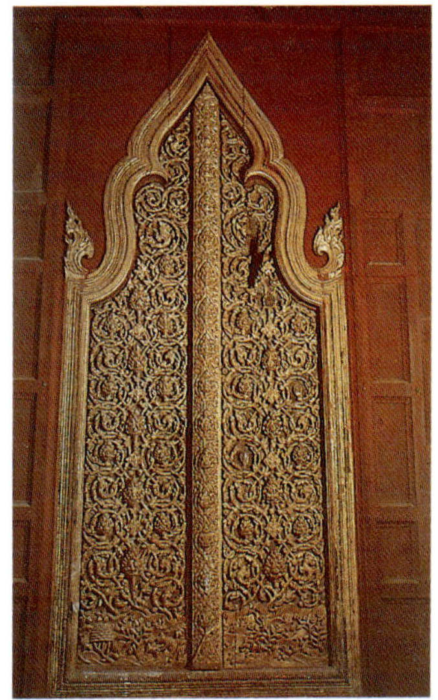

Figure 16.
The carved central door of the teaching hall at Temple Yai Suanaram in Petchaburi Province showing the spiraling vines and floral designs characteristic of the Thai folk art contribution to temple design.

Like its counterparts elsewhere in the world, Thai folk art involves a merging of the decorative and the functional, e.g., the artistic elaboration of a wide array of utilitarian items such as food and garment containers, house supports, clothes, swords, buffalo yokes, manuscript cabinets, betel nut boxes, and the like. However, especially important are those items defined as sacred or meant to convey a ritual attitude toward their use. Thus, the windows, doors, gables, pillars and ceilings of most of Thailand's Buddhist temples are covered with elaborate decorative elements drawn from the folk tradition which are meant to beautify and reinforce the sacredness of the temple environment. In fact, these elements are so much a part of the ambience of the temple setting that any distinctions that might be drawn between the "classical" and "folk" components of temple art are essentially irrelevant. Frequently these elements are modified to make them even more "classical," such as when they are painted gold, the color of Buddhism, or red, the color of heaven and of those who reside there.

The concept of "folk art" refers primarily to a wide variety of craft skills and secondarily to an array of distinctive styles. Perhaps the most widespread of all Thai folk styles are the intricate arabesques of spiralling vines, leafy tendrils, floral and flame-like designs that are used to beautify and honor material objects of value. While these arabesques are always associated with religious structures and objects (see figures 16–19) they also appear in more secular contexts, typically as a way of highlighting the status of the object's owner. Thus, garment containers made of lacquerware, food containers inlaid with mother of pearl, or embossed betel boxes made of silver were traditionally covered with these designs as a demonstration of their owners' wealth and good taste. Antique versions of these arabesque decorated items—or, more realistically, newly crafted reproductions that are treated to look like antiques—represent a major segment of the contemporary folk art market, a market that now caters as much to indigenous Thai collectors as to foreigners.

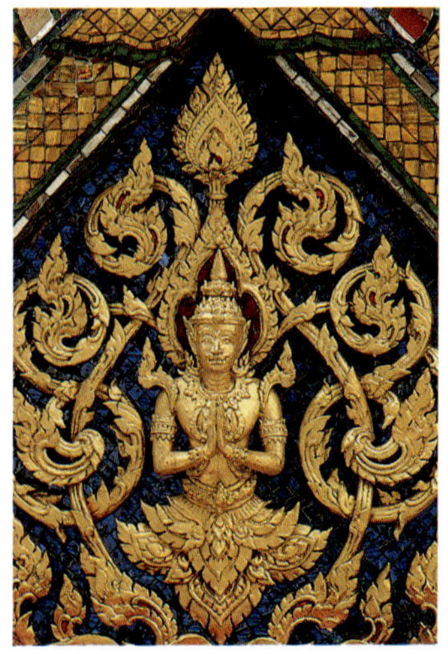

Figure 17.
Restored facade of a 19th century temple gable showing folk mosaic work and spiral vines surrounding a godling from the Buddhist pantheon.

These folk arabesque designs also find their way into contemporary Thai art. Sometimes they are used directly as in the flame (plate 30) and vine (plate 4) designs of Angkarn's work or in the garments worn by the figures in Panya's (plate 3) and Arunothai's (plate 25) paintings, and sometimes more

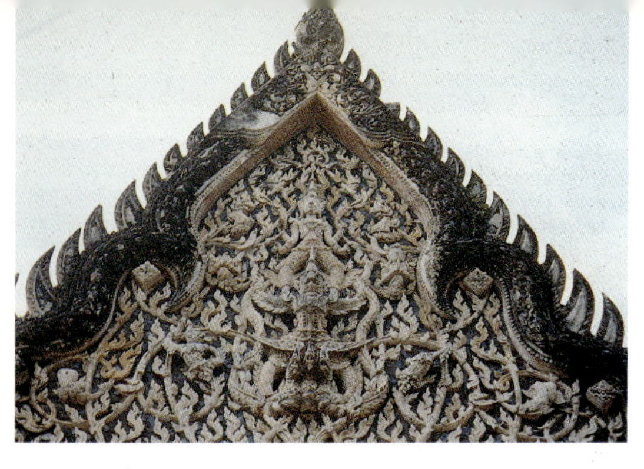

suggestively as in the dense, convoluted patterns that characterize Thawan's drawings (see plates 7 and 33). Many Thai say that they favor this *raa-la-iad* (fine lined, tight, repetitive) style because it shows how much time, labor, and commitment that an artist gives to his work.

Figure 18. Stucco gable of a scripture repository displaying the folk spiral vine motif surrounding a god astride garudas and nagas drawn from the Hindu pantheon, Ayuthia, circa 15th century.

In addition to this use of folk designs, contemporary artists incorporate folk concepts, objects, and materials directly into their work. The demons shown in Panya's "Three Concentrations" (see plate 3) are a visual representation of the *phii* and other malevolent spirits that inhabit the Thai supernatural world. The belief in these spirits is pre-Buddhist in origin and in fact represents the oldest and most widespread religious tradition of Southeast Asia (see Spiro 1967 and Tambiah 1970). Similarly, the lingam shown in Arunothai's "Homage to Siva Lingam" (see plate 27) relate to a parallel set of folk beliefs, although over the centuries lingam have become more closely associated with the Brahmanic elements of Thai religious practice.

Of a different order is Kamol Tassananchalee's use of Thai folk objects and materials. The *nangyai* or large puppet shadow-play form that unifies of much of his current work (see plates 1, 42, and 54) was in part "borrowed" from Thai folk culture because of its aesthetic flexibility and freshness. But it was also used because of Kamol's intense nostalgia for Thailand and his need to assert his Thai identity. This symbolic use of the *nangyai* was particularly apposite because *nangyai* is a folk entertainment that appeals to all classes, is found in many areas of the kingdom, and is often seen by Thai as a symbol of cultural unity.

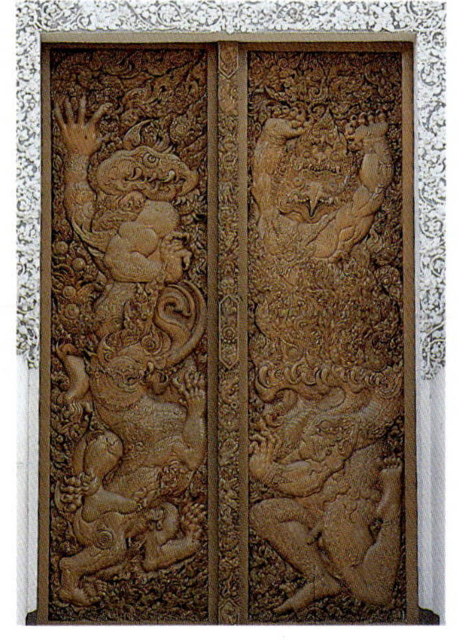

Figure 19. A temple door designed by Thawan Duchanee showing mythical creatures drawn from the Thai folk tradition, Chiengrai, 1988.

Kamol's use of handmade Thai paper, *kradad saa,* is significant historically. During the past century, *kradad saa* had almost ceased to be used in Thailand for any purpose other than gift wrapping. On a trip to Northern Thailand in the mid 1970's, Kamol learned the old techniques for making the paper, and he began to make and use it in California as a symbol of his own Thai roots. A few years later, Thavorn Ko-udomvit visited him in Los Angeles, and Kamol proudly introduced Thavorn to his modern applications of this traditional, but almost obsolete, material. Thavorn, a faculty member at Silpakorn University, also became enamoured with *kradad saa,* and on his return to Thailand he both used it in his own work and taught its applications to his many students. Now, a decade later, *kradad saa* has become one of the most commonly used art materials in Thailand.

The rediscovery of *kradad saa* may be special in that it involved international travel and its re-creation in a foreign setting. However, Thai artists are continually experimenting with folk materials and techniques—sometimes for ethnic identity reasons, but sometimes for possible solutions to age-old technical problems. Thus, a few artists have recently tried to reduce mildew damage to their canvases by using the old folk technique, used on stucco and plaster walls, of bonding onto the painting surface a thin translucent paper that has been coated with mildew-resistant natural extracts. Although it is too early to judge the long-term effectiveness of the technique, some artists speak approvingly of how the procedure makes their surfaces more reflective, muted, and aged in appearance.

Finally, although "folk art" must be distinguished from "classical art" on the grounds of its non-Buddhist sources and uses, its greater age, and its closer links to village (as contrasted to court) culture, most indigenous Thai in fact deal with the two traditions as if they blend into one another and represent mutually reinforcing facets of a single, unified "traditional Thai art." The distinctions of provenience we have discussed here are known to most Thai, and are important to some artists and collectors. But for the majority of Thai, these distinctions represent minor emendations on what is a single integrated artistic tradition—a tradition in which contemporary art, as exemplified in this exhibition and catalogue, is simply the latest phase.

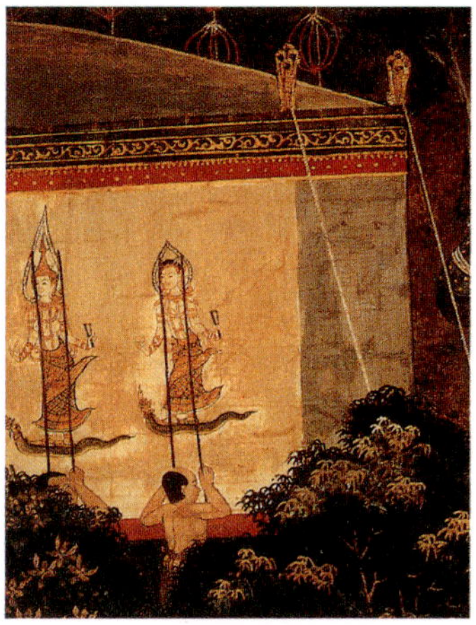

Figure 20.
Detail from a cloth painting, dated from the mid-19th century, showing a nangyai, *or large puppet shadow play performance. (From the collection of M. C. Piya-Rangsit.)*

Tourist Art

Tourist art differs from all other artistic genres in Thailand in that it is designed to address the collecting and decorating preferences—real or imagined—of foreign buyers. Also, because it is typically meant to be a souvenir of the tourist's short-term visit, it frequently reflects the tourist's vision—a restricted, but happy, one—of what is interesting about Thailand. The dialectic of souvenirship is further complicated by the fact that the foreign traveller typically seeks art and artifacts that will not only be attractive in his home setting, but that he hopes or imagines were culturally authentic in their Thai setting. Offsetting this seriousness of purpose, there is in the tourist art situation a streak of frivolity as well (as there is in the tourist experience as a whole); travellers will sometimes buy objects they never would favor or display at home—except perhaps as conversation pieces.

With more than five million tourists visiting annually in recent years, "tourist art" has considerable economic impact on Thai artistic activity and spans an extraordinary range of artifacts. Its simplest and least expensive expressions are the mass-produced—but hand-made—lacquer bowls, native dolls, wooden or brass replicas of turtles and elephants, ceramic and wooden models of village homes, and silk flowers that are sold at airport and other government tourist shops. Somewhat more sophisticated in their craftsmanship and design are the headgear, costumes, and weapons of Thai classical dancers that are also sold at these shops, or the Christmas ornaments done by tribal people and periodically available from Western missionary organizations. Thousands of similar items, more and less elaborate, are produced by the weavers, wood carvers, and bronze specialists of the kingdom.

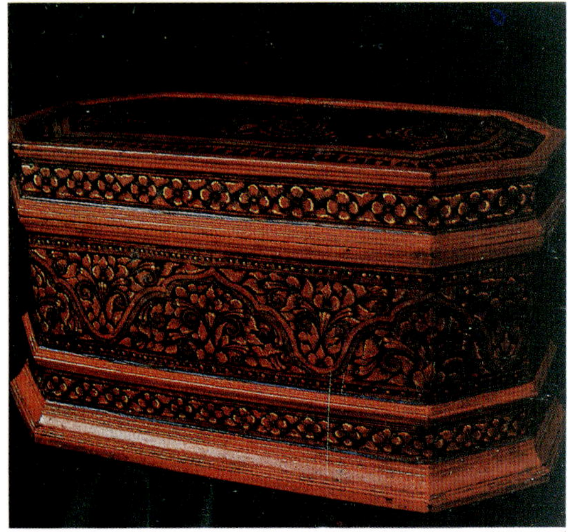

Figure 21.
A heavily embossed lacquerware clothes box which typically accompanied a new groom when he took up residence in his bride's family's home.

Of an entirely different order are the bronze, stone, wooden, and stucco replicas of Buddha images, temple lintels, and statues of godlings and mythological animals that are sold in the "antique" shops of Bangkok, Chiengmai, and other provincial centers. The Bangkok English-language yellow pages list eighty-nine such "antique" shops and another twenty-seven that call themselves "art galleries," most of which are located in or near tourist hotels.

The nature of these "antiques" must be contexualized. Like many locales in the ancient world, Thailand has been ravaged of most of its genuine classical and prehistoric art. Some of the finest expressions of this art are still safeguarded in the National Museum, certain temples, and private homes, but much of the kingdom's artistic heritage disappeared from Thailand in the late 1950's and early 1960's when Thai art was "discovered" by the international art market. Thai law had since 1933 prohibited the export of any religious antiques or objects without the permission of the Department of Fine Arts, but this law was no challenge to the combined resourcefulness of bronze- and stone-cutting thieves, corrupt or incompetent Thai officials, and foreign collectors who were reputed to have used diplomatic pouches to remove their stolen treasures.[2]

One result of this activity has been the development of a broad scale industry for producing and selling modern replicas of these classical works—some of which are superior in craftsmanship to their historical models. Techniques have been developed for accelerating the aging process—burying bronzes underground and having water buffalo urinate on the covering soil; using rolling pins to crack the paint surfaces of oil cloth paintings. There is of course no tourist protection law requiring shop owners to inform buyers of the modern origin of this classical art. Thus, while many tourists leave Thailand fully aware that they have obtained contemporary reproductions, others leave with prized "antiques" they think they have purchased at bargain prices.

---

2. The "discovery " of classical Thai art by the international art market during the 1950's–60's period was related in part to the declining availability of Khmer art and in part to the entry into the marketplace of such new collectors as Doris Duke, the American tobacco heiress, who began to collect classical Thai specimens en masse for her newly created Southeast Asian Art complex in Hawaii. Also, a public confrontation between the then premier of Thailand, Sarit Thanarat, and Jim Thompson, the Thai silk entrepreneur, over who "owned" the art objects in Thompson's home, sharpened the public's awareness of the monetary value of Thai classical art. Other collectors soon followed the examples of Duke and Thompson, and within a very short time the prices of genuine classical artifacts began to skyrocket. Hundreds of thousands of fallen Buddha heads started to disappear from Ayuthia and Sukothai, and all over the kingdom famous Buddha images began to disappear from their bases. Such activity has had all kinds of ironic consequences. Thus, in one of the earliest instances of his emerging notoriety, Thawan Duchanee had several of his art works slashed by protesting students who objected to his portrait of flies crawling over the head of a Buddha image. Thawan's intent was to portray the character of those who for profit would behead Buddha images; his protestors falsely assumed he was vilifying Buddhism. Perhaps the most complex case of artistic theft of a classical relic involved the mid 1960's disappearance—perhaps involving a U.S. or Thai military helicopter—of a lintel from the Phnom Rung temple area in Buriram Province in the Northeast. By the late 1980's, the lintel had become a prize possession of the Chicago Art Institute. After long and intense negotiation between representatives of the Thai government, the Institute, the Chicago City Council, and the Thai community of Chicago, the lintel was returned to Thailand.

In addition to the "antique" shops are the "art galleries"—or more accurately, picture shops—that cater to the tourist trade. Since tourists themselves are extraordinarily varied in their tastes and budgets, these shops carry a vast array of genres and styles at a broad range of prices. Particularly favored are modern copies of Thai classical art, Thai pastoral scenes, semi-nudes, still lifes, seascapes, religious subjects, and scenes of canal life and village festivals. While most of the merchandise of these shops emphasizes Thai themes and scenes, shop owners claim that they could not exist on the tourist trade alone. Thus they also carry locally executed copies of 19th century European pastoral art which are especially popular among Thai and Sino-Thai who have been tourists in Europe and who want to decorate their homes with what they judge to be European taste. Like tourist-oriented Hong Kong tailors, many of these picture shops can also reproduce in less than 24 hours facsimiles of paintings by Van Gogh and Rembrandt, as well as portraits of family members from wallet-size snapshots—often with extraordinary felicity.

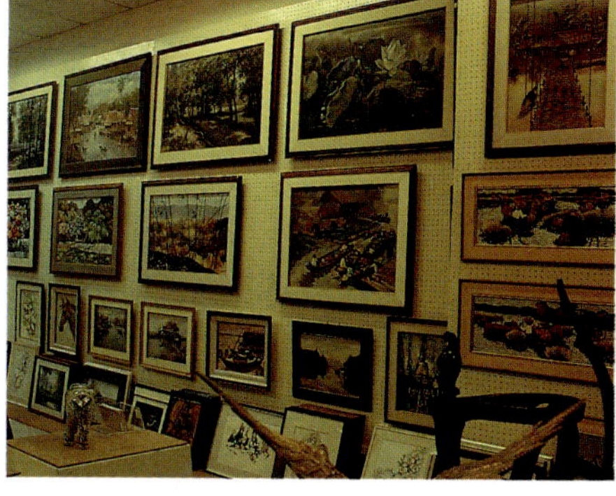

Figure 22. A wall of a typical tourist art shop.

As might be expected in such a bazaar-like setting, these shops pay little attention to individual artists—their position in the Thai art world, the distinctiveness of their work, or even their identities. In fact, almost all the works shown in tourist picture shops are unlabelled as to artist (who, it is assumed, most potential customers would neither know nor care about) or even price (which is inherently negotiable). Unlike the situation in a genuine gallery where an art work is typically sold on a thirty percent commission and the gallery owner works on behalf of both the artist and collector, almost all the works in tourist picture shops are purchased outright from artists or prior owners, and are resold at the maximum prices the market will bear—sometimes with profit margins of 300–400 percent. Because the essence of the process is a quick sale to a transient, anonymous buyer, the shops do not maintain catalogues or brochures of the works of individual artists, although some may have on hand clippings of favorable reviews of a few of the artists they are showing. Certainly the shops do not perceive themselves as representing the work of specific artists, and the concept of "exclusive representation" is completely alien. Some shops do favor certain genres and styles, and some shop owners say that they might adjust their stock to fit the preferences of certain classes of foreigners. Thus, North Americans are said to prefer paintings of quiet villages, children jumping into canals, or color saturated landscapes, while Japanese reputedly prefer still lifes and Buddha images. However, most tourist picture shops appear to be strikingly similar to one another in the works they carry, competing mainly on the basis of price and their access to the undifferentiated tourist public.

The artists who stock these shops are for the most part competent, fast-working artisans who have no pretentions about the nature or purpose of their work. Indeed some of the art is produced in tourist art factories where members of a family may produce as many as 600–800 works a month, which are then sold to many different shops—all signed by the group's key member, a single "well-known artist" whose renown obviously is based as much upon the quantity and distribution as the quality of his work. However, it would be incorrect to think of these shops as containing only tourist kitsch. Some shop owners are well educated in art and some customers are highly discriminating, and thus some shops carry at least a few works of high quality. Too, individual works of some of Thailand's most accomplished contemporary artists—often from earlier periods in the artists' careers—find their way into these stores, sometimes bought from private owners but just as frequently from the artists themselves. Further, during periods of financial stress or nonproductivity, some of Thailand's finest artists will not hesitate to use such shops as sources of income. At least six of the twenty-eight artists whose works appear in this catalogue have sold some of their work through tourist shops, and one artist regularly earns extra family funds through them by selling under his own signature the work of his older children.

The existence of these shops represents a paradox for most of Thailand's better contemporary artists. On the one hand, most do not want to display their work in such an aesthetically indiscriminate, crassly commercial environment—particularly one in which they have no knowledge or control over how much the shop owner has profited from their skills. They also feel deprived of any contact with the party who bought their work, and the aesthetic or cultural reasons for the sale. Thus, the simple circumstances of purchase deny them all opportunity for critical feedback from those most interested in their work. Too, most realize that the distinctive nature of their art is not likely to appeal to the souvenir-oriented interests and budgets of the majority of tourists. On the other hand, these artists also know that, despite their bazaar-like ambience, tourist shops serve as convenient conduits to an international world which has a rich and remunerative interest in the aesthetically different or exotic—which defines a large part of the commercial value of their own work. They realize that if tourist shops are not the most prestigious venues in which to show their work, they are certainly the most accessible—at least for casual or first-time buyers. And at least a few of these artists find something irresistible in the notion that using such shops can result in getting their works into homes and offices literally half the world away.

Commercial Art

As used here, "commercial art" is a residual category referring to those commercially produced items—photos, posters, commissioned works in a variety of materials—that Thai use to decorate the interior and exterior spaces of their homes, work places, hotels, restaurants, banks, and similar environments in order to make them visually more attractive or interesting. Certainly the contemporary integrative, classical, folk, and tourist arts are also used for ornamental purposes. However, the enhancement of a particular living or working space is usually not the defining feature of these other genres—at least from the point of view of the aesthetic conceptions that inspire them or their artists' purposes in creating them. The decorative purposes we are speaking of here have to do with objects specifically designed to contribute to the ambience or a particular space and the visual pleasure of those occupying it.

In the Euroamerican context decorative items are ordinarily given short shrift as "artistic" representations. However, in the Thai situation where ideas about the nature and functions of "art" are neither widely shared nor institutionalized, and where there is no clear consensus about matters of artistic excellence and taste, such commercial items loom large in people's conceptions of the "beautiful." Equally important, because many Thai draw little or no aesthetic distinction between commercially produced art and the other artistic genres, commercial art genuinely dominates the artistic market place—not only in the quantitative and financial sense, but also in setting standards of aesthetic fashion and acceptability. In the broad scale of Thai society, commercial art may not represent the most creative, elegant, or imaginative art forms, but it certainly represents the most popular.

Primary among these decorative forms is the photograph—principally of family members and important personages. In fact, family photographs—which are ritually necessary for domestic altars and cremation books[3]—represent the single most widely used decorative item in Thailand. Even the poorest peasant household will have a series of small, ID-type photos of each family member pinned to a wall of their home. Considerably more elegant are the novelty photographic portraits of family members dressed in-turn-of-the-century Western garb that have recently become very popular among elite and middle class Thai families as symbols of Thai grace and sophistication. The clothes and attitudes shown in these portraits are almost identical to those shown in photos of members of the royal family during the reign of King Chulalongkorn (1868–1910), and although the modern portraits are meant to be amusing, they are also meant to convey the family's identification with this golden era of Thai history. (A similar sentiment is expressed in the paintings of Arunothai Somsakul. See plates 25–27.)

More widespread and less costly than these novelty family photos are the sepia colored photographs of King Chulalongkorn and members of his royal family. In fact, framed versions of these likenesses represent the single most frequently displayed photos in contemporary Thailand and, like Buddha images and the Thai flag, they have essentially become icons of Thai culture. Many homes, shops, and offices also contain photographs and paintings of King Bhumibol Adulyadej, the current monarch, and of other members of the current royal family, particularly the Crown Princess, but they are greatly outnumbered, perhaps as much as two-to-one, by the photos of the king's grandfather. A few commentators believe there is some kind of oblique political message in this kind of distribution, but sellers and buyers

---

3. Virtually every Thai home has a family altar, usually located adjacent to the head-of-household's sleeping area, on which there is a Buddha image, photos of recently deceased family members, and sometimes receptacles containing the ashes of these persons. "Cremation books" refer to a wide variety of books, honoring the deceased, that are distributed to guests attending a funeral. The books typically contain poetry, favored sections of the Buddhist canon, and photos, a biography, and eulogies to the deceased.

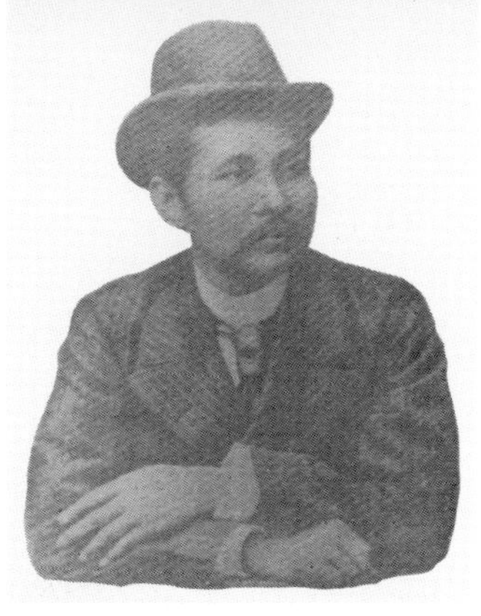

Figure 23.
A turn-of-the-century photo of King Chulalongkorn, dressed in Western garb.

say that the popularity of the Chulalongkorn photos is a result of their antique qualities, the fact that they were the first widely available photos of any Thai monarch, that they portray a king who was a handsome and endearing man, and that he was the king who most clearly embodied the glory of the nation's past and its readiness to adapt to the modern international world. While obviously serving patriotic motives, the photos are evocative expressions of a time now seen as the most cultivated and elegant period in Thai history. To display such photos in one's home or workplace is to partake, however derivatively, in that elegance.

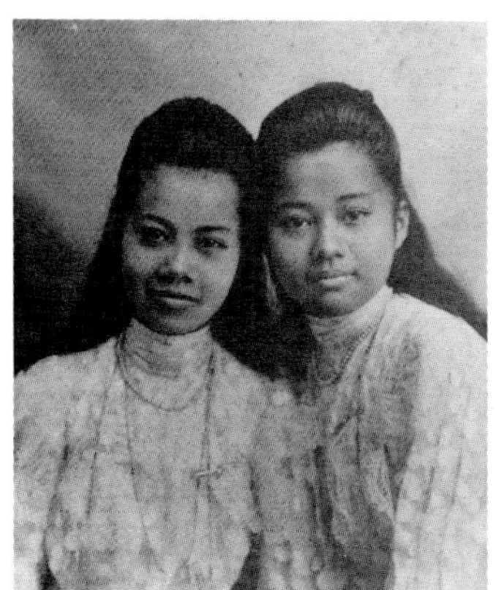

Figure 24.
Princess Malini Nopadara and Princess Nipha Nophadol, daughters of King Chulalongkorn, wearing Western hairstyles and blouses, circa 1907.

Different from these photographic materials are the posters, fabrics, wooden and metal inlays and carvings, mosaic designs and portraits, logos, and personal colors that comprise some of the major elements of the world of Thai interior decoration. Two of these merit special attention. First, the creation of logos—for firms, governmental departments, private and public organizations, as well as individuals—is a major focus of Thai decorative activity. Because they are permanent symbols of one's corporate or personal distinctiveness, an immense amount of time and attention is devoted to their design. Over and above their aesthetic qualities, many are ritually meaningful—and some even ritually powerful—and consequently are integrated into the design of one's working or living space in ritually determined ways. They are also widely used on the banners, vehicles, stationery, invitations, publications, and almost any other surface which might be used to express publicly the identity—and implicitly, the power—of the individual or his institution.

Thai colors have similar attributes, although they are linked primarily to individuals rather than to organizations and institutions. Unlike their use in the United States and Europe, colors are defined not only in terms of their decorative and cosmetic value, but also in terms of their cosmological significance. Thus, the distinctive colors that many Thai take on—in their choice of clothes, decorative fabrics, wall colors, art works—are a function not only of personal preference but also of supernatural factors (the person's hour or date of birth, unanticipated or unexplained life-cycle events) with which those individuals are indelibly identified and which the colors are believed to symbolize. Although not all Thai have such color consciousness, they understand its significance to those who do. Too, they assume that although the decorative and cosmological attributes of colors are mutually reinforcing, the latter always has priority in the individual's aesthetic selections.

Finally, there has emerged in recent years considerable interest in what, for the lack of a better term, might be called "Thai Hallmark card art"—gentle landscapes, still lives, and paintings of familiar house-hold collectibles like bencharong pottery, antique Thai vanities, and other items expressive of elite feminine interests (see figures 25 and 26). Although the subject matter of this art covers a tremendous range, almost all of it is designed to be muted in color, unobtrusive in tone, and capable of blending into almost any domestic or working environment. Some of this art, particularly the landscapes, has found its way into bank lobbies and hotel rooms to become, like visual equivalents of Muzak, the most familar decorative forms of commercial Thailand.

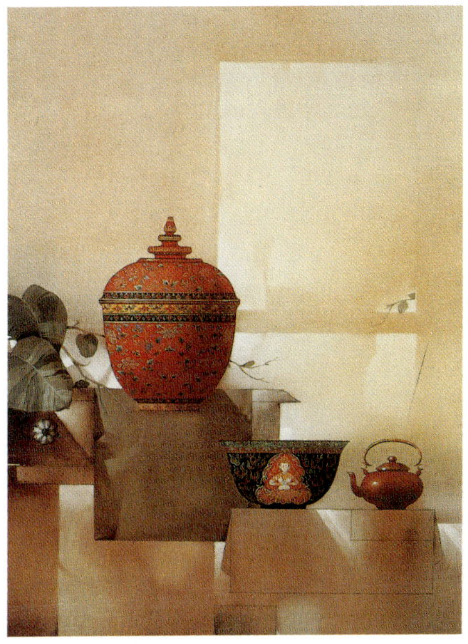

In contrast to contemporary integrative art—which is designed to stimulate, educate, and provide new meanings—this "Hallmark" art is meant to be sentimental and essentially soporific. It is perceived as helping to make the environment in which it is located a retreat or haven from the chaos of the real, contemporary world, primarily by displaying tokens of a time and place (or perhaps only a state of mind) that is felt to be more simple and stable.

For all of its popularity, commercial art is really not an alternative to contemporary creative art. The people who buy commercial art are much more interested in its decorative values than in the issues of aesthetic power or cultural meaning which preoccupy contemporary integrative artists. With the exception of persons like Uab (see figures 25 and 26) and Chakrabhand (see figures 8 and 9), who over the years have become society artists, few commercial artists are identifiable by name or are otherwise acknowledged for their skill or originality. Too, commercial art is recognized by both decorators and buyers as intrinsically ephemeral: the notion that such work could be sustainably stimulating or interesting, that one might wish to "collect" it, or that it might over time increase in value as a result of the artist's developing stature is foreign to its nature. It represents a genre that creates a relaxed ambience and that is pleasant to glance at, but as "art" it is an inherently transient, peripheral phenomenon.

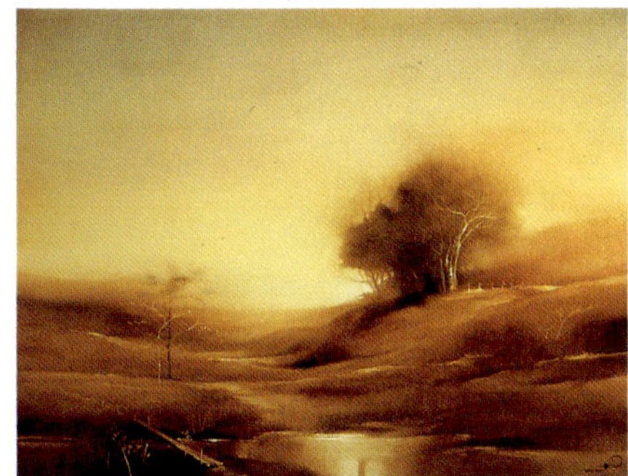

Figure 25 and 26. Two examples of "Hallmark"-type decorative art by Uab Sanasen, one of Thailand's most celebrated commercial artists. "Bencharong," above (oil on canvas, 23.75"x31.5", 1982) portrays a ceramic tradition, adapted from the Chinese, which over the years has become a symbol of Thai elegance and skill. Thai decorators consider landscapes such as Uab's (oil on canvas, 23.75"x31.5", 1985) to be among the most versatile of decorative items.

THREE:
THE ART COMMUNITY

Social Process and Family Influence

To be an artist in Thailand is to participate in a long and complex social process. Thus, irrespective of one's artistic talents, one must—from almost the very beginning—become involved in a web of social relationships that will shape the direction of one's career. In conducting the research that resulted in this exhibition, the investigators collected detailed life-histories of all the artists whose works are shown here. The vast majority of these persons report that while their artistic skills began to emerge at an early age (sometimes as young as three or four years old), they each had the support of some significant adult—a family friend, a teacher, a monk, an older sibling—who actively encouraged their rather special skills. These adults were especially important when, a few years later (typically between the ages of twelve to sixteen), the aspiring artist applied to be admitted to art school, or to be apprenticed to a senior artist, and arrangements had to be made for the long-term costs of room, board, and tuition. Since few artists had either wealthy or supportive parents, some kind of external sponsor or liaison to a government scholarship had to be found.

Upon entry to art school, and later the university, the artist began in earnest that excruciating balancing act between being a loyal, obedient, and conforming student on the one hand and an innovative and perhaps even daring one on the other. Later, the stakes would get higher when the student began to participate in campus and national art competitions, and perceived the possibility of being recommended to study overseas—but again, only if he or she had endorsements from influential teachers. Too, for all of its excitement and experience-expanding possibilities, overseas study also involved the reality of enduring long months of loneliness and confusion—particularly if one were serious about relating the artistic heritage of the world to one's own Thai traditions. And still later, upon one's return to Thailand, one had to cultivate gallery owners, fellow artists, and clients to determine what would or would not sell in Bangkok[4] and how such realities traded off against one's own artistic passions and abilities.

---

4. With a population of more than 7,000,000 people, Bangkok is the focal point of virtually all artistic activity in Thailand. (Cholburi, the kingdom's second largest city, has a population of only 180,000.) The capital contains most of the nation's art galleries, exhibition halls, and art schools, and it is where most Thai artists and collectors live. Chiengmai and Chiengrai in the North have rich artistic traditions and a disproportionately high number of the kingdom's finest artists are born and reared there, but the majority of these Northern artists eventually settle in or near Bangkok.

Too, to establish oneself as a creative artist one had to develop an array of non-artistic talents. One had to have a clear conception of the nature, power, and uniqueness of one's art, and one had to be able to speak about it—or find somebody else to speak about it—in an articulate way. In fact, a readiness to explain or justify one's artistic vision, and the capacity for self-awareness that underlies it, characterizes almost every artist we encountered. (Of course, a few artists dissemble outrageously in their after-the-fact explanations of their aesthetic intentions while others have difficulty in clarifying the subtleties of their representations. But all seem to have a coherent intellectual position about the thrust and overall purpose of their work—a position that in all cases is intimately linked to some of the most cherished values of Thai culture.) Additionally, to be successful at one's calling one had to develop the interpersonal skills that would enable one to negotiate with patrons, gallery owners, critics, publishers and the printers of one's brochures and posters—or at least find persons who would serve as agents to such parties.

While such considerations may characterize the nature of the artist's experience almost everywhere, they are nevertheless for Thai artists central elements of their professional identities. In fact, most Thai artists are convinced that these kinds of non-aesthetic factors are just as important as the quality of their artistic talent in determining the trajectories of their careers. Some of this attitude undoubtedly derives from the fact that it is simply not easy to become a successful artist in Thailand, and those who have done so have overcome formidable social and cultural obstacles.

The obstacles are in fact multiple. Despite Thailand's two-thousand year old artistic tradition, being an artist in Thailand is neither a high-status nor a well-rewarded profession—at least in terms of such standard Thai rewards as money and power. A few artists are famous, and a few have become wealthy through their art. Many are also well-travelled and, although it may take a lifetime, a few have even been honored. Those who are teachers are also not without a modicum of power, or at least influence, over their students. But despite the spirit of empowerment that Bhirasri, decades earlier, tried to impart to them, artists are seen by most members of Thai society as craftspersons in the service of others. To face the reality of being in the service of others—particularly in the contemporary art world where one must be a servant who does creative and original things—requires considerable love of one's work, as well as a generous measure of self-confidence.

The sense of overcoming obstacles begins at an early age. We earlier noted that most artists report having an adult in their childhood who encouraged them in the pursuit of their artistic interests. But the supportive adult was rarely the artist's father, mother, or primary caretaker. In fact, parental attitudes toward their child's somewhat peculiar interest ranged from indifference (tinged with the sense that "he'll grow out of it") to downright hostility (particularly at that point when the child announced that he or she wanted to go to art school). Too, the child's intentions often resulted in parental conflict, typically with the father obdurate in his objections ("How can he make a living being a painter?") and the mother willing to defer to her child's wishes ("But he has won a government scholarship.")

There are of course always cases with special circumstances: one of Thailand's more respected integrative artists has a history of mental problems and is also the son of a Thai general. The father saw his son's interest in art as a way both to deal with his episodic breakdowns and as a means to do something valuable with his life, and he has supported his son, psychologically and often financially, over the course of his career. Family circumstances can also take a very different form: Misiem Yipintsoi was born to an elite Indonesian-Chinese merchant family that had earlier moved to Thailand, and led an uneventful upper-class life until one of her own daughters came down with polio. She and her child then travelled to Europe where they searched in vain for a modern medical cure, but where Misiem also had her first encounter with art, in the homes of family friends and in the museums of England and the Continent. On her return to Bangkok, she took up painting at the age of 42, and over the next four decades developed into one of Thailand's most prolific artists—the bulk of her work being done in sculpture. She is currently the only Thai artist to have her work in the permanent collection of New York's Museum of Modern Art.

Of course, few Thai artists have the advantages of such elite backgrounds. The majority are children of farmers or fruit and vegetable gardeners. Those who come from Sino-Thai backgrounds are typically children of urban or provincial merchants or functionaries (clerks, accountants) in larger firms. Beyond that there is a broad range: a few are children of schoolteachers or lower level Thai bureaucrats; one is an orphan; one is the son of an army officer father and a shaman mother; another the son of a village silver worker; yet another the son of a famous local wood carver. The father of one artist is a deep-sea diver for the Thai Navy, who, with the other men in the family, also carves vegetables in his spare time for use in cremation rituals.

The point that must be made is that most Thai artists come from unexceptional families. For the most part, their parents are neither poverty-stricken nor well-educated. Even those whose parents have been folk artists hesitate to allow their children to be modern artists, if only because they cannot understand the practicality of such an occupation: while they know, for instance, that people pay good money for silver jewelry and wood carvings, they have never known anybody to pay anything for a modern painting. It is not until much later, when a child sells his work at a National Gallery exhibition or writes home from London, that a parent may become reconciled to the child's occupational choice.

However, it must also be said that if artists' families are unexceptional in a status or occupational sense, they are also families which seem richly steeped in Thai culture, folk wisdom, and religion. In our interviews, artists frequently alluded to parents who kept books and magazines (luxury items in a peasant household) in the home, who enjoyed telling tales and stories, who knew their Buddhism and their cultural myths and taught them to their children, and who dealt with their children in an attentive and companionable way. If the artists' reports are to be trusted (and most Thai ordinarily do not discuss such things) their parents were people who actively stimulated their curiosity and imagination as an integral part of their growing up.

This type of environment perhaps laid the foundation for the kind of self-direction and resilience that artistic activity requires—an activity that, while admirable, is also regarded by fellow Thai with uncertainty and wariness. In fact, perhaps the most widely shared public perception of artists is that—like folk theatre (*likee*) performers, shamans, and fortune tellers—they are among the more unorthodox members of Thai society. To be sure, there are numerous artists who are seen as thoroughly ordinary in their demeanor, dress, and compliant responsiveness to others. But many more artists are viewed as individualists who always do what they want to do rather than what they have agreed to do. More importantly, unlike ordinary people (but like shamans and seers) they are perceived as individuals with secret talents. The fact that they work completely alone, with materials that others can neither handle nor understand, and are driven to create things that have never before been made or seen, also does not help public understanding. For many Thai, there is something suspicious, but also quite marvelous, about such behavior.

Some artists enjoy building upon these public images, and over the years they develop distinctive personae of their artistic temperaments. These personae serve, on the one hand, to mark their eccentricities, but on the other, to define and amplify the value of their contributions. Thus, although he is a man of many parts, Thawan Duchanee (see plates 7, 8, 33, and 34) has no hesitation to have himself displayed in Thai socialite magazines as a caveman dressed in wild animal skins surrounded by the skulls of the cobras and bobcats he keeps in his Bangkok home—all of which helps to reinforce the expression of his deeply held views on the oneness of humans and beasts. Prateung Emjaroen (see plates 6, 35, 36, and 40) is more muted in his public imagery, but he and and his spouse try to make sure that almost everything written about him speaks of his preoccupation with the beauty of nature, his current Garden of Eden lifestyle, and his personal struggle to achieve that state. Angkarn Kalayaanapongse (see plates 4, 30, and 32), now officially recognized as one of the kingdom's greatest living artists, was in his younger years strongly influenced by Bhirasri's notions of the bohemian life of European artists. One consequence of Angkarn's bohemian passion was to get himself expelled from Silpakorn University when, in a moment of personal pique, he used fecal matter instead of paint on a Silpakorn ceiling mural. During the same period, he also created the first and most productive artists' commune in the nation's history. Currently at the apex of his career as both artist and poet, he lives in a home where the walls are completely covered by pencil sketches by his young daughter and thousands of books are stacked in middens all over the house.

The Education of Thai Artists

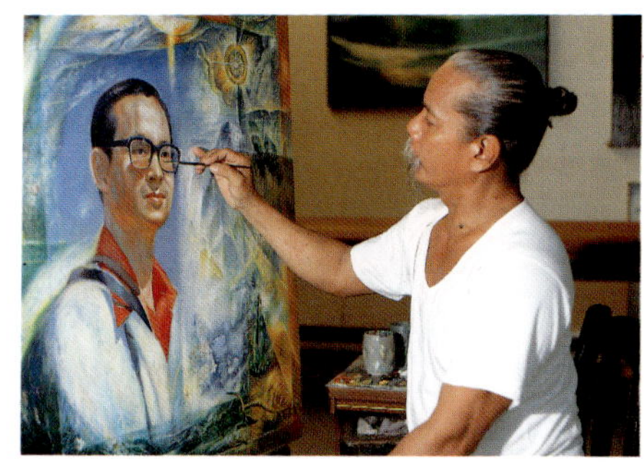

Figure 27. Prateung Emjaroen at work on a portrait of King Bhumiphol Adulyadej.

Every artist included in this exhibition received some form of art education. Prateung Emjaroen is often considered by some of his peers to be "self-taught," but in reality he underwent a long apprenticeship as a painter of movie posters, and after turning to creative art, studied with several established artists on a part-time basis. Misiem Yipintsoi also did not attend art school, but she studied privately with Bhirasri for a few years and worked with some foreign artists who lived in Bangkok for varying periods. Although formal art training tells us little about the talent of an artist, it seen by members of the art community as providing the individual artist with a basis of professional respectability.

Thailand has six major art schools, five of which are located in or near Bangkok. Two of these—Poh Chang (the College of Arts and Crafts) and Chang Sil (the College of Fine Arts)—have traditionally provided the equivalent of a high school art education, but Poh Chang has recently been upgraded and now also confers an Associate of Arts degree. Established in 1913, only a year after the creation of Thailand's first university, Poh Chang is the oldest formal art academy in the kingdom. Chang Sil was created in 1933, in part to reflect the European interests of Corrado Feroci, but has also offered training in classical Thai dance, drama, and music. The typical pattern of most aspiring artists is to gain government scholarships or independent financial sponsorship to attend one of these schools as a teen-ager, and having demonstrated ability, to gain admission to one of the universities for more advanced programs. Thus, artists as varied as Chalood Nimsamer, Chamreung Vichienket, Thawan Duchanee, Sawat Tantisuk, Kamol Tassananchalee, Chalermchai Kositpipat, and Damrong Wong-Uparaj all began their formal art education at Poh Chang.

Among the universities, Chulalongkorn and Chiengmai Universities and the Prasarnmitr campus of Srinakharinwirot University each have highly visible programs leading to the B.F.A. and M.F.A. degree. Students admitted to these programs typically enroll in these art departments as undergraduate majors and may or may not go on to professional artistic careers. However, virtually all of the faculty are professional artists. Among these three schools, Chulaklongkorn University, the kingdom's premier university, is unique in requiring all of its art faculty to have M.F.A.'s or Ph.D.'s from abroad, and consequently places great stress on teaching Euroamerican artistic traditions. Chiengmai, founded in the early 1950's, has an extremely active program in the artistic traditions of Northern Thailand, and consequently their teaching of contemporary art is imbued with influences from the folk, music, and dance traditions of the Northern region. Prasarnmitr, although the smallest university art program in the kingdom, is one of the most experimental.

The most comprehensive and influential art training program in the nation is at Silpakorn (the Fine Arts) University. Founded in 1943, in part through the efforts of Feroci, Silpakorn has over the past half century developed into a general liberal arts university with the original campus located next to the Grand Palace in Bangkok and a second campus in Nakorn Pathom, 55 km. to the south. In addition to teaching the history and practice of every branch of the visual arts, Silpakorn also has extensive programs in archaeology, architecture, history, and European languages and literature. One measure of the university's impact on contemporary art is the fact that almost 80% of the artists included in this exhibit attended Silpakorn.

Whatever school they may have attended, certain features of the educational experience are shared by almost all art students, and are integral to their self-image as artists. First, a central part of their vocational identity is that they have been well prepared in the technical fundamentals of their profession, particularly in subjects such as anatomy and composition. This view is expressed especially strongly by artists who later studied abroad and feel that their initial education in Thailand was superior to that of their foreign peers—some even claiming that they encountered few skills overseas that they did not already know. However, these artists also acknowledge that the foreign experience was profoundly mind-expanding, providing them with direct access to a vast artistic tradition—including museums, galleries, and publications—that before they had known only in a secondhand way, and to an artistic culture driven by the values of exploration, innovation, and criticism.

Second, the relationship that most students have with their teachers is essentially one of master (or mistress) and disciple. Students deal with their instructors with unwavering respect, obedience, and even an attitude of awe, while teachers—at least proper ones—reciprocate with a spirit of unconditional patronage. In the incessant competition that characterizes the Thai art world—for prizes, sales, fame, and influence—the reciprocal support that teachers and students accord each other is sometimes almost embarrassingly blatant. Thus, art teachers who are judges in university or national competitions are expected to select their own students as winners (sometimes year after year), and students are expected to campaign for their teachers in the perennial conflicts that arise over university budgetary allocations or the creation and reorganization of art programs. Occasionally these conflicts and the coalitions that form around them take on a life of their own. Thus, three decades after his death, the students of Feroci (Silpa Bhirasri) still disagree over the legitimacy of his successors, and several generations of their own students continue to do battle against each other.

Whether through this kind of carefully crafted socialization or through influences from their classical past, almost all Thai artists learn the obligation to pass on their knowledge and skills to others. For many this takes the form of becoming art professors themselves. However, among those who make their living solely through the sale of their creative work, there is also a compulsion to teach their craft to others. Thus, Thawan Duchanee freely instructs novice artists in programs organized periodically through university extension programs, and Prateung Emjaroen, himself a product of such training, has long had a coterie of disciples whose work he freely guides. Angkarn Kalayaanapongse's "artist's commune," cited earlier, was also shaped by such non-profit motives. Sometimes the very nature of the artistic task requires long-term teaching obligations, such as when Panya Vijinthanasarn and Chalermchai Kositpipat undertook, without salary or commission, the design and painting of the dramatically modern wall murals at the Thai Buddhist temple at Wimbledon, England, and for a four-year period were completely dependent upon the assistance of nine student artists—all of whom also worked only for room and board. Other than the training they received and the experience of living in England, their sole reward for this commitment was the Buddhist merit that they each accumulated.

Third, in accord with a widespread cultural pattern, the classmate relationships that students initiate with each other at their art schools and universities are considered among the most significant relationships of their professional lives: it is these ties which over time become memberships in *klum,* the mutual support groups that loom so large in the lives of artists. It is within their respective *klum* that artists join together to exhibit their work, form pressure groups for and against certain critics or dealers, receive friendly criticism of their most recent work, gain financial assistance during times of difficulty, or simply join together for a dinner or party. Klum memberships are rarely permanent, and *klum* comprised of classmates are often supplanted by considerations of geographical origin, artistic skill, access to wealthy collectors, or other such factors. However, having attended university or art school together, or having studied under the same instructor at different times, provides an inherent legitimacy to any *klum* affiliation.

Most *klum* rarely have more than 8–12 active members, although each of these persons can usually draw on a much larger pool if the occasion arises, such as a collective need to protest a political attack against one of the *klum*'s members or the putative misrepresentations of an unfriendly critic. Most *klum* are voluntary associations of peers, with leadership typically going to the oldest member of the group or to members with special artistic, rhetorical, or organizational skills.

Some artists avoid *klum* affiliations, if only to assert their artistic independence. Others avoid *klum* pressures in order to be free of the inevitable conflicts that arise between friendship obligations on the one hand and judgments of artistic excellence on the other—although it must be said that when caught in such conflicts, most Thai artists opt for maintaining the strength of their personal ties. In preparing this exhibit, the curators were repeatedly approached by artists urging us to exhibit the work of their classmates or to reject works that they or their classmates considered to be unacceptable. Such is the moral leverage that artists assign to the classmate relationship.

Figure 28 to 31.
Four Facets of an Artist's Work

The works of Thongchai Rakpathum represent the artistic range of contemporary Thai artists. The classical painting on the top left (oil, 38"x25") was a student work completed in 1962. Just six years later, Thongchai won the silver medal in Thailand's 1968 National Exhibition with his abstract vision (top right, tempera, 44"x30") of the nature of chaos and order. From 1973 to 1976, he spent three years in Rome, where, working in pastels (bottom right, 26"x19") he discovered that the skin tones of Europeans reflect color very differently than the skin tones of Thai. On the bottom left, his 1986 watercolor, "Windy Day on Cholburi Beach" (14.5"x22") returns to the theme of chaos and order, here as natural phenomena.

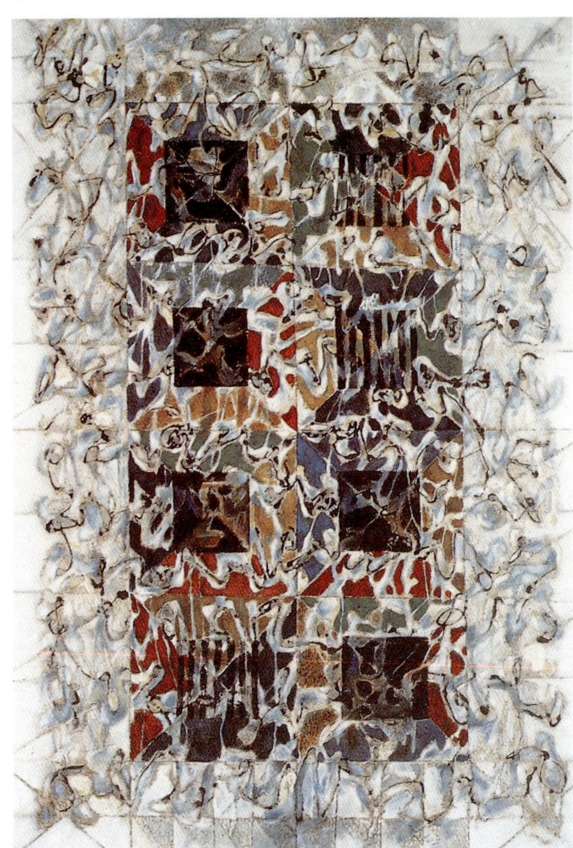

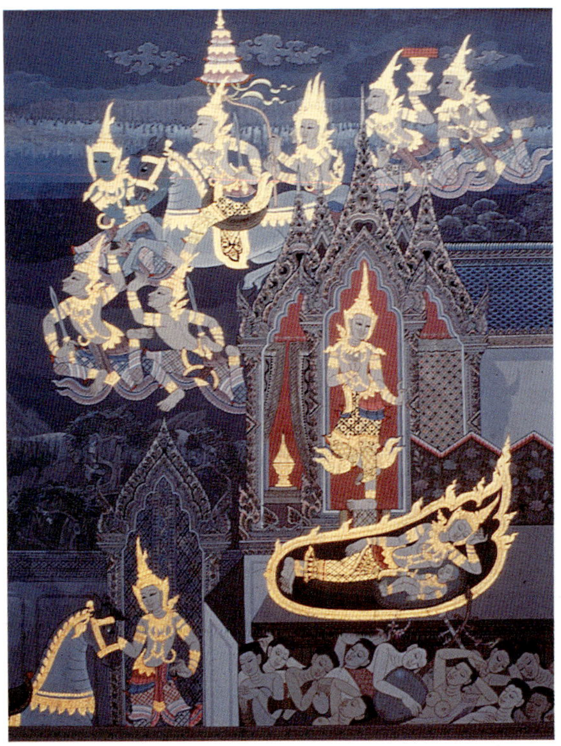

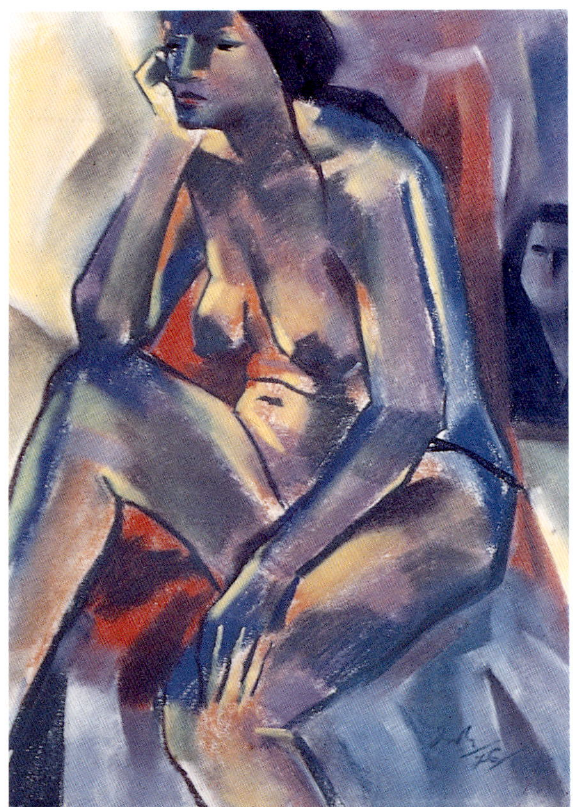

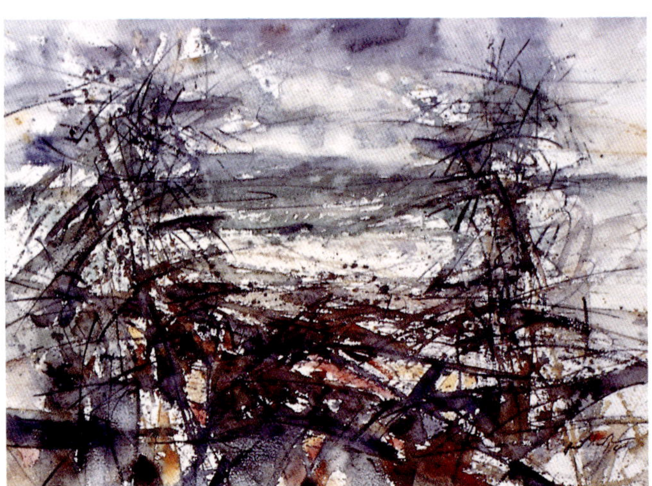

Thai Art Publics

Despite its institutionalized nature—its art schools, galleries, the attention it receives from the media—contemporary Thai art is neither a mass phenomenon nor even a highly public one. Most art exhibitions, both in museums and private galleries, are rarely installed for more than two weeks, and most collectors—governmental as well as corporate and private—perceive their purchases as mainly for their private pleasure rather than for the commonweal. Art is not even widely available in the form of inexpensive, commercially produced posters and prints, although public exhibitions frequently do sell posters of work by featured artist or artists during the course of the exhibition.

Nevertheless, Thailand does have a highly viable art community—those people who, for many different reasons, are involved with art in many different ways. While it is impossible to calibrate all of these variations, they seem to fall into three general modalities.

Out on the periphery are people—perhaps 75,000, perhaps as many as 300,000—who may read the occasional art columns appearing in *Matichorn* and *Siam Rath Sabadaa Wicaan,* the nation's two most respected weeklies, or who may be fascinated by the presentations of individual artists appearing on the television program *Nyng Naj Rauauj* (*One In A Hundred,* meaning the most accomplished representatives of various professions—artists, classical dancers, prize fighters, physicians). If their English is sufficient, these persons may also read the detailed reviews of newly opened art exhibitions that appear regularly in the English language dailies, the *Nation* and *Bangkok Post.* (Reviews in the latter are currently written by a professional art historian.) Since these newspapers also publish weekly calendars which list the art installations at Bangkok's five public galleries, at major hotels and malls, and at the principal private galleries, readers may also consider dropping in at one or more of these exhibits—always calculating the likely nature of Bangkok traffic and their proximity to the venue at the hour they hope to visit. Many of these people will also calculate whether they would feel welcome at these venues. Virtually anybody, dressed in any manner, would feel free to enter the exhibition halls at Silpakorn University or the National Gallery, but in the class-conscious environment of Bangkok many would think twice before venturing into the Dusit Thani hotel or the Gallerie Lafayette shopping mall.

These persons might dress up their walls at home or workplace with photos from the free art calendars that various corporations and public agencies distribute as gifts. Some might also cut out and mount the photos of art works reproduced in the Thai Airways cabin magazine, *Sawadee,* which regularly runs stories on contemporary artists. Although there are no shops that sell Thai art posters or prints, some of these individuals might regularly make the rounds of exhibitions in search of posters and catalogues that are on sale during the tenure of an exhibit.

Whether people on this outer-periphery would actually buy an original art work is quite another matter. Contemporary art—the nature of its value and the standards applied to it—is for most members of the public still so fundamentally inchoate that it takes a certain confidence, passion, or eccentricity to commit oneself to investing money in it, even a modest amount. Equally important, it takes time and effort to find personally meaningful, or economically rewarding, art works. One of our most frequent experiences in conducting the research upon which this exhibition is based was being approached by individuals, often well-educated and well-off, who had heard about our research and wanted advice on where and how to buy art, who the "best artists" were, what kinds of standards to use and questions to ask, and how to judge the value of various works. Art seem to be perceived by them as something good and pleasurable, but also as something alien and nonrational. Like novice gamblers, they wanted to try their hand at the new game, but did not know quite how.

Somewhat closer to the center of the Thai art world is another population of indeterminate size—perhaps 20,000 to 75,000 people—who are much more constant in the time and attention they give to artistic activities. They are persons who read, and may subscribe to, magazines like *Silpa-Wattanatham* (*Art & Culture*) and the English language decorator and society magazine, *Living in Thailand.* Many of these persons are likely to be students or graduates of one of the kingdom's art schools, or have taken courses in art or art history while studying abroad. Others may be employees of or otherwise connected to the Department of Fine Arts or the National Identity Board, the government agencies charged with preserving and celebrating officially favored aesthetic activities. Other members of this population may be employed in art-related industries like architectural and interior design, advertising, and tourism—especially tourist activities concerned with the glorification of the the Kingdom's historical and aesthetic achievements. Some might also be among or related to the approximately 300 teachers a year who take special courses qualifying them to teach art in Thai public schools. However, the most significant element of this population is made up of those persons—most of them women—who consider themselves, and want to be considered by others, to be *phuu dii*—people of cultivation, manners, and taste. For them, the possession and appreciation of Thai art and artifacts is symbolically essential.

It is these persons who most frequently attend art exhibitions, lectures, and auctions; who know the details of and enjoy visiting archaeological sites (some on group-charted buses or with domestic tourist groups); who travel to villages famous for their weaving, ceramics, or silverwork; and who attend festivals in honor of members of the royal family that celebrate the arts of certain regions or ethnic groups. However, *phuu dii* are not unified in their aesthetic preferences. Those who are older, particularly older women, are more interested in the inherently conservative forms of Thai classical, folk, and decorative art than in contemporary integrative art. By the same token, they also prefer the art of people whom they do not know or from whom they can maintain some social distance. Some Thai suggest that the *phuu dii* who prefer the conservative genres—avoiding, or even disdaining, contemporary art—do so because they perceive contemporary artists to be undisciplined, eccentric, or inherently anti-establishment. However, there are other members of this elite—men, younger women, and those who identify with international values and Thai versions of post-modernism—who much prefer the eclectic and synthesizing features of contemporary integrative art or even the culturally alien modernism of the Euroamerican world. Sometimes consciously, but more frequently unconsciously, they identify with the freedom, boldness, and spirit of experimentation that so clearly distinguishes contemporary work. Also, they are curious about the artists as persons and and are intent on knowing the meanings of their artistic creations. Most importantly, they perceive their commitments to contemporary art as expressions of their own cosmopolitan self-image.

In contrast to those who live with photos or posters, persons in this population typically insist upon owning original art works, and are guided by both budgetary and decorative constraints in their selections. Some often buy art on approval or on an exchange basis so that they can determine its appropriateness to their home or work environments. If they are wealthy, they may well use an interior decorator and buy a range of works by a variety of artists, in part to demonstrate their liberality and worldliness. Many, particularly businessmen, are keenly aware of the prestige value of displaying "a Thawan" or "an Angkarn" on one of their office walls—often with knowledge of the place of the work in the history of Thawan's or Angkarn's career.

The aesthetic sophistication of the collectors in this middle group is varied. Some have been educated in the history of art and are preoccupied with styles, originality, and the formal features of works (line, color, balance, composition). However, the majority are much more interested in subject matter and require that their works be attractive, amusing, or didactic. They appreciate a subject that is visually or cognitively provocative, so long as it is not unpleasant. Such viewers expect that their art will engage them in an environmentally friendly way, but that, as cynosures of an environment that they have created, these works will not reproach them on the inadequacies of the human experience. It is precisely for these kinds of reasons that the more lurid work of Thawan Duchanee, while tantalizing to many Thai intellectuals, is not easily accepted in the home by their wives and children. Too, many of the collectors in this middle group use the traditional Thai standard of judging a work primarily in terms of its *raa-la-iad* qualities—the fineness, detail, delicacy, and intricacy of its lines and composition—all of which is to them *prima facie* evidence of the time and labor that the artist has given to his work.

Finally, there is a third group, comprising at least 5,000 and perhaps as many as 20,000 persons, who are at the center of the contemporary Thai art world and who represent its principal actors. They are the individuals and organizations who give time, attention, funds, and a relatively constant commitment to the pursuit of their aesthetic or cultural interests. Included in this group are the artists themselves and their teachers, colleagues, and students, major collectors and their families and business associates, museum and gallery owners and personnel, and critics. Associated with this group is a number of foreigners—some with an intimate knowledge of Thailand or of Buddhism, and others who are simply steeped in art—who buy the very finest Thai art to add to their own collections, often as long-term investments. Some are dealers and collectors who regularly travel the globe in order to buy Third and Fourth World art, perceiving it as the last frontier of high quality, but still inexpensive, 20th century art. (See Graburn 1976 for the definitive discussion of Fourth World art.)

The Center of the Contemporary Art World

The twenty-eight artists whose works are included in this exhibition are drawn from a population of approximately three hundred and fifty persons who define themselves as working, contemporary Thai artists.[5] It is impossible to determine what proportion of this population makes their living exclusively or partially from their contemporary art or what proportion also makes their living from classical, folk, tourist, and commercial work. However, it is clear that the members of this larger group serve the aesthetic and decorative needs of thousands of clients and, like the smaller number of more distinguished artists, represent a broad range of talents and styles.

At the same time, they also represent a central element of the art public itself, in that significant numbers of them always show up at exhibition openings (as supporters, but sometimes as detractors, of the featured artists), are students or teachers of the exhibitors, and are certainly among the most highly informed members of the viewing public. Some are *klum* associates or opponents of those who are exhibiting, and may serve as informants to critics reviewing the exhibits, or may be critics themselves. On occasion, some of these artists may buy a colleague's work—perhaps by paying for it, but usually by bartering one of their own works. Most importantly, through their word-of-mouth assessments of the kinds of work being done, and because their own work always represents a palpable alternative to what is being exhibited, priced, and perhaps sold, they have considerable influence in defining the nature and parameters of the art world.

Together with the artists themselves, the most critical participants in the Thai art world are the collectors and such go-between institutions as dealers, galleries, and museums. The relationships between

---

5. This figure is an extrapolation from the 1982 volume by Paothong, Piriya, and Pisanu which lists the identities and provides examples of the work of 296 individuals defined by the authors as "contemporary Thai artists." Given the inevitable flux—some of those persons have died or stopped working, others have taken their place—as well as the increasing public interest in art during the intervening years, the figure of three hundred and fifty artists seems a reasonable approximation for the current situation. Our own search for the identities of Thailand's "most distinguished living contemporary artists" used a peer selection procedure in which 88 persons were named at least twice by their own colleagues. The 28 artists included in the exhibit were among those most frequently identified by these 88 peers as "most distinguished," although some highly ranked individuals were not included in the exhibit on the grounds of their stylistic similarity to other artists, the unavailability of their better works for the exhibition, or the fact that they worked solely in the Euroamerican tradition or primarily in another genre. No effort was made to include or exclude artists on the grounds of ethnicity, gender, age, regional or class background, or any other socially discriminating standard, although such criteria may have influenced the decisions of some of the Thai artist judges.

these principals is not easy to characterize if only because they are always a function of a complex array of factors: the age and stature of the artist; whether the collector is new or established, a private individual or a corporate entity, indigenous or foreign; the collector's knowledge of art and/or his dependence upon expert advice; and the kinds of obligations that have been established between the artist, buyer, and go-between institution. Too, like most public phenomena in Thailand, the buying and selling of art—and ideas about the value of art itself—are extremely faddish, and what is true for one brief historical period may be irrelevant to the next. This is particularly true for large corporate collectors whose passions for or indifference to art may be at the whimsy of executive officers of the moment, or of the passing preferences of public relations directors or company designers.

The collecting of contemporary art really did not begin as a cultural movement until the early 1960's, and was a serendipitous result of the converging interests of six critical members of the Thai elite. (That all of these persons had spent considerable time in Europe or were foreigners themselves was clearly not fortuitous.) One was M.R. Khukrit Pramoj, publisher of the kingdom's most respected newspaper, the nation's leading intellectual (Phillips 1975: 345–346 and 1987:104–112), and a long-time collector of classical artifacts, who later was to become Prime Minister. Through his daily newspaper column, Khukrit began to comment on the emerging art movement, criticizing most artists as copyists of modern Western art, but approving and even buying the work of a few to hang in his sumptuous, classical style Thai home. Another was Princess Chumbhot of Nagara Svarg who opened her own park-like residence, Suan Pakkard Palace, to the public and who later provided the land for the Bhirasri Institute of Modern Art, Thailand's first contemporary art museum. A third was Dr. Puey Ungpakorn who, as Governor of the Bank of Thailand, the nation's national bank, instituted the bank's practice of regularly buying or commissioning art works for a permanent collection—a practice which became a model for the heavy institutional buying later pursued by Thailand's largest privately owned banks. There were also two foreign residents who were crucial to this process. One was Achille Clarac, who had been French Ambassador to Thailand for several years, and who through personal example and the local Alliance Française, stimulated members of the large international community to buy contemporary Thai works—a support function that was also taken on by the British Council and the Goethe Institute. The other was Darrell Berrigan, an expatriate American who published one of Thailand's two English language newspapers, and who unabashedly used the Sunday magazine section of his *Bangkok World* to publicize the works and lives of Thai artists. Most important to this entire process, however, was King Bhumiphol Adulyadej, who would occasionally make unannounced visits to group art exhibitions. Although the king assiduously avoided making any public purchases or public statements of approval of particular artists, his sheer presence at these events dramatically increased the public's awareness of the work of Thai artists and the desirability of patronizing them. Word also occasionally emerged from the Palace that the king was taking art lessons, and although he later turned his aesthetic interests to other matters (back to an earlier interest in playing and composing music) his personal involvement with the visual arts served to legitimize and enhance the entire value of the enterprise.

The role of these figures was principally to provide an impetus to the production and sale of modern art, and during the next few years the collection of such art did indeed become one of the most fashionable activities of the elite and international communities of Bangkok. Literally scores of art galleries opened to serve this newly-identified cultural need, and although the art-buying binge of the period soon simmered down and was transformed by the development of more discriminating artistic tastes on the one hand, and by the emergence of the tourist art industry on the other, it did serve to establish the aesthetic and economic viability of the contemporary movement. It is not surprising that much of the creative modern art of the 1960's—which focussed on depicting village life, canal activities, and the charms of a disappearing "old Bangkok"—became a major, if less imaginatively crafted, part of the tourist art of the 1970's and 1980's.

During the 1970's, corporate and organizational Thailand seemed to discover contemporary art. In 1975, the Bangkok Bank, the largest bank in Southeast Asia, instituted a program of art collection, the center of which was an annual art exhibition and competition which awarded a then-unheard of first prize of 50,000 baht (US$2,000). Motivated principally by public relations concerns, the program was the personal project of a high officer of the bank, Bunchoo Rojanasathien, and was justified on the basis of providing a constant flow of art that would eventually be displayed in the bank's numerous branch offices and that would be both educational and attractive to the bank's customers and staff. Although the purpose of the program has changed significantly since its inception, the bank continues to support the annual exhibition and contest, a weekly TV show that frequently shows the work of contemporary artists, and a music and art center in Bangkok which occasionally mounts public exhibitions.

A similar arts program was soon instituted by the bank's principal rival, The Thai Farmers Bank. However, because the founder of the latter, Bancha Lamsam, had a personal interest in art, the bank undertook the sponsorship of other art contests (e.g., one celebrating the king's birthday). Other financial institutions soon followed suit. The Thai Investment and Security Company (TISCO) has held no annual contests, but because of the personal interests of its president, Sivaporn Dardarananda, it has become the largest investor in and collector of contemporary art in Thailand, most of which has been displayed in the firm's offices in Bangkok's financial district. Some of the works have also been used in the company's advertising, and have been reproduced in a desk calendar regularly distributed to the firm's clients. Sivaporn typically visits as many as a dozen exhibitions a year and buys wherever his complex, but finely honed, artistic tastes take him. Similarly, the CEO's and high officers of virtually every other leading financial institution in the country have taken to buying at least a few works for display in their own or company offices. It is as if the purchase of contemporary art has over the years become one of the defining features of being a banker in Thailand.

Among non-banking organizations, *Thai Rath*, the nation's most widely circulated newspaper, became a major collector and contest sponsor, with a penchant for works by Sino-Thai artists. In the public sector, Chulalongkorn University has had a major continuing program in purchasing and displaying modern art, and for a period of time Thai Airways purchased numerous works for display in its various airport VIP lounges. Too, the Bank of Thailand has in recent years greatly expanded its collecting activities.

Several points must be made about the nature of this type of corporate and organizational collecting. First, with the exception of such persons as Sivaporn or Bancha, much of the art chosen by these institutions as contest winners or for direct purchase is the result of decisions made by committees of advisors—typically senior artists or art professors. This inevitably introduces a host of considerations relating to *klum* links, teacher-student obligations, and other strictly non-aesthetic criteria.

Second, although there are some corporate collectors who are explicitly motivated by investment considerations in their purchases and prizes—they all know about the dramatic increase in the value of world-class art during the 1980's—they are much more concerned with the public relations, public service, and self-image features of the collection process. For most of these organizations the amount of money given to art collection is a pittance of their total operating costs, and the prestige that redounds to them as art patrons—modern equivalents of the royalty and nobility who built the palaces of Thailand's past—is an extraordinary return for their modest expenditures.

Third, despite its public relations and cultural service justifications, most of this collecting activity has ultimately been for almost the exclusive use of those who have purchased the art. After Bunchoo resigned from the Bangkok Bank to go into Thai politics, most of the bank's art disappeared from its public areas and went into the private offices of its higher officials or became favored gift items from these officials to their clients and associates in the business world. Similarly, despite its continuous sponsorship of art contests, virtually all of the Thai Farmers Bank collection is installed in the executive office area of the bank's Bangkok headquarters—to be enjoyed by the executives and their guests, but denied to their ordinary customers and the vast majority of their staff. Even the Bank of Thailand has removed its best works from its public areas, and has installed them in the offices and corridor areas of their senior officials. While such behavior is very much in conformity with the traditional Thai practice of using public service interests for private purposes, it clearly runs counter to the rationale originally used to justify such expenditures. Chulalongkorn University and TISCO represent significant exceptions to this practice—in part because of the sheer quantity of their collections, but primarily because of their continuing commitment to creating stimulating working environments for their clients and staffs.

The role of museums, galleries, and exhibition halls is obviously quite central in all of this, if only because they exhibit the most recent work of Thai artists. It is through such exhibitions that corporate and individual collectors learn about new artistic developments and gain a comparative perspective on current and emergent trends. Further, collectors attend most exhibitions—even those installed at non-profit venues—on the clear expectation that all the works will be for sale. Because of the lack of a curatorial tradition and trained curators, there are almost no public exhibitions (other than student exhibits) that are concerned solely with educating the public or that organize contemporary Thai works in terms of periods or styles, unified aesthetic or cultural themes, or that even depend upon established collections or prior research. This is a strange omission because museums and universities regularly host travelling international exhibitions that are organized in precisely such terms and that attract large local audiences. Too, the notion is not alien to those museums that have been developing their own collections—obtained as gifts from private collectors or from exhibiting artists who have "paid" for exhibition space in the form of one of their unsold works.

Whatever the venue, most exhibitions are either one-person shows or are organized by a *klum* or other group whose members feel that they either have something in common ("Three Women Artists," "Four Northern Thai Artists") or that they complement one another ("Thailand's Fifteen Greatest Artists"). There are several groups ("The White," "The Vane," and "Art of Arts") that have established their own public identities and exhibit almost annually. Established artists typically do one-person shows or may join a group show as a favor to a friend, while up-and-coming artists do group shows, in part to benefit from sharing the costs of brochures, invitations, and opening receptions.

The choice of venues is always a function of a number of carefully calculated factors: availability and time of year;[6] the reputation, status, size, and attractiveness of the venue and how it treats its viewers; its accessibility to the public, including the nature of local foot traffic, surrounding street traffic, and availability of parking; the cost of the space, whether in terms of rental fees or gifts of art work; and the interest and cooperation of venue managers. Because the choice of venues often serves to define the artist's status in the art world and in society, artists weigh these various factors with extreme care. Installing one's exhibit at the Bhirasri Institute of Modern Art may add substantially to one's stature as an artist, but because of its impossible parking situation and lack of foot traffic it is not going to attract as many impulse viewers or buyers as would an installation in the River City Shopping Mall.

Exhibition venues fall into four general categories: publicly chartered museums and galleries; exhibition areas provided by foreign embassies; privately owned galleries; and temporary exhibition space rented from or operated by hotels or malls. The first three categories are especially critical to the maintenance of the art world as it is currently constituted.

6. March to May is "Hot Season" when schools are out and art buyers are most likely to be away on vacation.

At the present time, there are five publicly chartered venues: the National Gallery, Bhirasri Institute of Modern Art, the Art Gallery at Silpakorn University, the National Cultural Centre, and the Queen Sirikit Exposition Centre. Each has its own special position in the Thai art world.

The National Gallery has been housed in the old National Mint, a turn-of-the-century wooden structure which constantly vibrates as a consequence of passing traffic. The building also has air conditioning which is turned on and off at the beginning and end of every working day, resulting in the gallery's permanent collections being subject to twice daily temperature swings of 20–30 degrees. Nevertheless, the rear portion of the building—which does not vibrate and has open windows—has recently been dramatically upgraded and now represents some of the finest exhibition space in Southeast Asia. The gallery's central location, its long history as a government-operated public museum, and its relaxed ambience make it particularly attractive to members of the art community. Because almost none of its staff is professionally trained, visiting artists have to provide their own support people when installing an exhibition.

The Bhirasri Institute of Modern Art (BIMA) was founded in the mid-1970's as the first institution devoted to housing Thailand's contemporary visual and performing arts—the latter including dance and drama. The establishment of BIMA was an extraordinary effort because it was really only the second time in memory that members of the Thai elite worked in cooperation with one another to create a non-governmental, public institution that would serve the commonweal—the other instance being the early 20th century creation of the Siam Society, the nation's principal scholarly and historical organization. BIMA thrived for more than fifteen years, and during a typical year hosted ten to fifteen contemporary art exhibitions. However, as time passed the original founders of the Institute retired to private life or passed on, and BIMA's broad-scale support among the elite slowly began to fade. After the recent death of Princess Chumbhot, upon whose land BIMA was built, the future of the Institute became uncertain, principally because of family disagreements about the future use of the land and the hesitation of any publicly-minded donors to try to buy the family out or interfere in what is essentially a family matter. The BIMA staff was let go, and until the matter is resolved the Institute remains closed. At best, BIMA might reopen housed in the top floors of a newly constructed high-rise condominum, or at worst, may close forever.

The Art Gallery of Silpakorn University is perhaps the most dynamic and liberal exhibition venue in the country, with frequent changes of shows. However, it suffers the reputation of hosting an inordinate number of student exhibits and of favoring the art of members of the Silpakorn community—both of which are inherent to its mandate. On the other hand, because it is adjacent to the Grand Palace and a host of other cultural institutions (Thammasat University, the Pramane Grounds park, and Thailand's National Museum, National Theatre, and National Gallery), it is considered to be the perfect locale for attracting large numbers of viewers.

The National Culture Centre (built largely with Japanese funds and initially intended to be a venue for bi-national cultural activities) has the most up-to-date exhibition space and facilities in the kingdom. But because the Centre is in an inconvenient area of Bangkok, and is mandated to exhibit Thai folk art and develop art programs for children, it has come to be defined as the venue of last resort by most members of the contemporary art community. However, the addition of some bus lines and a change in exhibition policies could quickly alter these attitudes.

The Queen Sirikit Exposition Complex, completed only this past year, was built to host international conventions in Bangkok, and this will undoubtedly become its full-time function in the near future. However, until its international reputation is more firmly established, the complex is being used for domestic functions, including the mounting of art exhibits. The space is extremely popular because of its central location and its spick-and-span ambience, although an extremely conspicuous modern carpet design—appropriate for a convention center but brutally intrusive for an art venue—interferes with the art works on exhibition. Members of the art community are attempting to get the carpet covered with a more neutral floor carving during exhibitions, but the matter remains unsettled.

For reasons that derive historically from the early 1960's activities of Achille Clarac and his ambassadorial colleagues, the Alliance Française, the British Council, the Goethe Institute in Bangkok, and the Library of the U.S. Information Agency in Chiengmai, have a strong tradition of providing space for a wide variety of art exhibitions. Artists enjoy exhibiting in these spaces because they almost always attract viewers from the international community and also provide free advertising, although in most cases the actual exhibit space is rather limited. Certain artists have through old-boy networks developed close relationships with some of these institutions and often give free lectures, or even have some of their work on permanent display.

Because of their very nature, all of the above venues make art available to the public only episodically and virtually always at the instigation of the artists themselves. In contrast, gallery owners—whose livelihood or reputation depends upon it—are constantly in search of good art and artists on the one hand, and buyers and collectors on the other. Gallery owners differ fundamentally from tourist art shop owners in that they almost all charge thirty percent of the sale price of a work (as contrasted to the outright purchase and maximum resale price method used by tourist shops), and they work long hours both stimulating their artists to produce and educating their clients to buy. Too, because much of their business depends upon repeat sales to satisfied customers, they must be genuinely responsive to the latter's personal needs, and artistic and decorative values.

Because it is not an easy role to play, most galleries and gallery owners do not last too long in Thailand. Also, the idea of "exclusive representation," so commonplace and understandable in the

Euroamerican world, is virtually unworkable in Thailand. Young artists, or those who are just starting, are delighted to be exclusively represented by a gallery, if only because they know that in order to make his own profit the gallery owner will devote himself to finding appropriate clients and to obtaining a maximum price—often at levels the artists themselves never imagined. But once artists achieve reputations and clients begin to solicit them directly, they will typically break away from the gallery and keep the thirty percent gallery profit for themselves—rarely acknowledging that with many clients the gallery could well have obtained a considerably higher price.

These kinds of realities make the lives of art galleries extremely precarious. Those that do last usually do so as a consequence of some special situation. Occasionally *klum* members establish their own galleries and divide the profits, although this typically results in certain members selling very well and others hardly carrying their own weight. One of the finest and longest-lasting galleries in Thailand constantly loses money, but because it is a labor of love for its owner (a former graphic designer) and is also the elegant entry area of one of Thailand's finest restaurants—operated by the owner's spouse, and patronized by the nation's business elite—its continued existence is almost assured. Still another special situation is the gallery owned by an Austrian expatriate that over the past decade has become the principal conduit of contemporary Thai art, largely Buddhist art, to serious European collectors. Deeply knowledgeable in the history of art and impeccably honest in his dealings with both artists and collectors, the owner has kept the gallery going by constantly searching for new artistic talent and providing his clients with excellent prices and accurate information. Among the artists in this exhibit, he has at one time or another been the principal agent for Angkarn Kalayaanapongse, Pichai Nirand, Thawan Duchanee, Prateung Emjaroen, Chalermchai Kositpipat, Panya Vijimthanasarn, Montien Boonma, Sompop Budtarad, and Kamin Lertchaiprasert.

Once an artist has achieved distinction his professional life becomes more secure and he begins to represent his own work to collectors. As one of Thailand's most productive artists, Prateung Emjaroen typically holds bi-annual sales in his own home (which is also his studio), to which he invites all of his favorite clients, and to whom he typically sells 70–80% of the work on display. Because he has numerous clients and does not want to offend anybody, he posts his prices rather than leaving them unspecified and subject to individual negotiation. Additionally, Prateung often joins with members of his own *klum* (comprised mainly of junior colleagues and students) to mount exhibitions in shopping malls where, again, all his prices are publicly posted. Thawan, on the other hand, does not participate in many exhibitions, and when he does, it is usually as a favor to a friend or in a venue outside of Thailand. Instead, his clients come to him individually, and he negotiates a price that he considers appropriate to the status and wealth of the client, the nature of the work, the time and effort that has gone into its completion, his judgment of how it compares with his other recent work, and his past and likely future relationships with the client. Often he informs clients about work in progress that he thinks will be particularly to their liking. And like Angkarn, Prateung, Panya, Chalermchai, and a few others, he almost always has more requests for his work than he has works for sale. The result of this direct negotiation is a price range that is extraordinarily variable.

Because of the great range in the nature and quality of their work, their pricing methods, and their access to clients, it is impossible to generalize about the economic situation of artists. Almost half the persons in this catalogue make their living as fulltime artists, the other half being, in addition to artists, university faculty members, art teachers, or, in one case, a Fine Arts Department official. But whatever their primary source of income, all artists view the pricing of their work with utmost seriousness. Like artists everywhere, they consider the income they receive from their art the most accurate index of their creative abilities, and ultimately their social value. Only rarely will they accept a lower-than-expected fee because of the stature of the patron (a member of the royal household) or the historical importance of the project (the wall mural at the Thai temple in Wimbledon, England).

During the latter part of the 1980's, the prices of the work of a few of Thailand's senior, most accomplished artists (Angkarn, Thawan, Prateung) began to rise dramatically—as much as 20 percent a year. Some of this economic rise has trickled down—or in a few instances, splashed down—to younger or less famous artists. It is difficult to pinpoint the precise cause of the increase, but members of the art community say it is a result of an increase in the number of first-time collectors and the spreading awareness that art—particularly the best art—is a special marker of social status and a valuable subject for social discourse and exchange. Evidence from other locales in Asia and the recent emergence of a trans-Asian contemporary arts publication (*AsianArtNews,* published in Hong Kong) suggests that this phenomenon is by no means unique to Thailand. In fact, it may well be that like skyscraper offices and condominium apartments, international vacations and foreign home ownership, and an appreciation for classical music, contemporary indigenous art is finally emerging as one of the primary symbols and cultural pleasures of the new Asia.

Finally, we should note that we have dwelled here on venues, *klum,* clients, gallery owners, and prices because, although they are ancillary to the actual creation of art, they are matters that are uppermost in the thinking and decision-making of almost all Thai artists and are critical in providing the rewards of an artistic career. They represent the pragmatics of the artistic enterprise, without which the institution of contemporary art would not exist.

FOUR:
INTERNATIONAL INFLUENCES

The most overarching fact of Thai society over the past 150 years has been its active, willing, and accelerating participation in an international culture. Whatever the domain—law, technology, politics, agriculture, religion, even cuisine—the Thai have been involved in an exorable process of adapting themselves to the practices and standards of the international world. However, having said this, it must also be said that their adaptations have been highly selective and have always involved significant modifications of the foreign practices they were taking on so that these practices would fit with or enhance Thai cultural needs. Further, while the foreign origin of the new practices has been readily acknowledged as an historical reality, once taken on and amended they quickly have come to be experienced as integral elements of Thai culture. Many of these new practices were viewed not as replacements or substitutions of functioning cultural elements, but rather as ways to enrich the nature of Thai experience.

With this exhibition we have tried to show these processes occurring in the domain of the visual arts. They were accelerated by the role that Bhirasri came to play in Thai educational and political circles and, more recently, by the increasing numbers of foreign-educated Thai returning home with a dual sense of identity, and with the need to possess artistic symbols of their bi-cultural commitments. What is remarkable is that despite the increasing flow of international influences—particularly in terms of styles, materials, colors, and techniques—the thrust of contemporary Thai art remains true to the central meanings and values of Thai culture in its conceptions and subject matter. Many artists have pointed out that foreign influences have actually aided this process, in providing innovative ways to express old ideas.

Foreign influences have entered Thailand through at least four routes: through Thai artists who were sent overseas for more advanced training; through the continuing input from those Thai artists who remained overseas; from the selective interests and pressures of foreign collectors; and from the participation of Thai artists in international exhibition and exchange networks.

The Role of Foreign Education

Thai artists began to study overseas in significant numbers over forty years ago,[7] and these numbers have increased almost exponentially in the intervening decades. In fact, there are now so many artists who have studied overseas, and who then have taught about both Euroamerican art and the personal impact

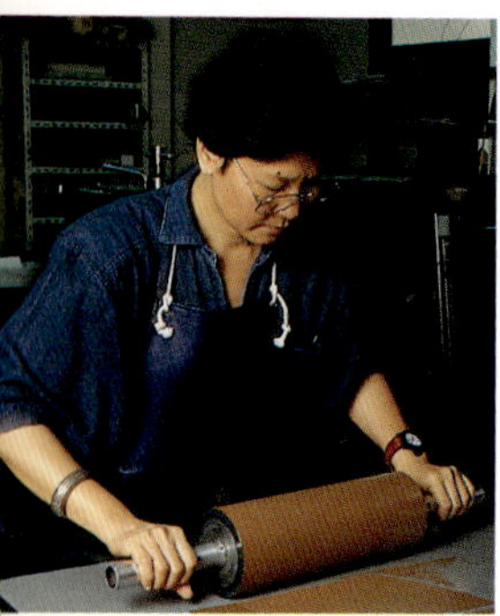

Figure 32. Kanya Charoensupkul studied at the Art Institute of Chicago. She is a student of Chalood, who studied in New York and Rome, and teacher of Kamin, who studied in New York.

their foreign experience has had upon them, that it is essentially impossible to separate the indigenous and international components of Thai art education. Equally important, because most Thai students work with a number of instructors who have had strikingly different foreign experiences and who themselves are students of foreign-trained Thai teachers, they no longer attach any significance to the provenience of their instruction. Kamin Lertchaiprasert recently spent a year studying in New York, but even before leaving Bangkok, he had already studied under three instructors trained in Thailand and America, whose own roots reach back through two generations of instructors who had studied in Italy. However, for all this genealogical baggage, Kamin claims that the artist who most influenced him while he was still in Thailand (and solely through publications and accompanying photos) was an Austrian, Arnulf Ranier, and that the inspiration to do his own work on the Thai alphabet, "Living Letters" (see plate 56) came to him while he was living in New York.

The foreign experience itself has affected Thai artists in a variety of ways. Thawan returned from his five years in Amsterdam with extraordinary pride in his own powers—he compared himself with his Dutch student cohort—and an awareness that he could draw upon the art history of the entire world in fashioning his own work. However, he was particularly enriched by his encounter with Hieronymous Bosch and the latter's 15th century preoccupation with the nightmares of religious suffering and human evil. For Thawan, Bosch opened up an area of Thai religious thought that, although conceptually elaborated in Thai folk beliefs, had never before been visually explored. Over the past twenty-five years Thawan has been working through various renditions of this vision, admixed with memories of the jungle creatures he encountered when, as a child, he accompanied his mother on her herb foraging expeditions through the rain forests of Northern Thailand.

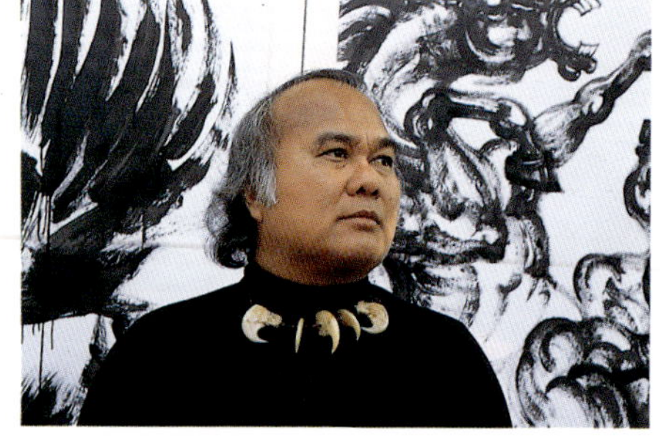

Figure 33. Thawan Duchanee

Piriya Krairiksh, on the other hand, had a strikingly different foreign experience. He had studied with Kokoschka in Salzburg, and his own early work had defined him as potentially one of Thailand's greatest artists. He had also studied at the University of Indiana and Harvard, but he was so dismayed by the cut-throat, pretentious, and implicitly racist qualities of the New York art scene—a scene to which he felt all world-class artists aspired—that he returned to Bangkok, gave up painting altogether, and has since become one of Thailand's most controversial art historians.

The experience of the vast majority of foreign-trained artists has clearly fallen somewhere between these two extremes. Damrong Wong-Uparaj studied at the Slade School in London and at the University of Pennsylvania in Philadelphia, and later spent a year in Kyoto as a visiting faculty member. He

---

7. The first artist known to have studied overseas was Phra Soralaklikhit who was sent to Italy as early as the reign of King Chulalongkorn. He returned home to become a court portrait artist (his frequently reproduced painting of an imagined Rama I being his single most famous work) but he is not known to have had any long-term impact on the development of Thai art.

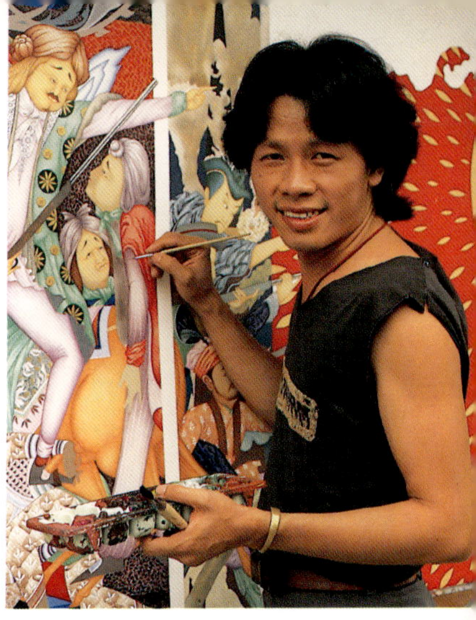

Figure 34.
Panya Vijinthanasarn

remembers that during his years in the English-speaking world he was enthralled by his visits to museums and the direct encounter with great works of Euroamerican art. He also recalls receiving intense training in Western abstract expressionism and in the modern use of color—neither one of which, however, has had any long-term impact on his own work, although "in Philadelphia I did discover blue as a splendid color for expressing meditation." His year in Kyoto, however, was dramatically different. The Japanese love of nature, the subdued qualities of their landscapes and colors, their concern with line and form, all led to major modifications in his own style, and to richer and more complex paintings (see plate 16). Panya Vijinthanasarn also graduated from Slade, but he was more deeply affected by it than was Damrong. It was there that he discovered medieval illuminated painting and the 18th century print-making techniques of William Blake, both of which had a major impact on his developing style. At a simpler but more unconscious level, he also discovered the triptych as a basic pattern for presenting the story-telling features of his art; it appears repeatedly as a motif of his works in this exhibit (see plates 3, 46, and 49). The impact of the foreign experience on Chalood Nimsamer was less specific, but ultimately perhaps of greater consequence. It was as a student in both Italy and New York that Chalood encountered the reality of Euroamerican art and artists constantly changing, and the necessity to utilize this dynamic in his own career. His application of this principle resulted in his gaining control over painting, sculpture, printmaking, and drawing, and becoming recognized as Thailand's most versatile artist. Similarly, his willingness to experiment with virtually every new foreign style—from Fauvism at the beginning of his career to conceptual art toward his retirement—marks him as one of his nation's most innovative artists.

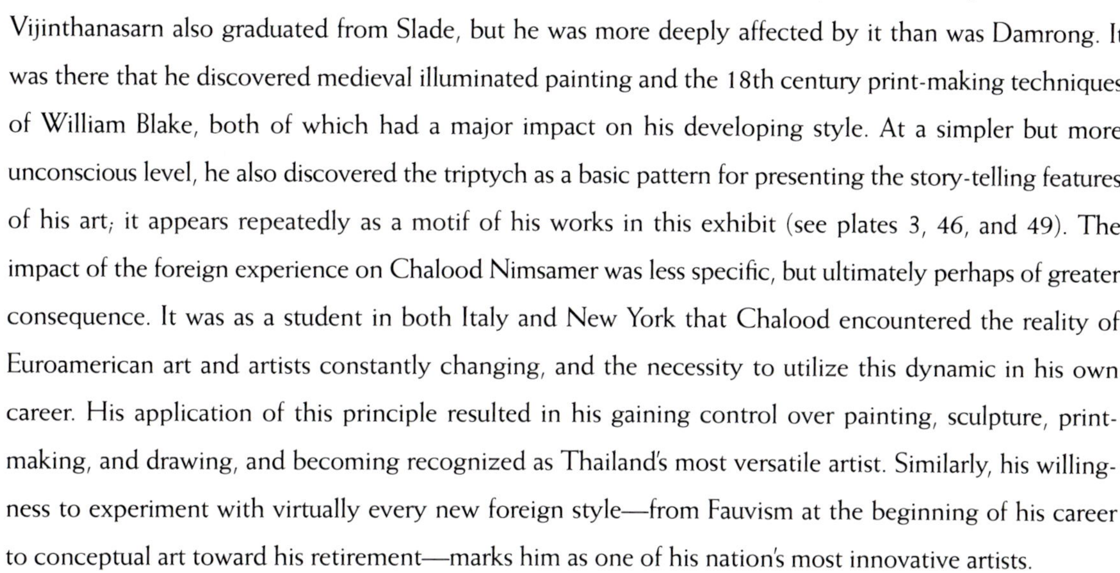

For many artists the most memorable feature of the foreign experience was not the influence of specific mentors or styles, but rather the encounter with the infrastructure of the Euroamerican or Japanese art worlds—the galleries, publications, museums, museum visitors, art supply shops, critics, curators, collectors, conservateurs, appraisers, and other specialists who collectively represent the perduring institutional nature of the artistic enterprise. A critical element of this encounter was the Thai artists' expanding awareness of the value assigned to art and artists in the Western and Japanese worlds and the critical role that artists have played as both historical figures and historians of their culture—a role that some imagined might eventually be assigned to them in Thai culture. Inevitably some were also dismayed by this foreign model—in part because it reminded them that upon their return to Thailand they would hardly find such large-scale institutional supports, and in part because it made them realize that the competitive nature of the enterprise meant that such supports would always be limited to the very few, best practicing artists. However, whatever their views, this encounter with the international art world, particularly with original works in museums and galleries, was a profound lesson in international aesthetic standards and the possibility of meeting or exceeding those standards in their own work.

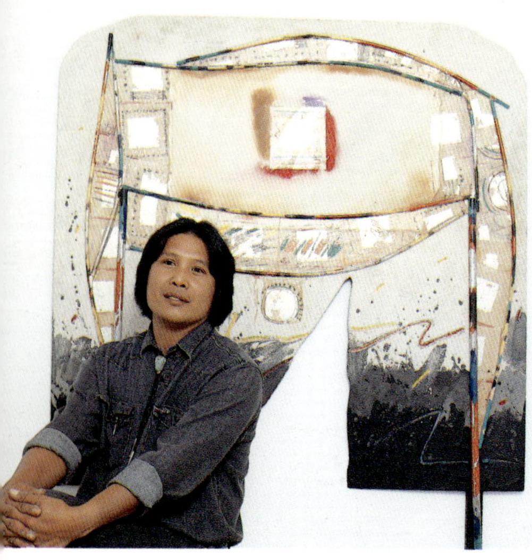

Figure 35.
Kamol Tassananchalee

Those Who Stayed Abroad

The role of Thai artists who went abroad and who, for a variety of reasons, stayed abroad is a much more diffuse feature of the contemporary Thai art scene. Although these artists are few in number—we currently know of only four in the United States and one in Holland—they loom large in Thailand for having successfully pursued their talents in a foreign setting while maintaining their professional and personal connections with their colleagues and friends back home. When they visit Thailand, they are attended to and often celebrated, and when living abroad, they are perceived as critical contacts for travelling artists, art students, and other members of the art community. Above all, they are considered the most reliable, up-to-date sources of knowledge on what is happening in the Euroamerican art world—if only because (unlike returning students) they are successful and active participants in that world, and can interpret the realities of that world in terms that are most apposite to practicing artists and other actors in the Thai art scene.

Whether they are inherently more venturesome or talented than those who opted to return home is debatable. Among the artists we know, three have foreign spouses; one was supported for a lengthy period by an American art dealer; and one was patronized for virtually his entire career by a governmental agency. Almost all say that they suffered through long periods of loneliness and uncertainty about whether or not they wanted to remain abroad, and they view their foreign residence principally as a matter of luck or as a result of the unpredictable circumstances of life. The four who live in the United States have all retained their Thai citizenship.

Of the five, Kamol Tassananchalee (see plates 1, 42, and 54) has perhaps been the most assiduous in retaining his Thai identity—both professionally and personally. Living in Southern California, he is surrounded by an expatriate community of approximately 200,000 Thai-Americans (after Bangkok the largest concentration of urban Thai in the world), to whose more affluent members he sells some of his works. He has also attracted his parents and other family members to reside in California—all of whom live successful Thai-American lives. His elderly father has become renowned within the Los Angeles Thai community as one of the finest Thai vegetable gardeners in the United States.

While Kamol has been in Los Angeles for more than twenty years, has sold his work to some of America's major museums (the California Palace of the Legion of Honor in San Francisco) and collectors (Vincent Price), and acknowledges his deep artistic debts to Jasper Johns, Robert Rauschenberg, and the motifs of American Indian cultures, he nonetheless still sees himself as a Thai artist. He repeatedly uses in his work Thai motifs (the *nangyai* and *thammachak*), concepts (the Buddha Footprint), and materials (gold leaf and handmade Thai paper)—and, as indicated earlier, recreated the use of handmade paper within Thailand. Since the early 1980's, he has every few years brought five or six Thai artists to work in his Los Angeles studio for several months, has arranged exhibits of their work in Los Angeles galleries and, in turn has learned an immense amount from them about the changing nature of contemporary Thai art. But most important, he has returned to Thailand approximately every five years to exhibit his own work, to lecture on art on national Thai television, at universities, and in provincial towns, and to reconfirm his own sense of Thai-ness. From a Thai point of view, he is, despite his Janus-like posture, considered to be a native artist—a perception that was legitimized in 1990 when the National Gallery of Thailand hosted a retrospective exhibition of his twenty years of work in the United States. He has since been commissioned to do works for Chulalongkorn University and several other institutional collectors in Thailand. Certainly colleagues like Thawan, Prateung, and Chamreung judge his work to be as central to the history of contemporary Thai art as they see their own to be.

Wattana Wattanupun's situation and his impact on Thai art have been very different. Unlike Kamol, he spent several years teaching art—sometimes "oriental art"—at the American colleges Haverford, Oberlin, and the Rhode Island School of Design, and later taught in Seattle and at Chiengmai University. He also had a separate career doing abstract expressionist and decorative works for American clients. His university situations affected him deeply as he became increasingly preoccupied with explaining the differences and similarities between Thai and Euroamerican artistic traditions, and equally important, with trying to make sense of the revolutionary cultural changes occurring in Thai society. Early in his career he had bought a home and studio in Chiengmai, and since 1975 he has repeatedly returned to Thailand to regenerate himself. These trips, however, have also intensified his awareness of Thai culture's becoming dominated, perhaps even ruptured, by the processes of modernization. The bifurcated nature of his own life paralled these larger cultural events, and his work turned more and more to depicting the conflicts and uncertainties resulting from this inexorable historical movement (see plates 43–45). This intellectual purpose is itself more apposite to Euroamerican than to Thai aesthetic traditions, and not surprisingly, his efforts to address these matters artistically have also had greater appeal to foreigners than to indigenous Thai: like Thawan, Wattana has over the years sold more of his work to foreign admirers of Thailand than to Thai collectors. Nevertheless, this very fact has bolstered Wattana's artistic stature within Thailand, and his style of social commentary—subdued irony, the use of trompe l'oeil devices, and other modes of visual suggestion—has increasingly influenced contemporary Thai conceptions of art.

The influence of Prawat Laocharoen and Thana Lauhakaikul has been much more indirect, undoubtedly because they have spent much less time in Thailand. Prawat came to New York in 1967, attended the Pratt Institute completely on scholarships, and specialized in printmaking and conceptual art. He collaborated for several years with such artists as David Hockney, Alex Katz, Adolph Gottleib, Larry Rivers, and most recently Dennis Oppenheim—with whom he did a site specific installation on how printmaking draws from and alters the environment. Although he did not often return to Thailand, Prawat remained in constant contact by hosting Thai artists visiting New York and by sending some of his best work home for teaching purposes and as philanthropic contributions. In 1991, he returned to Bangkok to participate in a major group exhibition on Thai printmaking at the National Gallery where, because of his international stature, he was one of the major attractions.

Thana Lauhakaikul had already established himself as a successful classical and commercial sculptor in Thailand when, out of professional boredom and a spirit of adventure, he left for further study at the Massachusetts College of Art in Boston. His career later took him to Austin, where for the past fourteen years he has been a faculty member at the University of Texas. Thana has over the years returned to Thailand to lecture and, more recently, to craft a light and sound installation in the town of Rayong, where almost twenty years ago he installed his first public work—a statue of Sunthorn Phuu, the most acclaimed poet in Thai history.

It is difficult to locate these artists precisely in the Thai art world. While they are a great source of pride to the art community, their success in the Euroamerican world acknowledged, and their counsel solicited whenever they return home, they are for much of their lives at the margins of the Thai art scene. Of the four, Kamol and Wattana are closest to center stage—in part because they return with sufficient frequency or retain a residence in Thailand, but most significantly because, wherever they are, they continue to address Thai issues or use Thai motifs or materials in their work. Wattana's teaching at Chiengmai University is also an essential part of his public identity. In the last few years, Panya (visiting in England, Australia, and Spain), Thawan (visiting in Germany, Japan, and California), and Kamin (visiting in New York) have spent almost as much time out of Thailand as have Kamol and Wattana, and certainly none of them would ever be defined as anything but a contemporary Thai artist. When Prawat and Thana visit Thailand, lecture in Thai, and are honored at receptions and in the press, their foreign affiliations—which are the very source of their celebrity—almost disappear from the public's awareness; they are viewed not as "American artists," but as "Thai artists" who are speaking on American artistic activities to Thai audiences. Their bicultural experience, and the multiple identities associated with it, is perceived as simply one more attribute of the postmodern nature of the contemporary art world.

The Role of Foreign Collectors

Contemporary Thai art has attracted the interest of two types of foreign collectors. One is that group of foreigners who have lived in Thailand for a period of time or who, if they now live elsewhere, have an abiding interest in both Thai culture and in Thai aesthetic representations. Many of them have come to Thailand with a finely honed aesthetic sense, and others have developed it after their arrival and their direct encounter with Thai artistic traditions. Some delight in the art as much for broad cultural reasons—

or for those no longer living in Thailand, for nostalgic reasons—as for its aesthetic value. The second group is comprised of collectors who know much less about Thailand, but who are attracted to Thai art either because of the excellence of its formal aesthetic features or because of its exotic contrast with Euroamerican art. It is precisely this sense of contrast that makes some contemporary Thai art seem so original in the eyes of certain foreigners (even if that sense is focussed on features—such as the flowing, androgynous Sukothai Buddha figures—which may actually be commonplace in Thai artistic tradition). The largest collection of contemporary Thai art outside of Thailand is owned by a collector in this second group, an American living in Beverly Hills who has never been to Thailand and who selected his works from catalogues and other publications.

Most Thai artists, in turn, perceive foreign collectors as gatekeepers of international aesthetic standards and, by virtue of that role, as arbiters in determining what works, styles, techniques, or aesthetic subjects meet or exceed those standards. Foreigners are also seen as much more likely than Thai collectors to select works for their aesthetic excellence rather than as markers of social status.

The net result of this mix of perceptions is that Thai artists take the views of foreign clients very seriously, but acknowledge that these views tend to be rather conservative. Foreign collectors overwhelmingly approve of works that demonstrate their Thai origins, and that do not venture far from traditional Thai aesthetic standards or subject matter. Foreigners clearly appreciate and reward artistic innovation (Panya's abstract rendition of the nature of "illusion," as in plate 3, or his representation of the great white chain of life, as in plate 49), but prefer to see such design elements as serving the contemporary expression of traditional Thai concepts, rather than as radically new or alien artistic forms.

Foreign collectors who live in Thailand often personally know and have warm, supportive relationships with artists whom they patronize. As art patrons they tend to be both more admiring and more critical than native Thai. Like many Euroamerican collectors, some have tried to accumulate the best works that a single artist has produced over a period of several years. Also, a few have become the principal sources of support for certain artists—a position that may give the patrons considerable leverage over the kind of work those artists produce.

Those who know Thailand only at a distance or through occasional visits influence artists mainly through the indirect pressures of the marketplace. In recent years, contemporary Buddhist art has become extremely popular in certain European art circles, and this has clearly had an impact upon the type of work produced by artists such as Pichai, Sompop, Chalermchai, Prateung, and Panya. In fact, Thawan recently spent almost a year in Europe painting several ceilings and walls of a medieval German castle with murals based upon Thai Buddhist and animistic themes, and the term "modern Thai spiritual art" is occasionally used by European visitors as a preferred category of Thai art.

Foreign collectors purchase far fewer individual works from far fewer Thai artists than do native

Thai collectors, but their aesthetic, economic, and psychological impact is by no means inconsequential. It is they who most clearly demonstrate to Thai artists that, however specialized, they are making a contribution to world culture and to the history of contemporary art.

International Exchange Networks

In recent years Thai artists have participated increasingly in international exchange networks which allow artists from other countries to visit, exhibit, and sometimes teach in Thailand, and Thai artists to visit and send their work for exhibition and sale in other nations. Because these exchange relationships are less institutionalized than are other forms of international linkage, and also differ from medium to medium—printmakers are much better organized internationally than are painters—it is difficult to determine the long-term impact of these international liaisons.

The least formalized—but nonetheless highly significant—type of international exchange involves European and American artists who come to Thailand as tourists, inevitably inquire about Thai contemporary art, and hit it off with a Thai colleague; soon the two find themselves working together on a collaborative effort. (Such collaborations have occasionally resulted in marriage.) If the visiting artist has sufficient stature in his or her own country, arrangements can sometimes be made for the Thai artist to visit and mount an exhibit in that nation. Such linkages have to date occurred most frequently with visiting artists from such nations as Poland, Czechoslovakia, and Israel.

Organizations such as the Fulbright Foundation occasionally fund foreign art instructors to spend a year in Thailand, but the visitors are rarely well-known artists and have not attracted much attention. More importantly, virtually every year the Cultural Affairs office of a foreign embassy—most frequently British, French, Japanese, or German—arranges a Bangkok stop of a travelling exhibition of contemporary art, or a visiting lecture, occasionally by artists themselves. These exhibitions and talks are usually very well attended, but their impact on the Thai art scene is primarily of a general educational nature.

The exhibition of the work of Thai artists in the Euroamerican world is still less institutionalized, with most shows arranged on an *ad hoc* basis. While he was a student, Damrong Wong-Uparaj arranged one-man exhibitions in Paris and Florence of his then most current work, as did Montien in Paris several years later. Also friends of Thai artists have over the years mounted one-man and group shows in a private London club and in Miami and Milwaukee galleries. A few years ago, the Thai Ambassador to Austria held a major exhibition of Prateung's work in the Thai Embassy in Vienna, and Kamol Tassananchalee has arranged group shows of contemporary Thai art at the Pacific Asia Museum in Pasadena.

As might be expected, Thai artists' most frequent network links are with art institutions and artists from other Asian nations. The Association for Southeast Asian Nations (ASEAN) sponsors an annual sculpture competition that moves throughout Southeast Asia, and the prize-winning entries from each nation have been installed in sculpture gardens in every capital city of the region. The competition has also resulted in the development of artistic links between sculptors from each country, although inevitably language differences have inhibited the potential impact of such ties. Japan also has a great interest in the arts of Southeast Asia, and Thai artists—Somsak, Thawan, and Montien among others—have recently mounted significant one-man shows in Tokyo and Fukuoka. Printmakers such as Itthipol have also had considerable success in exhibiting and selling their work in Singapore and Hong Kong, and in 1985 a major exhibit of classical, folk, and contemporary Thai art visited Beijing and Kwang Chow in China.

As indicated earlier, printmakers are best organized to take advantage of these forms of international exchange. This is partly a result of the relative ease with which they can package and deliver their artwork to virtually anywhere in the world, but it is primarily because the medium is often more decorative than it is representational or symbolic, and is thus less constrained by matters of cultural meaning. We suspect that as the years pass, the printmakers' networks will increasingly include other colleagues and outlets in the international world.

A Final Observation

The impact of the international world on Thai artists clearly will continue and perhaps even intensify. However, it is our view that contemporary Thai art—like all aesthetic expression—inevitably refers to the direct personal experiences, including imaginative experiences, of the individual artists. The numerous liaisons that Thai artists have with the international world are educational, stimulating, broadening, and extremely helpful in a practical sense. But for most artists, they are also diffuse and distant experiences—emotionally and cognitively, as well as aesthetically. When these foreign experiences and liaisons work their way into Thai art, what appears is frequently an unexpected or peripheral feature of these experiences—Thawan's encounter with Bosch's 15th century visions, Panya's encounter with William Blake's 18th century techniques, Kamol's encounter with the motifs of American Indian artifacts. Or if it is not totally unexpected—Chalood's encounter with Fauviste sources in Italy and New York, Somsak's with abstract expressionism in Tokyo—the international forms learned abroad are, once the artist has come home, thoroughly reworked to serve personal and local meanings. No matter the nature of international influence, it is difficult to imagine the Thai-ness of this artistic intent ever transformed beyond recognition—unless of course the Thawan's and Panya's of the future become culturally indistinguishable from their colleagues in Chicago, Caracas, Kyoto, or Cairo.

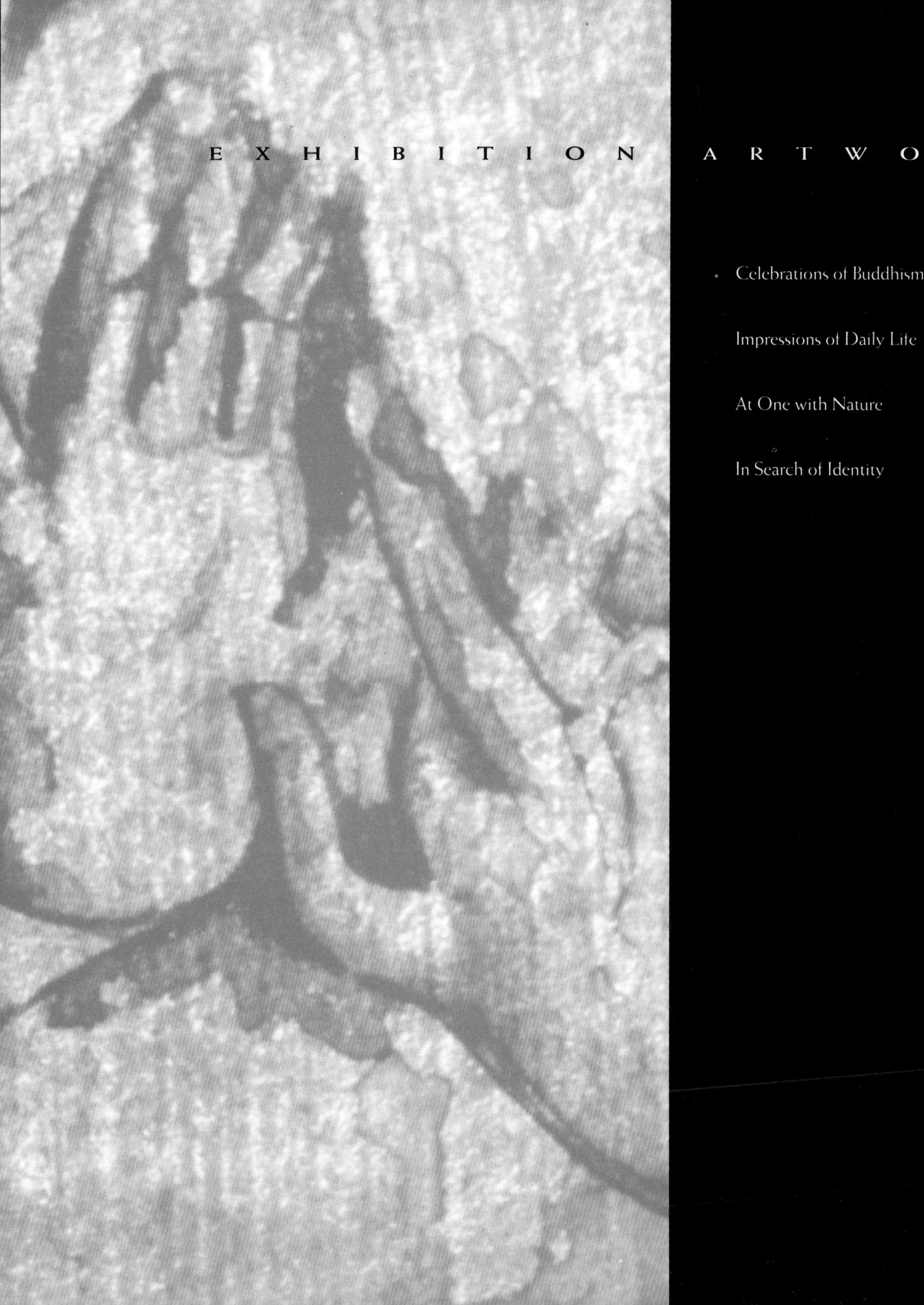
E X H I B I T I O N A R T W O
Celebrations of Buddhism
Impressions of Daily Life
At One with Nature
In Search of Identity

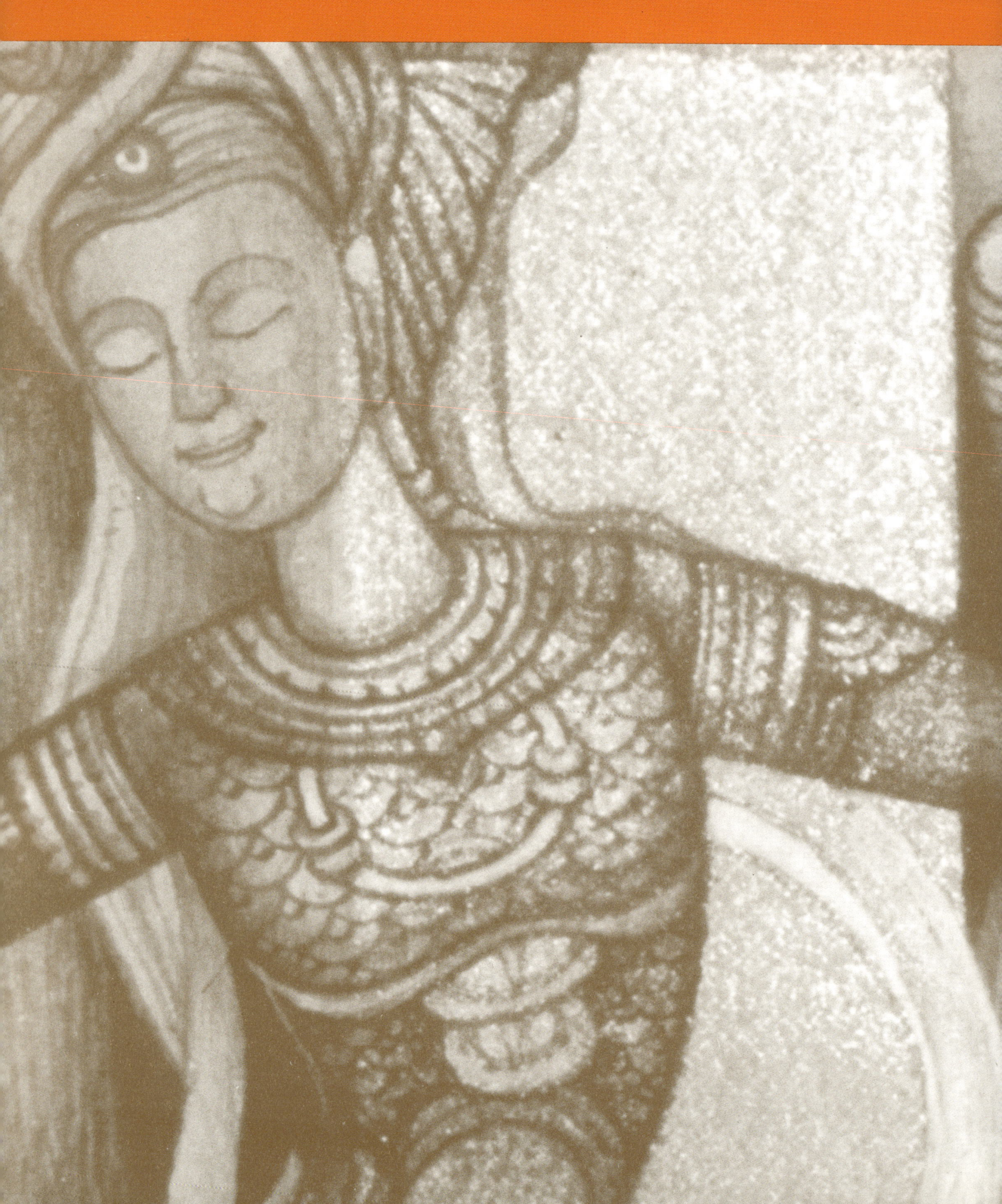

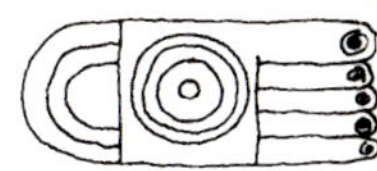

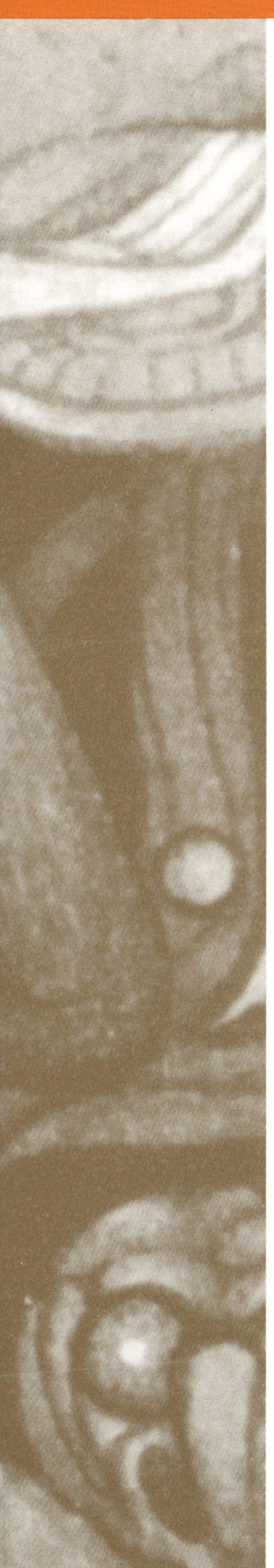

For more than a thousand years the paramount purpose of Thai art was to honor Buddhism—its teachings, practices, symbols, and above all, the person, career, and lives of the Lord Buddha. The strength of this tradition continues unabated into this century where Buddhist themes and aims still represent the most important features of Thai artistic expression.

The basic terms of modern Buddhist art—the meanings of its motifs and symbols— are well understood by most Thai. Equally important, they widely believe that the intent of this art should still be instructional, moral, and conceptual rather than aesthetic or decorative.

However, like many other things in Thailand, Buddhist art has in recent decades undergone transformation and experimentation. For many artists, the opportunity to express Buddhist ideas with modern designs and materials, and to do so in styles that are personally distinctive, is almost a form of artistic liberation. That some of these designs are modern modifications of traditional aesthetic forms makes them even more meaningful to Thai artists and audiences. Indeed, it is the extraordinary adaptability of Buddhist concepts and symbols to the contemporary world that so clearly demonstrates for most Thai their continued relevance, legitimacy, and timelessness.

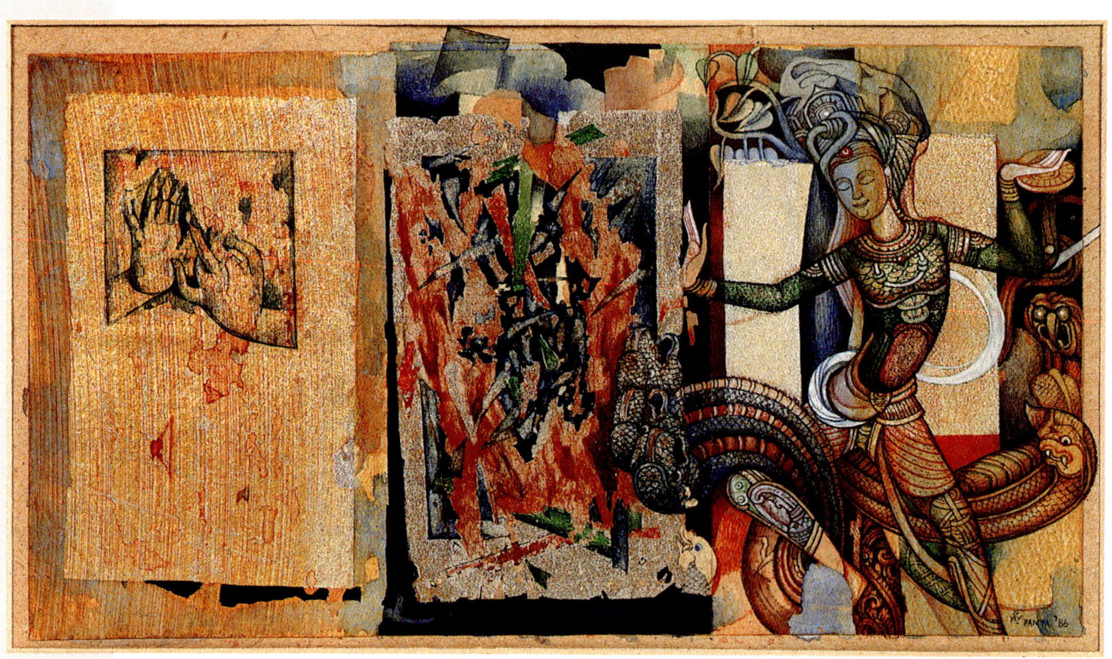

PLATE 3

PANYA VIJINTHANASARN

THREE CONCENTRATIONS, 1986

Acrylic, gold leaf, and silver paper, 4.5" x 7.63"

This work portrays a hero dealing with the three basic realities of the Thai Buddhist universe: that life is suffering (the demons on the far right); that experience is characterized by illusion (the abstract, Western-derived designs in the center); and that everything is impermanent (the broken fingers from the hand of a Buddha image on the left). However, the artist says that his hero is holding his own—maintaining a state of equanimity, balancing the responsibilities on his head, pushing away illusion with one hand while holding out the other to acknowledge his own human needs. The androgynous qualities of the hero are modeled on 13th century Sukothai Buddha images, while his tattoos—based upon folk practices—are meant to protect him against misfortune.

Loaned by Marc Bogerd

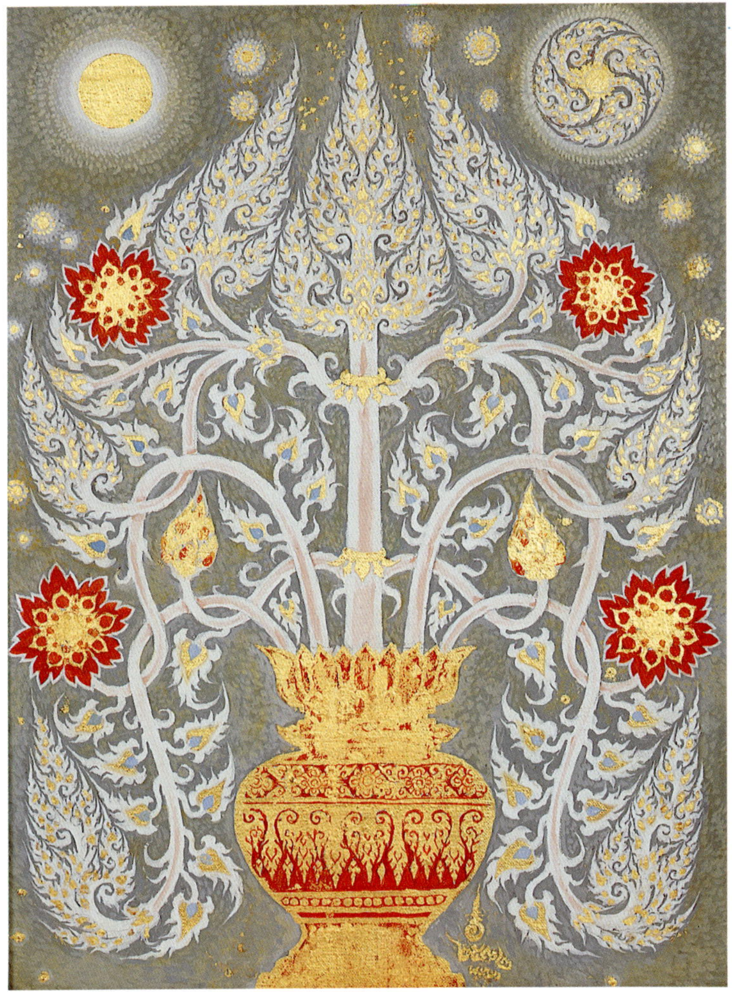

PLATE 4

ANGKARN KALAYAANAPONGSE

THE ROOTS OF ENLIGHTENMENT, 1989
Acrylic and gold leaf on canvas, 22" x 16.5"

The bho tree, or Tree of Paradise, under which the Lord Buddha achieved enlightenment, is one of the most revered icons of Thai Buddhism. Used repeatedly in the design elements of temple walls and ceilings, it has over the centuries become a generalized symbol of growth, happiness, and fulfillment. This version of the bho tree is in the form of a bowl of plenty overflowing with leafy tendrils. Every element of the plant—the individual leaves, the sweep of the tendrils, and the overall configuration of the tree—replicates the distinctive shape of the bho tree's leaf. As is the case in much of his work, Angkarn situates this Buddhist symbol in a cosmic firmament, surrounding the upper edges of the tree with the sun, moon, and stars. The gold and red buds of the plant are suggestive of lotus blossoms, one of the Lord Buddha's reincarnations.

Loaned by Chumpol Donsakul

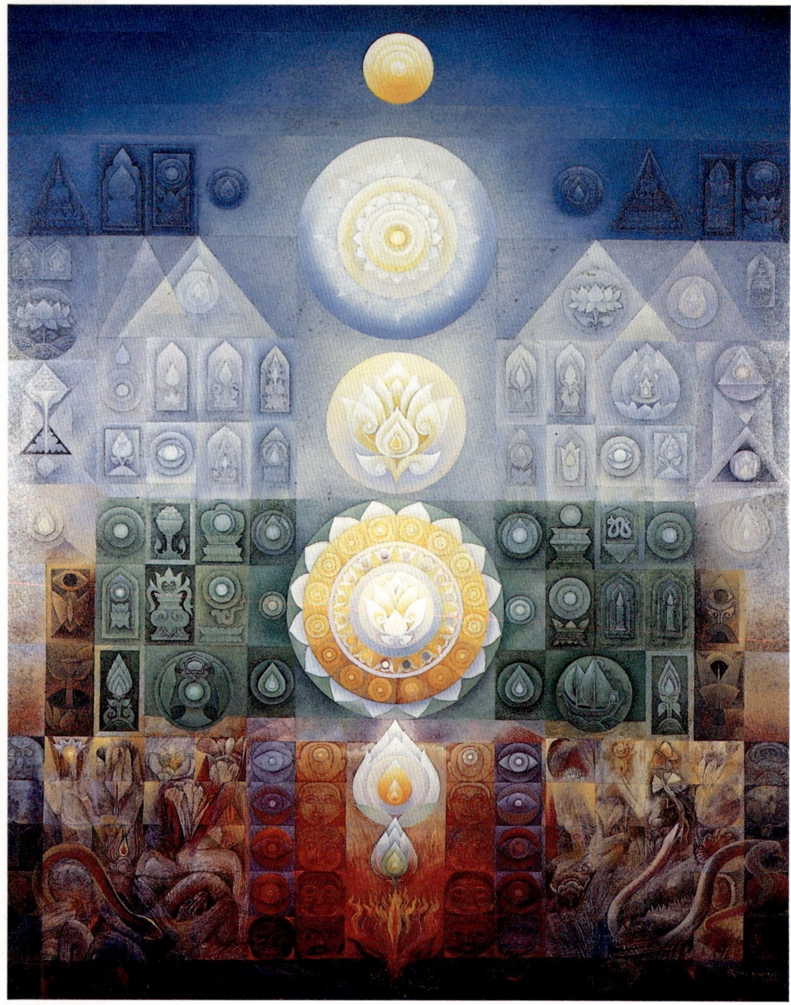

PLATE 5

PICHAI NIRAND

PATHWAY TO NIRVANA, 1979
Oil on canvas, 71" x 43.5"

The lotus is both a symbol of enlightenment and of moral progression: the bud rises from mud to bloom into a state of perfect natural beauty, as indicated by its symmetry and the purity of its white color. The central axis of this work portrays different versions of the lotus as it ascends through various environments and through levels of increasing abstraction. The color-saturated, lower region of the painting portrays the real, but amoral and immoral, world of animals and human beings. At this level, the artist likens the lotus to a person in ignorance. The green and gray amulet-like symbols in the grids of the middle levels represent aspects of the Lord Buddha's character, and here the lotuses represent those who have studied the Buddha's teachings. At the upper level, the lotus is transformed into an abstract sphere suspended in an environment that has no definition or limit, thus symbolizing the state of nirvana. While the message and symbolism of this work derive from the Thai classical tradition, its conception, color, and design are modern creations.

Loaned by Marjorie and Fred Lyte

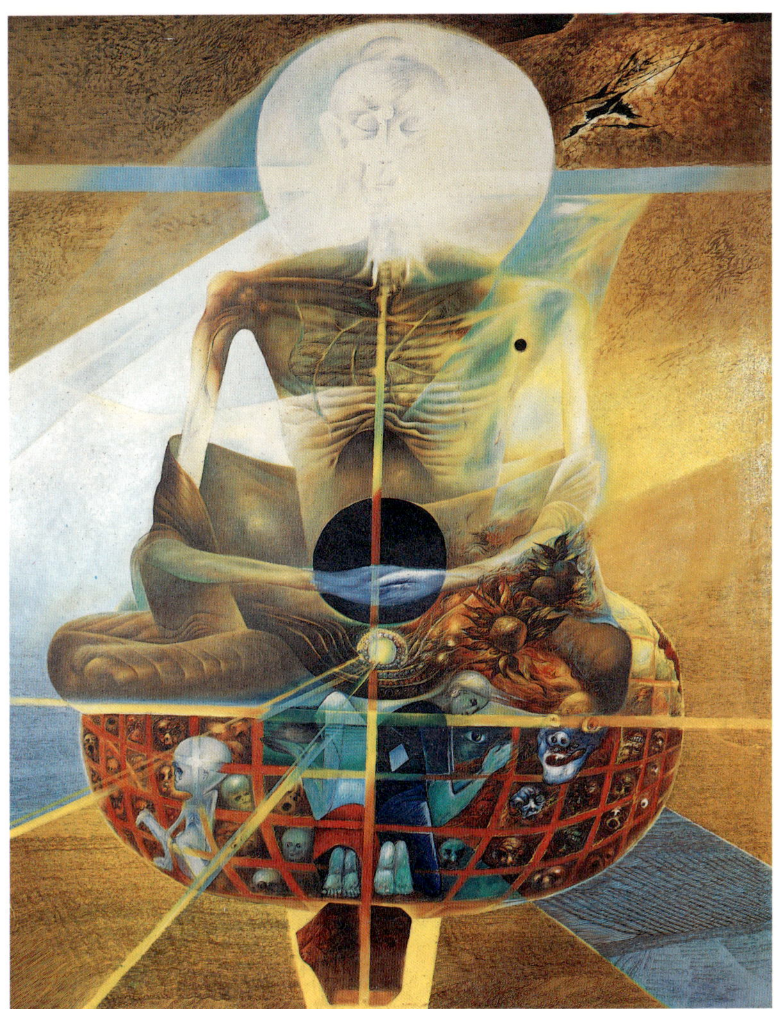

PLATE 6

PRATEUNG EMJAROEN

FASTING BUDDHA, 1976
Oil on canvas, 69" x 54"

One of the fundamental tenets of Buddhism is that all things change—not only living things, but inanimate substances such as stone and earth. The ephemeral nature of human beings and their experience has always been of special importance to Thai Buddhism. Even today, part of the advanced training of some Buddhist monks is to examine human cadavers in various states of decomposition—mainly to reinforce the immutable reality of the transient nature of all existence. Understanding this, many Thai find nothing inherently frightening or ugly about an old or emaciated person. Such conditions represent natural stages in the cycle of interminable change.

While this Fasting Buddha represents that fundamental tenet, it also depicts the nature of human suffering—and in the lower portion of the work, the suffering of the young, the innocent, and the incarcerated. The fact that the work was painted in late 1976 is also significant. This was a period of extreme political repression in Thailand. Although short-lived, it was perhaps the single most painful period of recent Thai history. Thus, the work is also a commemoration of the nature of suffering—which, in Buddhist terms, is another inherent attribute of human experience.

Loaned by the artist

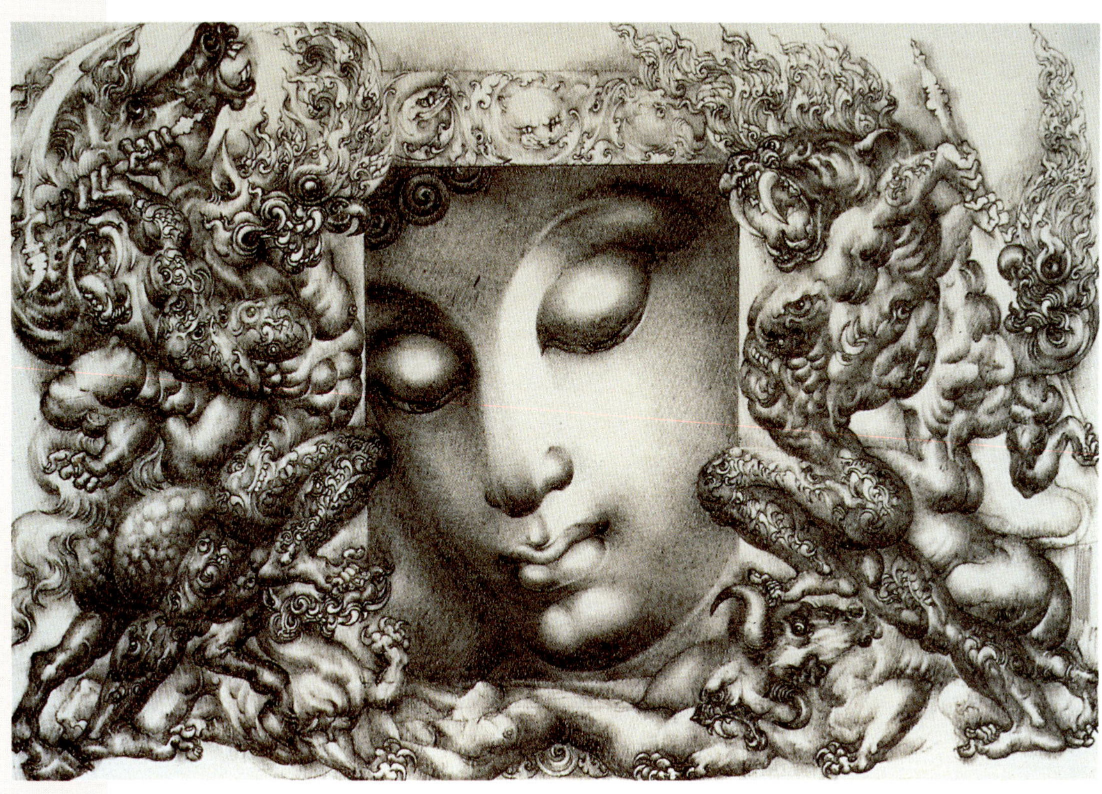

PLATE 7

THAWAN DUCHANEE

BUDDHA AND MARA'S ARMY, 1988
Ballpoint pen on paper, 9.25" x 13.25"

In Buddhist iconography, Mara's evil forces battled with the Lord Buddha and tried to dissuade him from attaining Enlightenment by tempting him with earthly delights, as represented by the female figure along the lower edge of the drawing. Thawan is distinctive in the Thai art world for the freedom with which he portrays the forces of violence and aggression. While these two works indicate no lessening of that interest, they do show a readiness, only recently displayed, to juxtapose and balance Mara's violence with the serenity and repose of the Lord Buddha. Comparing the two works on the same theme by the same artist, many Thai feel this rendition is the more successful, primarily because the visage of the Buddha is whole and complete.

Loaned by Prakas Yenanroong

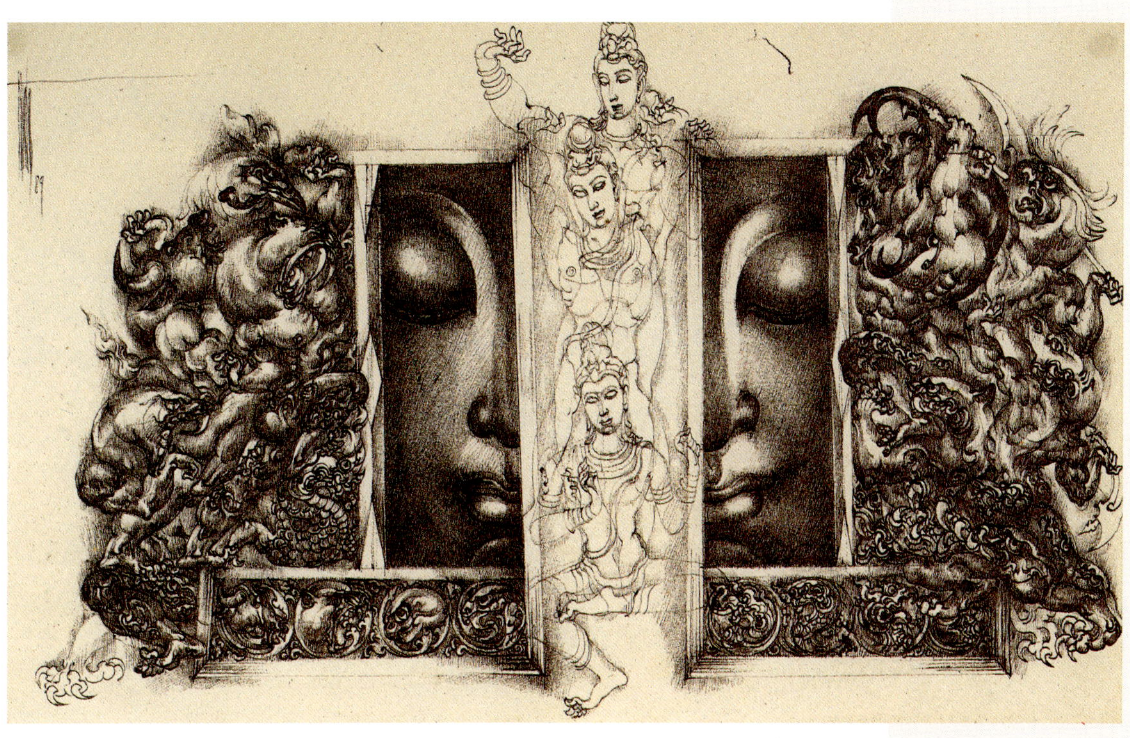

PLATE 8

THAWAN DUCHANEE

UNTITLED, 1988
Ballpoint pen on paper, 16" x 22"

This drawing is described by the artist as the forces of goodness, shown by the dual faces of the Lord Buddha in the center, combatting the powerful forces of Mara's Army, the embodiment of evil and temptation on the far right and left. The overlapping, unfinished figures in the center are reminiscent of the gods of the Hindu trinity, Brahma, Siva, and Vishnu—the last also being the preserver and the protector of the arts. The draftsmanship of the medallions along the lower border may reflect the influence of Renaissance art on Thawan, who spent several years studying in the Netherlands.

Loaned by Surachai Wattanaporn

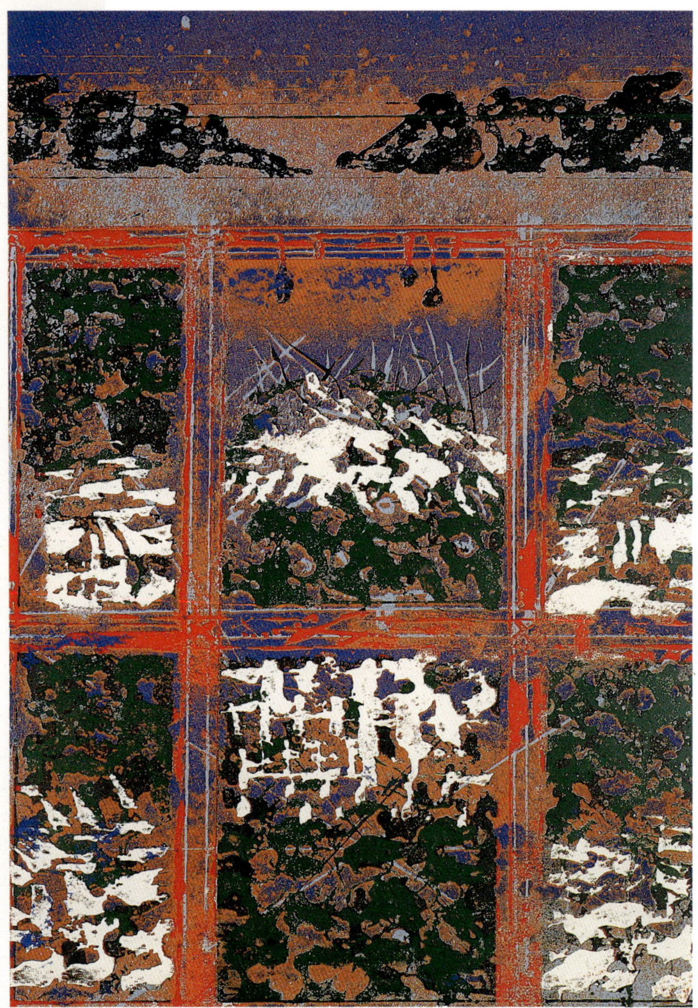

PLATE 9

VIBOON LEESUWAN

MEMORY NUMBER 3, 1984
Silkscreen print, 21" x 28"

Like many Thai, Wiboon is preoccupied with the relationship between life and death and how to make it understandable to people. Here the horizontal and vertical lines are window frames through which can be seen fossils of once living things and ancient stones. The colors that reflect and shimmer off one another and the white cross-hatching are meant to mark the vibrance that obtains between birth, life, and death.

Loaned by the artist

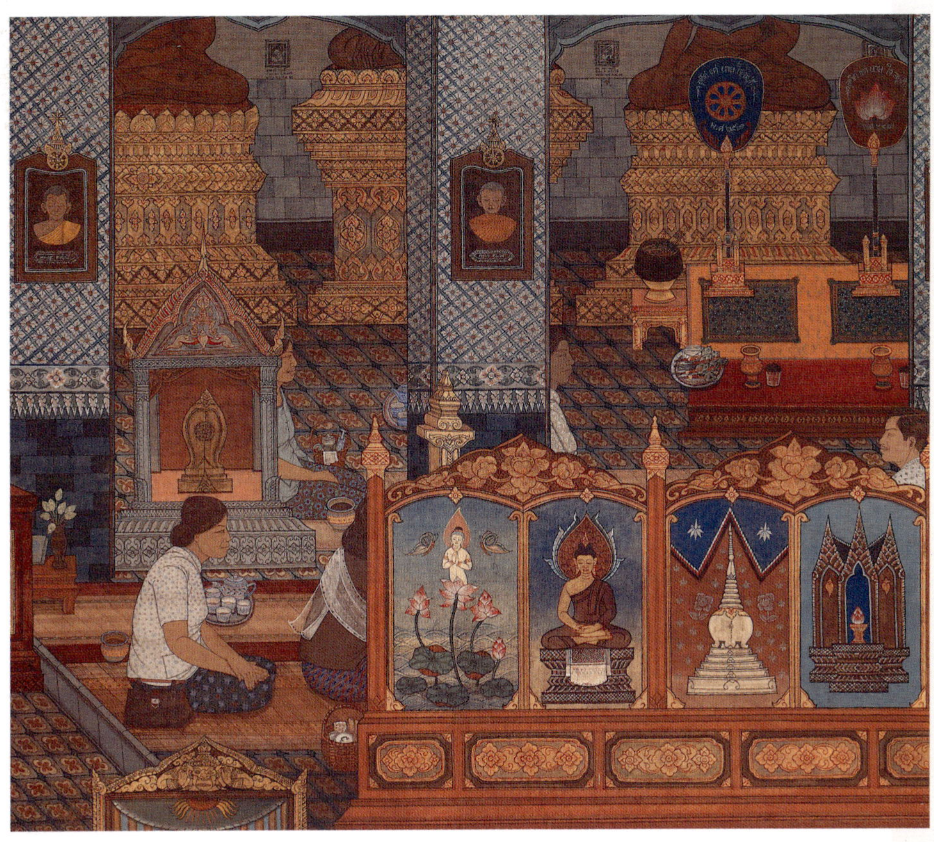

PLATE 10

CHALERMCHAI KOSITPIPAT

WAITING FOR THE MONKS, 1975

Tempera on paper, 45" x 51"

Despite the reduction in size and the use of paper instead of a stucco wall, this work is intended as a modern version of a traditional didactic temple mural. The subject matter is familiar—laypersons wishing to make merit waiting in the sanctuary hall of a temple for the monks to arrive. It is the very familiarity of the scene that underscores its historical depth, its cultural importance, the continuity of its social features, and the commitment of ordinary people to the expression of their devotion. The work's content is a celebration of the commonplace. The dark shade of the painting evokes the darkness of many temple interiors.

Loaned by Thai Airways International

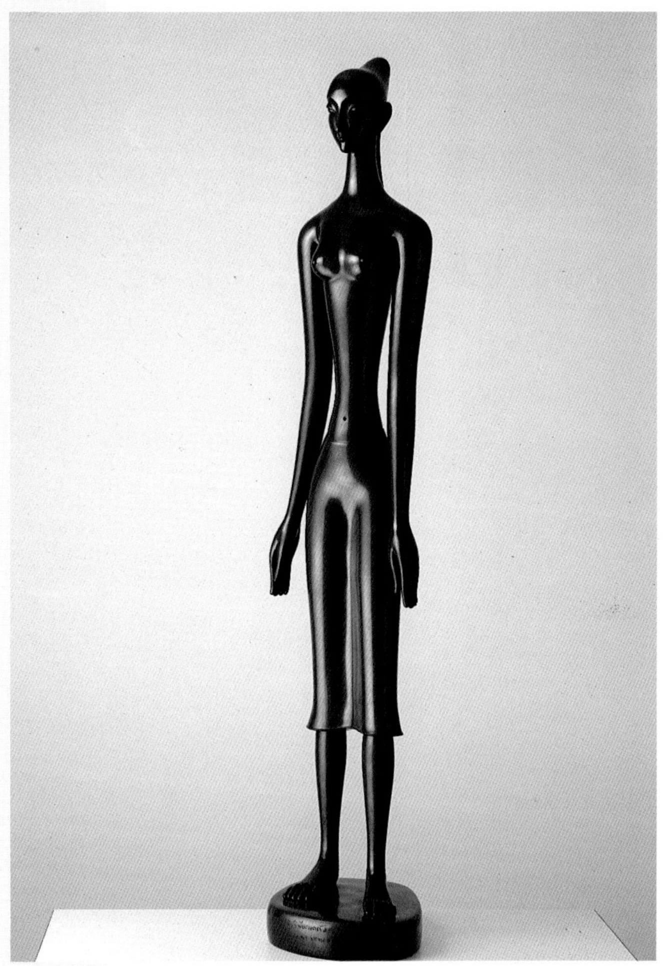

PLATE 11

CHAMREUNG VICHIENKET

SERENITY, 1978
Bronze, 2/3, 8" x 36" x 8"

The line, sweep, and perspective of this female figure are meant to convey a state of perfect repose—the state in which, in the Thai Buddhist view, one best comes to terms with the human condition. While the shape of the figure may suggest the influence of Modigliani, the serene facial expression and the elongated arms, hands, and ears are based upon Sukothai Buddha images. The folds of the figure's garment also reflect the Sukothai model.

Chamreung is the senior member of a family of sculptors. He was trained and inspired by Corrado Feroci, the Italian sculptor who came to Thailand in 1923 and stayed on to teach and develop Western artistic traditions in Thailand.

Loaned by the artist

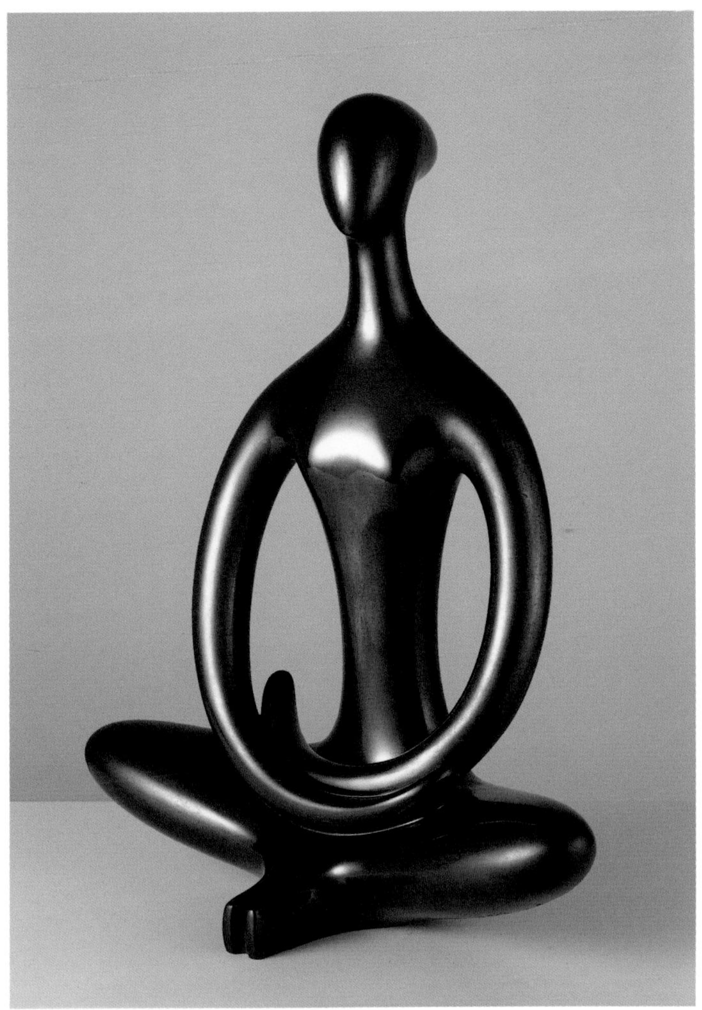

PLATE 12

SAOWAPHA VICHIENKET

MEDITATION, 1984
Bronze, 1/3, 14" x 18" x 6"

Seated in a ritual position, this figure conveys the peace and discipline of the act of meditation. While modeled on Buddhist ideals and prescriptions, meditation is a widely practiced activity of everyday life in Thailand. In much of her work, the artist focusses on women engaged in such daily activities as carrying infants or lifting their sarongs to cross a monsoon-flooded street. Saowapha is the spouse of Chamreung Vichienket.

Loaned by the artist

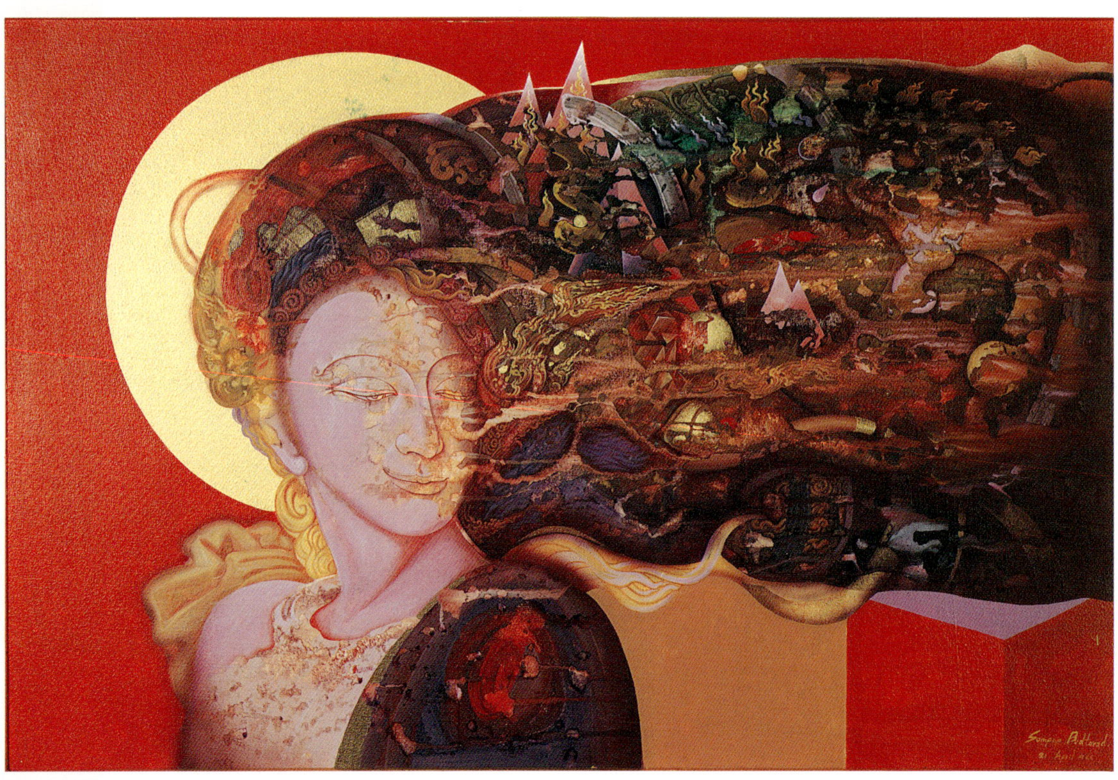

PLATE 13

SOMPOP BUDTARAD

FORMS OF THE MIND, 1988
Acrylic on canvas, 25" x 36.5"

One of the central practices of Buddhism is meditation, the religious purpose of which is to replace the normal confusions and distractions of the human mind with the clarity and certainty of Buddhist teachings. This work is a visual representation of that process, with the equanimity of the figure's face contrasting with the chaotic activity of his mind. The clarifying precepts of Buddhism—symbolized by the gold leaf and the small concentric circles at the figure's forehead—are located close to the center of the figure's mind, while his more murky thoughts are at the periphery. The elaborate, precise rendition of flames near the figure's left eye symbolizes mental energy that is ordered and focused; it contrasts with the cruder renditions of flames, and the less purposeful forms of energy, near the right upper edge of the work. The mountain tops express the figure's attempts to deal with abstract thoughts. The artist also uses the classical colors of Thai Buddhist symbolism, the gold behind the figure's head symbolizing Buddhism's purity and the red color field symbolizing Buddhism's nobility.

Loaned by the artist, courtesy of Visual Dhamma Gallery

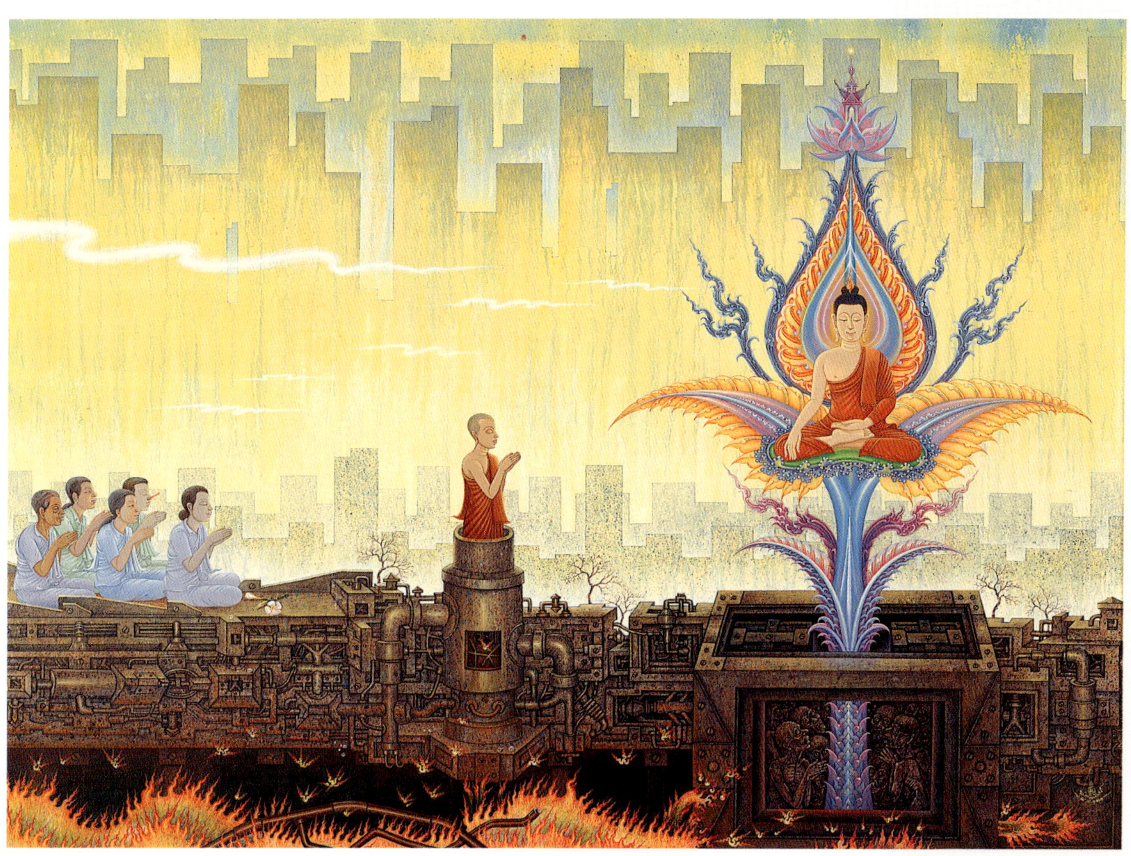

PLATE 14

CHALERMCHAI KOSITPIPAT

MIND AND TECHNOLOGY, 1990

Acrylic on canvas, 39" x 45.5"

This work portrays one of the fundamental oppositions of contemporary Thai thought: the conflict between the inner life of the spirit, Buddhist morality, and the power of the sacred on the one hand, and the uncontrollable consequences of amoral, secular technology on the other. Chalermchai recognizes that while there is no inherent incompatability between religion and technology, the uses to which technology have actually been put in Thailand have resulted in a deterioration of Thai life and of the legitimacy of Buddhist practice and belief. What were once grand, white skyscrapers are being overlaid by industrial pollution, and a monk, although paying obeisance to the Buddha, is being swallowed up by a modern boiler. The field of fire on the bottom edge of the work is modeled on a massive explosion of butane tanks that destroyed a section of Bangkok shortly before the painting was created, while those people already imprisoned by technology—with faces reminiscent of those appearing in traditional temple murals of sinners in hell—look up to the Lord Buddha for redemption. It is the five women on the left who may yet be redeemed. The simplicity of their devotion, and their being located under a white wave, a symbol of purity, that emanates from the Buddha, suggest that they are still committed to the sacred power of their religion.

Loaned by Song Watcharasriroj

MONTIEN BOONMA

BLACK STUPA, 1989

Soil, pigment, mashed paper, charcoal, rice flour, and rice grains, 110.5" x 78.75"

The Thai landscape is punctuated by more than 27,000 Buddhist temples, most of which also contain large stupas reaching toward the sky. Originally built to contain the relics of the Lord Buddha and his scriptures, stupas nowadays contain the ashes of distinguished monks, community leaders, and people who contributed significantly to the temple. Stupas are viewed by lay persons as symbols for propagating the faith and as a means for honoring those who supported the temple during their lives.

Montien has taken the concept of the stupa further by transforming it into a symbol of the Buddhist precept that all things change and take on different forms. This work represents a transformation of some of the most common elements of Thai life: grains of rice, soil, charcoal, and mashed paper. The panels of natural materials are mounted in the same alternating pattern in which bricks are laid in the construction of actual stupas.

Loaned by the artist, courtesy of Visual Dhamma Gallery

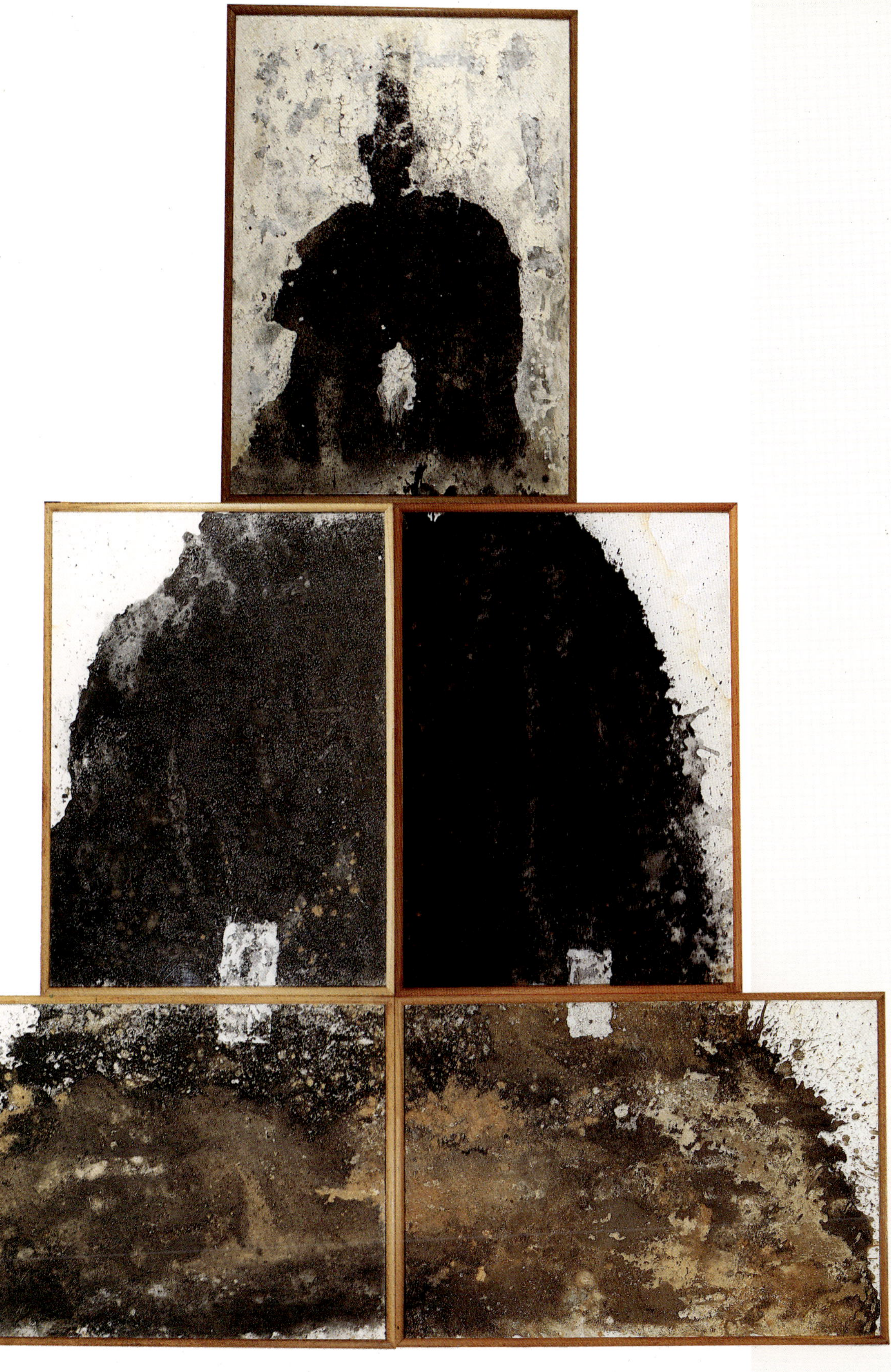

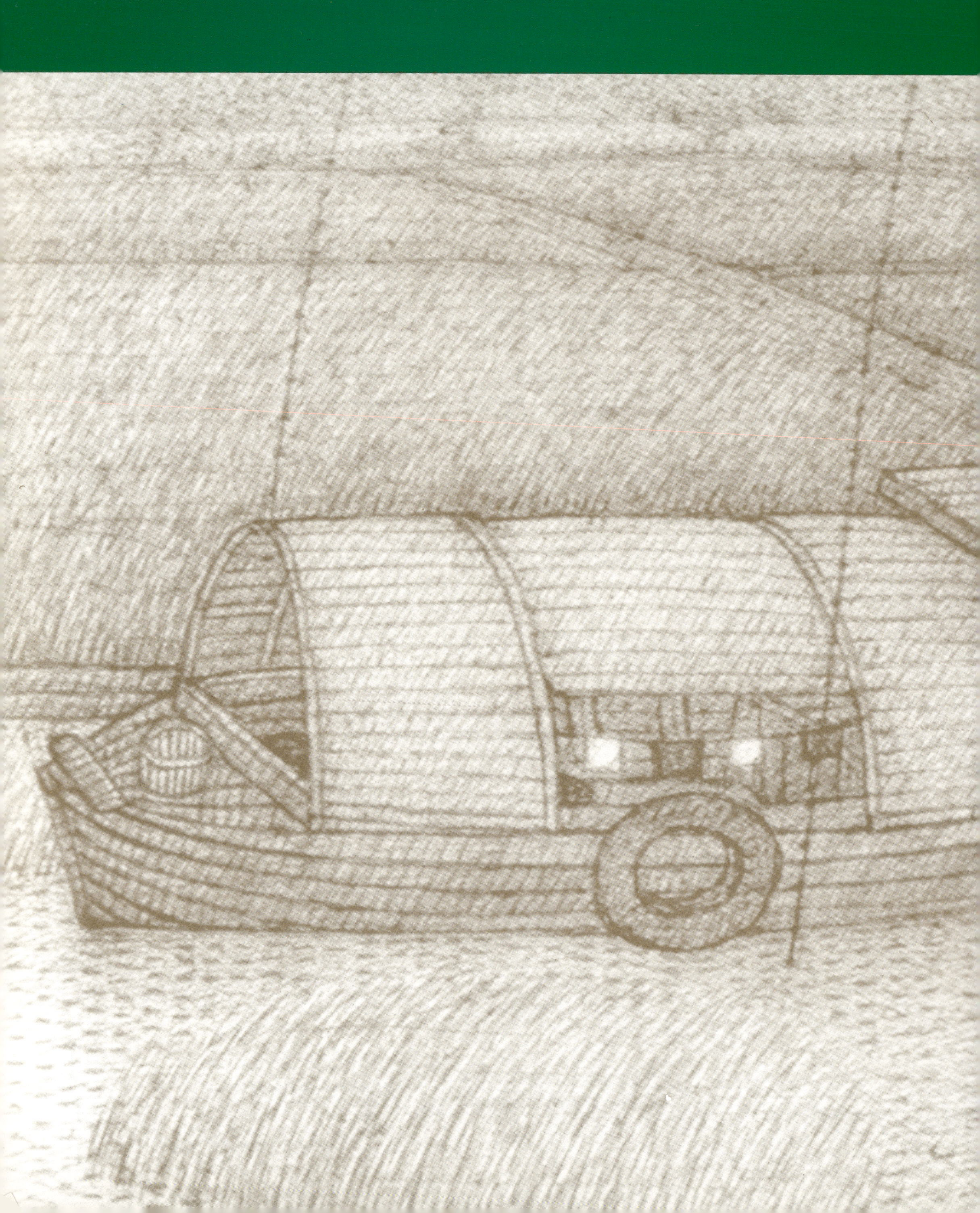

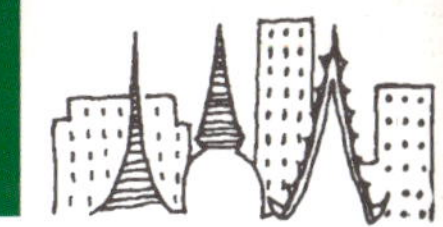

Although daily life in Thailand may be observed as throbbing with activity, bustling people, traffic and noise, this aspect of their environment is rarely portrayed by Thai artists. Artwork dealing with daily life tends to express a spirit and attitude about that life rather than to reveal it with precision or clarity. Artists' visualizations of the culturally familiar are mainly statements of suggestion, context, and atmosphere. Thus, while Thai artists do figurative work, their images of people are often faceless or without recognizable emotions. Some artists explain this preference on the grounds that their religion teaches them that appearances are illusions, that everything changes, and that it is folly to try to crystallize the ephemera of daily life (certainly the ephemeral nature of facial expression) into fixed aesthetic statements.

However, if Thai visions of daily life lack a certain directness, they have for native viewers the power to set the tone of an environment, a time of day or time of year, a temperament, a sense of things that may be happening or that may soon happen. There is in much of this art a celebration of the circumstances, and, in certain works, the rhythms of life.

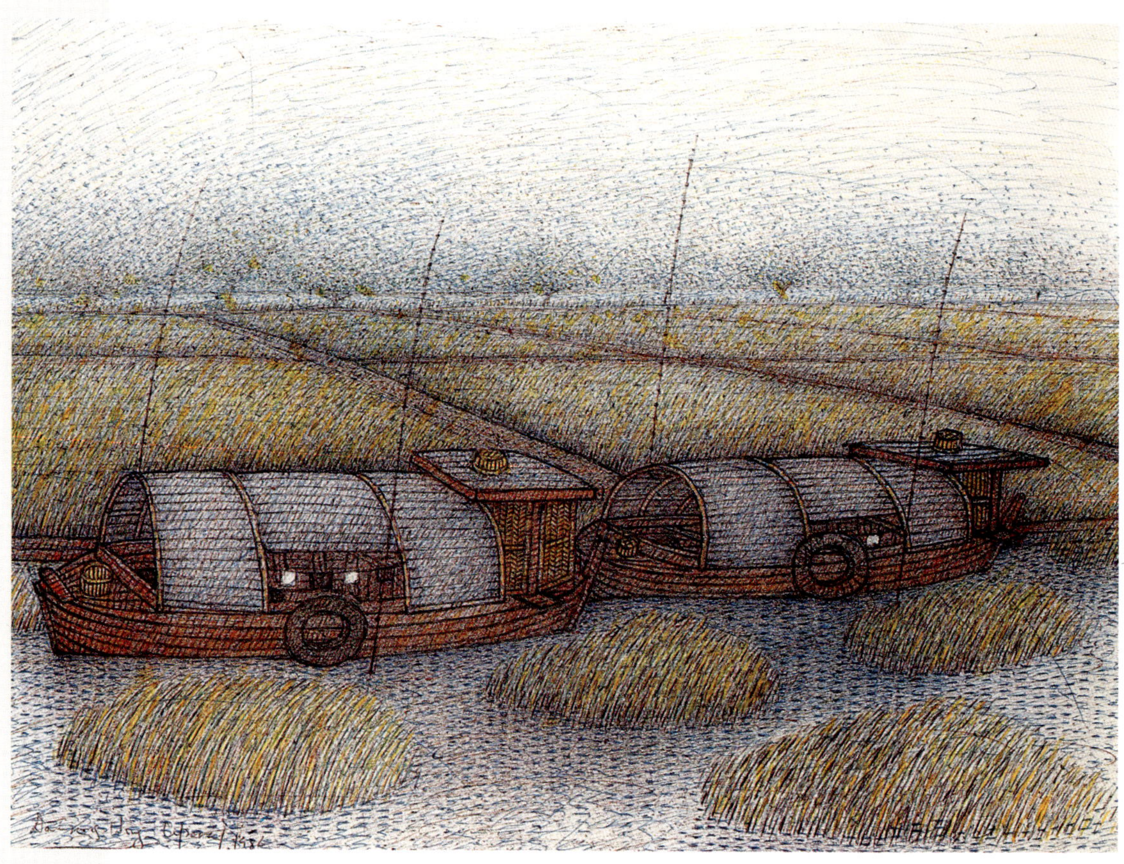

PLATE 16

DAMRONG WONG-UPARAJ

TWO BOATS, 1986

Watercolor and pen, 11" x 15"

"Two Boats" summarizes the spirit of Thai reflections on daily life. The time is dusk—or it could be dawn—and lights through the windows testify to the presence of human beings. They are perhaps preparing the evening meal, or if it is dawn, preparing for the work of the new day. But these ephemeral human acts are totally dominated by two fundamental realities of rural Thailand: the presence of water and the cultivation of rice. It is a setting of peace, plentitude, and comfort. The bamboo poles to which the boats are moored reinforce this spirit: they indicate that the boats are at rest, and for those inside there is also rest and relaxation. Damrong completed this work after his return to Thailand from a year in Japan where, living near Kyoto, he was influenced by Japanese conceptions of landscape and color; his sense of perspective may refer back to his earlier training in London.

Private collection

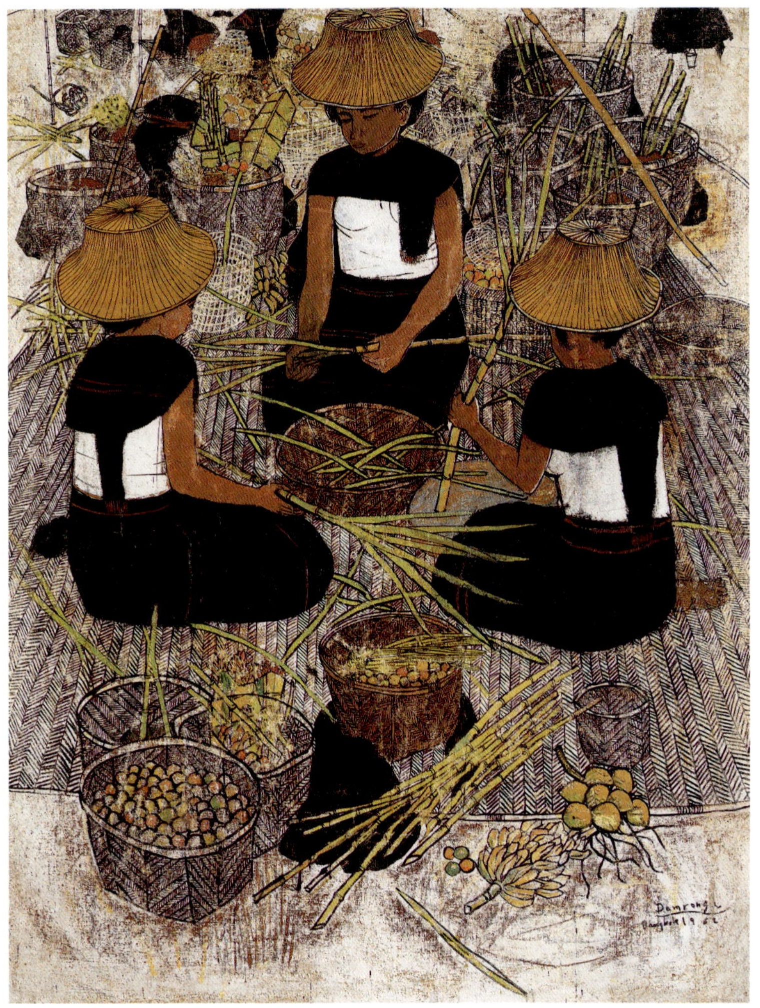

PLATE 17

DAMRONG WONG-UPARAJ

THREE WOMEN, 1961

Tempera, oil based enamel, and poster paint, on canvas, 48" x 34.25"

This portrays one of the most recurrent, personally satisfying situations in village life—three women, sitting, cutting sugar cane (the filled baskets suggesting that they are for sale at market) and gossiping among themselves. For Thai, it is the combination of work and sociability that is so pleasurable. In Thailand, a three-person group (with a member who can contribute diversion, an additional perspective, or a sense of witness) is considered more relaxing than a pair of persons with their greater potential for rivalry and misunderstanding.

Loaned by Faye G. Yoffa Stone

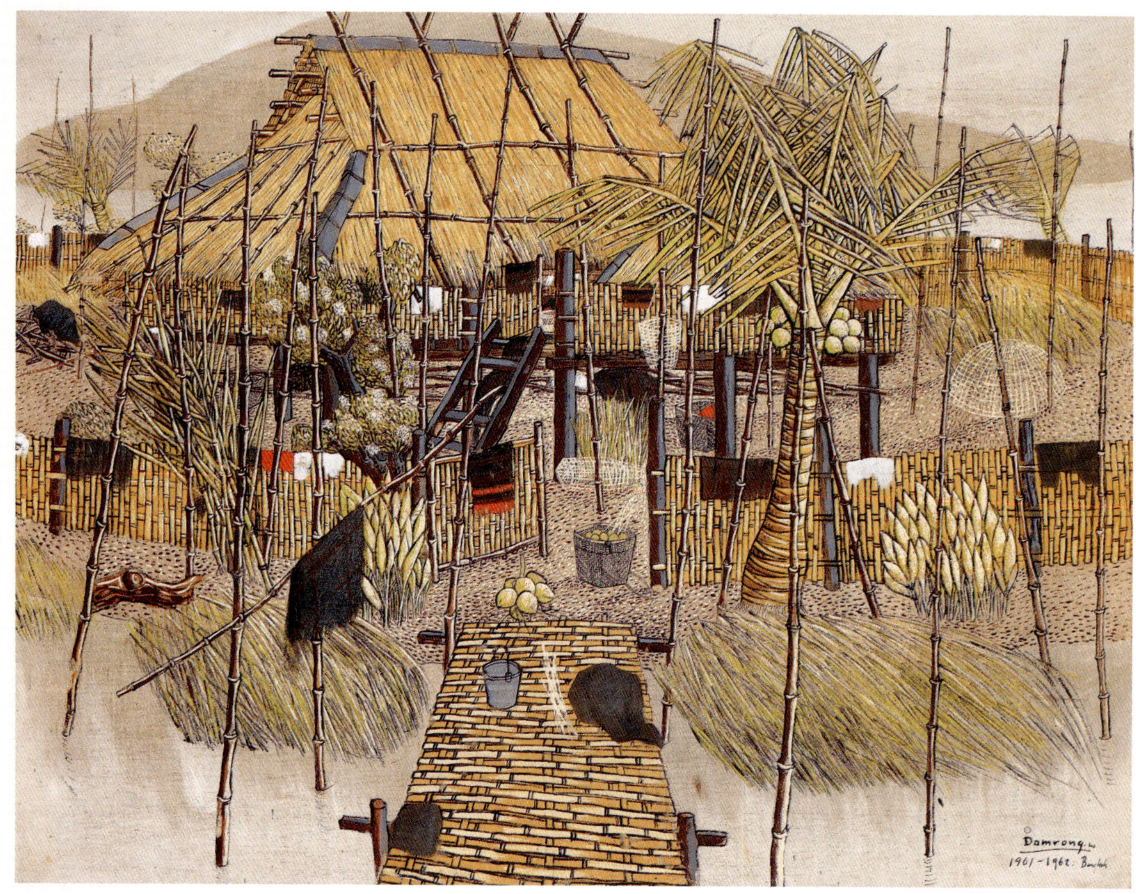

PLATE 18

DAMRONG WONG-UPARAJ

Fishing Village, 1961

Tempera and poster paint on cotton, 31.5" x 29.25"

Known in Thailand for his stylized landscapes and village scenes, Damrong paints in his studio inspired by memories of his environment in the North when he was a child and the fields near his current home in Nakom Pathom outside of Bangkok. This scene is rich with detail of the lives of Thai villagers. Sarongs and other traditional cotton clothing are drying on bamboo fences and poles. In the enclosure to the right of the house is a cage for confining poultry for market. The bamboo poles in the foreground serve to moor the fishing boats and the one against the tree is used in harvesting coconuts.

For Damrong painting is a meditative act—an act of personal focus and internal communication, unmonitored by external stimuli. He is concerned with portraying peace, silence, and moments of perfection that are independent of the flow of events.

Loaned by Faye G. Yoffa Stone

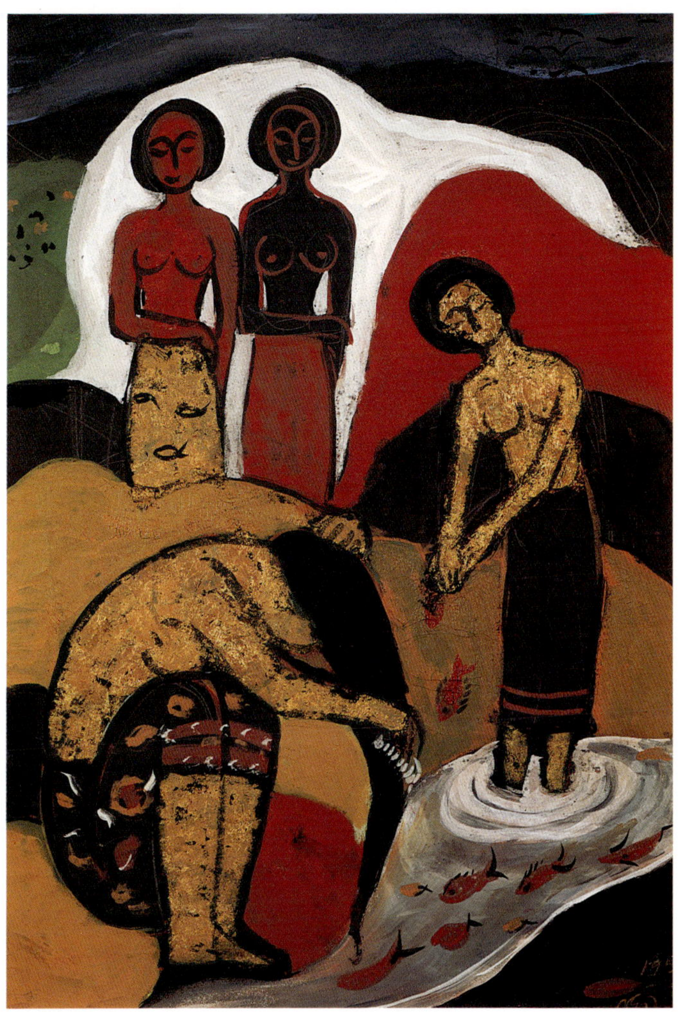

PLATE 19

CHALOOD NIMSAMER

Songkhran (New Year), 1957
Oil and gold leaf on canvas, 38.75" x 29"

The Thai Buddhist New Year or *Songkhran* is a time of reawakening, replenishment, and the performance of good works, such as releasing fish into a river as shown here. The water, the maidens, and the fish motif on the sarong all symbolize this celebration of gestation and growth. Some Thai identify the figure in the foreground as *Maeae Phra Toranii*, Mother Earth, a major figure in the Lord Buddha's struggle against the evil forces of Mara's Army. After victory, Mother Earth is said to have washed her hair to rid it of all vestiges of evil. Her posture is one of the recurring images of Thai art. The artist, however, says the figure is reminiscent of his own mother washing her hair in the nearby canal when he was a child.

Schooled in Bangkok, Rome, and the Pratt Institute in New York, Chalood Nimsamer has over his career tried to integrate international influences (in this instance, Expressionist and Fauvist sources, and through them, African or Oceanic masks) with Thai themes and sensibilities. Western viewers can easily identify such Western features as the abstract color fields in the background or the Matisse-like faces on the young girls. But this would miss what for Thai viewers are the painting's primary aesthetic qualities: the ceremonial subject matter and the two-dimensional nature of the figures, both of which are based on the stylistic conventions of traditional Thai painting.

Loaned by the family of Misiem Yipintsoi

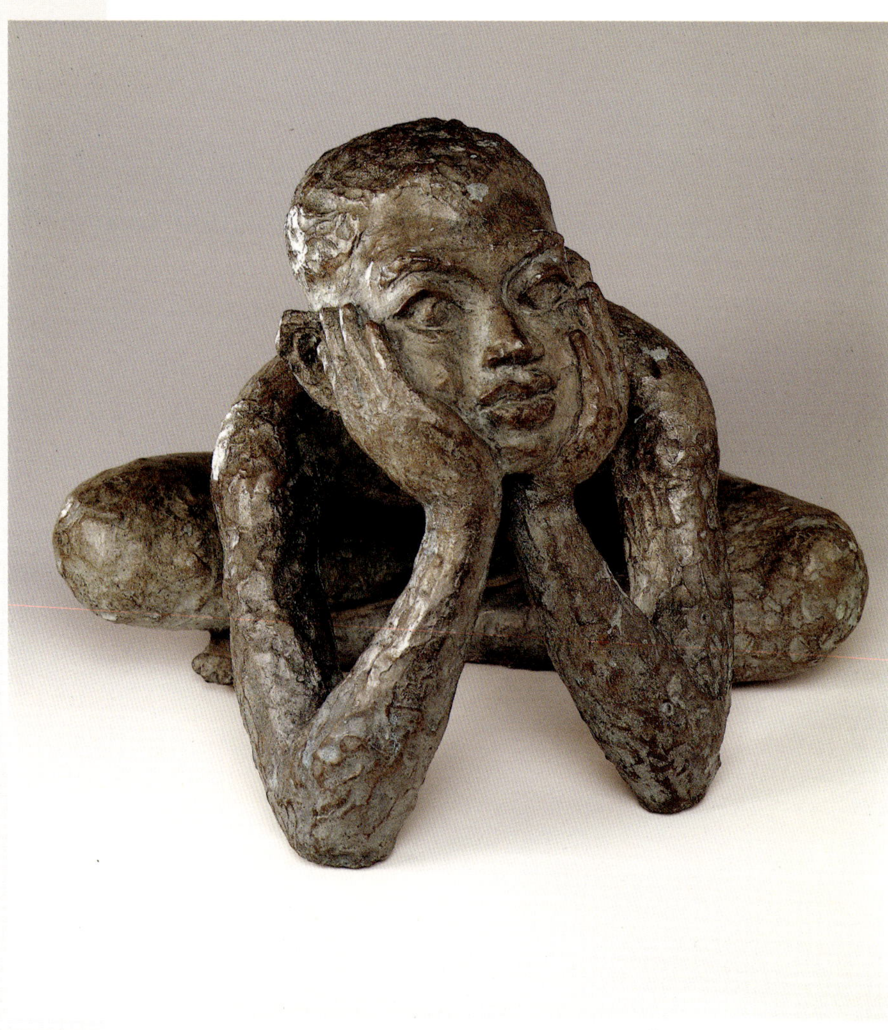

PLATE 20

MISIEM YIPINTSOI

WATCHING TV, 1975
Bronze, 1/1, 16" x 14" x 21"

Inspired by artwork she had seen on her travels in Europe, Misiem departed radically from her Thai contemporaries by eschewing the accepted "serious" subjects of Buddhism and nationalism. Instead, she focussed her attention on family members and friends, often portraying the activities of children. To American viewers accustomed to the figurative interests of Western sculptors, the selection of the commonplace activities and emotions of real humans as subjects may seem obvious, but in the Thai context Misiem's work is historically distinctive. The model for this work was the artist's grandson.

Born in Thailand to an Indonesian Chinese merchant family, Misiem first travelled in Europe after World War II seeking a cure for a daughter who had contracted polio. While the search was unsuccessful, she discovered art in the museums and homes of the Continent, and upon her return to Bangkok, she took up painting at the age of 42. She later studied under the transplanted Italian sculptor, Corrado Feroci, and at the age of 51, she shifted her attention to sculpture—to which she remained dedicated until her death in 1988 at the age of 82. While both prolific and varied in her career, Misiem felt her best work was on the pleasures of childhood.

Loaned by the family of Misiem Yipintsoi

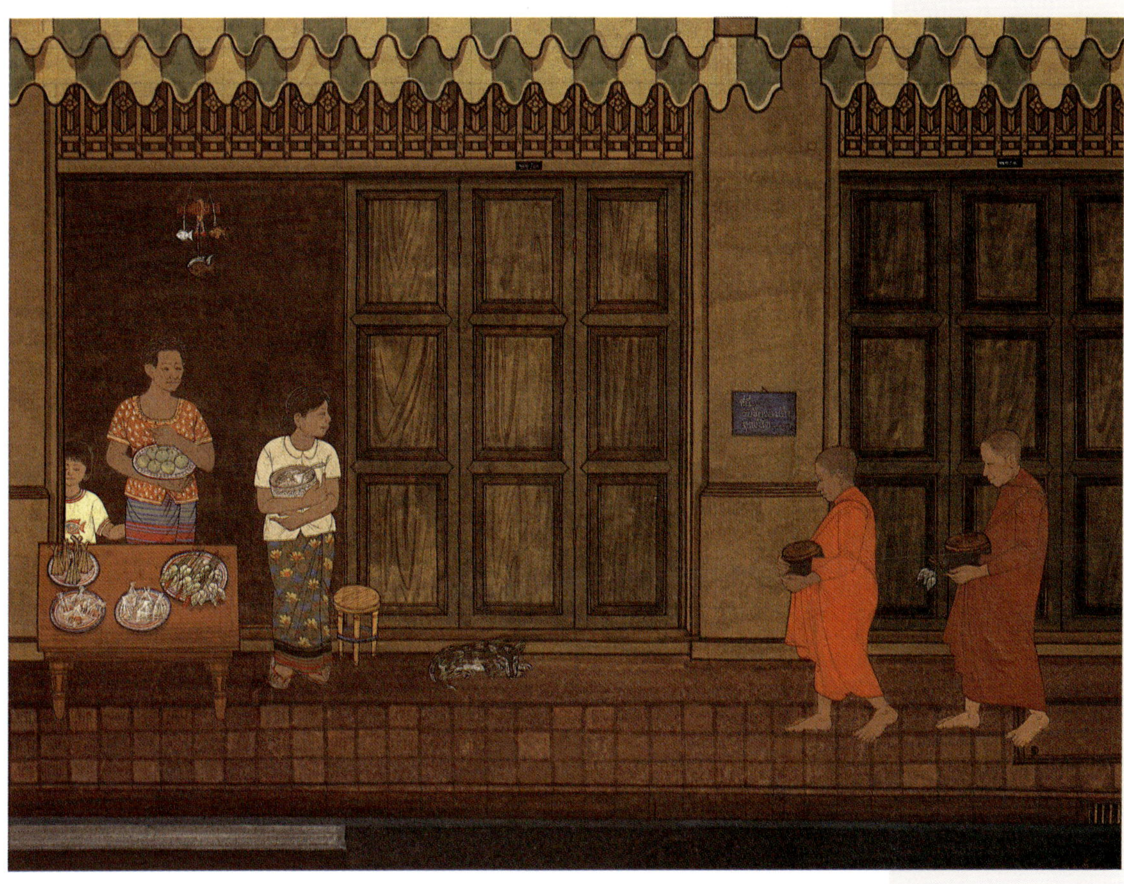

PLATE 21

CHALERMCHAI KOSITPIPAT

MAKING MERIT, 1975
Tempera on masonite, 21.5" x 28"

This work portrays one of the most recurrent scenes of early morning urban life—a family outside its shop house waiting to feed Buddhist monks on their daily begging rounds. Such activities make merit for each member of the family and serve to increase the participants' moral standing in both this life and future lives.

Chalermchai Kositpipat is perhaps more committed than any other living painter to merging the moral didacticism of traditional temple mural art with the realities of the contemporary Thai experience. He sees this as historically the most appropriate basis of a truly "unique Thai art." Here, the flat, two-dimensional quality of the painting (apparent in the table and sidewalk) is intentionally meant to replicate the two-dimensional nature of traditional Thai mural painting—explicitly linking the artist to that tradition. The work is also an expression of Chalermchai's belief that religious art should not be restricted to the walls of temples, but should be displayed in the home and workplace as well.

Loaned by Mr. and Mrs. Bart N. Stephens

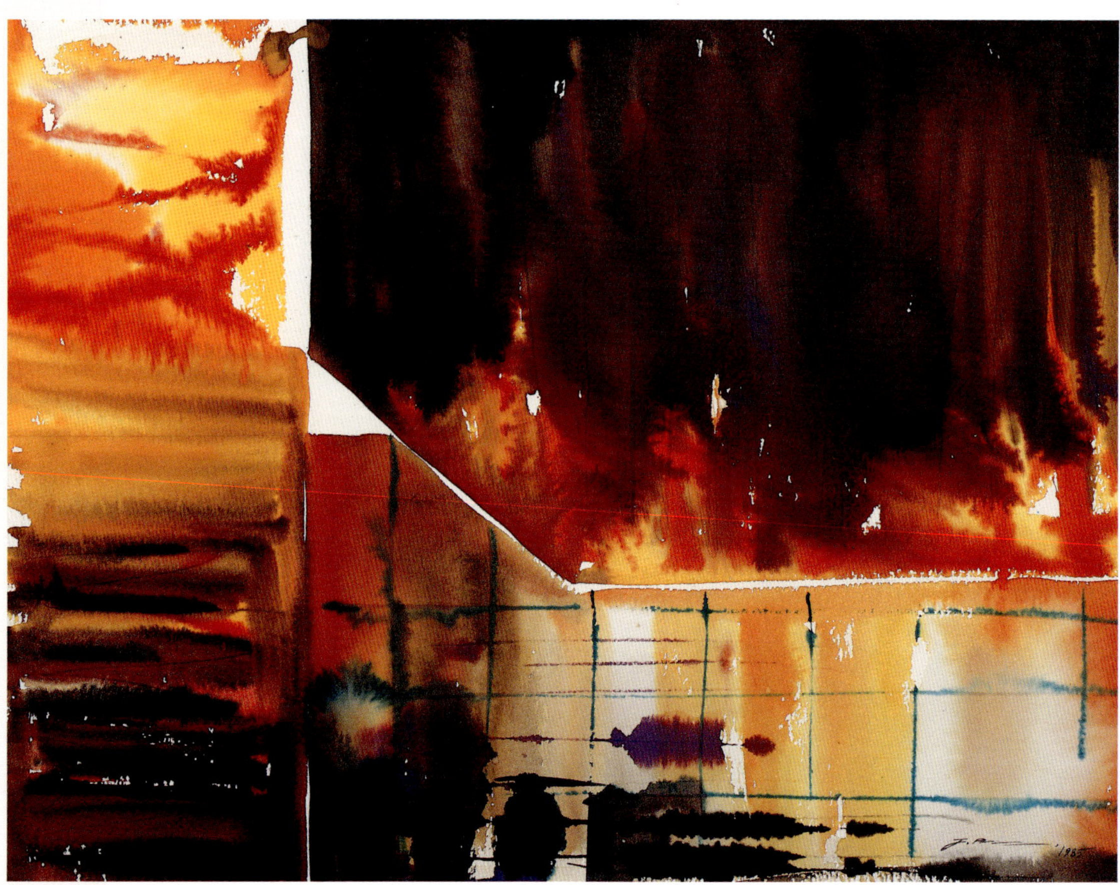

PLATE 22

JIRAPAT PITPREECHA

CITYSCAPE, 1986
Watercolor, 18" x 30"

This abstract work is meant to represent the ambience of Bangkok, the kingdom's capital and primary urban center. The artist explains that the yellow and orange express the tropical heat while the black expresses the filth and the oil residues seen everywhere on the city's streets. The green is meant to convey motorcycle tracks and the grid-like design of the metropolis, as well as the occasional greenery that can still be found in Bangkok.

Loaned by the artist

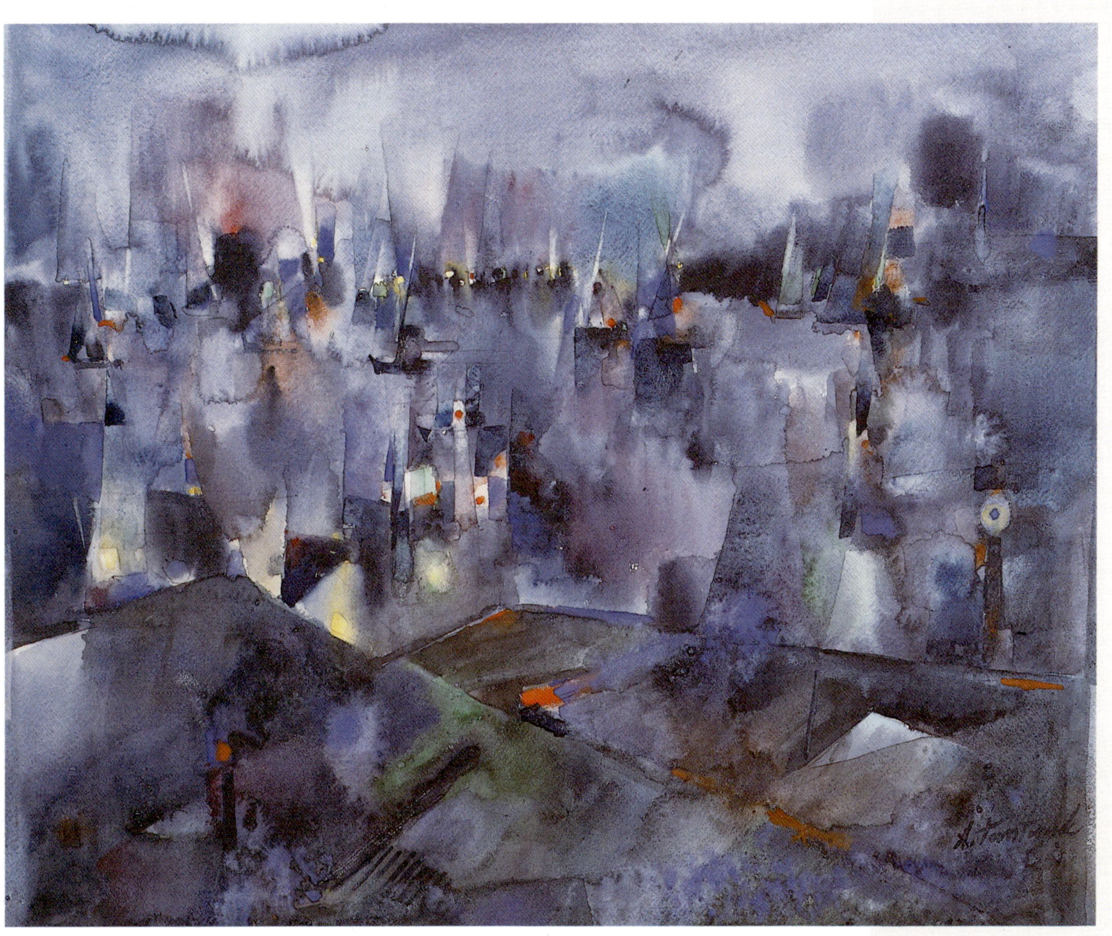

PLATE 23

SAWAT TANTISUK

CHOLBURI BAY AT NIGHT, 1986
Watercolor, 14.75" x 17.5"

This semi-abstract watercolor is the artist's vision of a night-time seascape. The subject is culturally significant because it demonstrates Thai attitudes about the night—a time for work, activity, and pleasure. Even the sea is alive with nocturnal activity.

Private collection

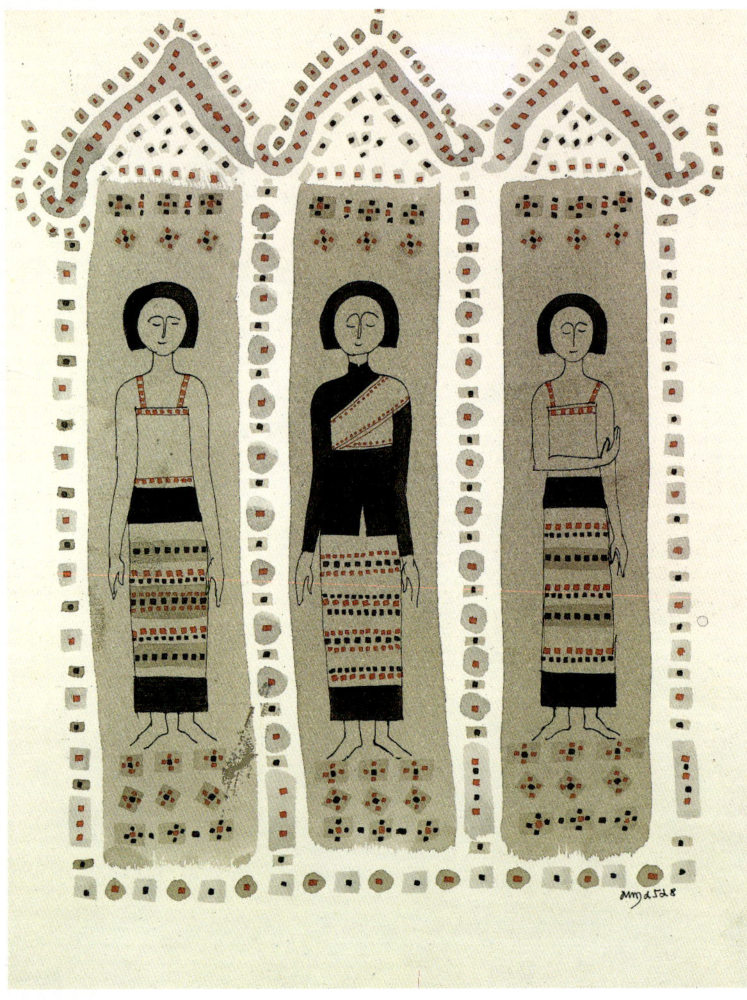

PLATE 24

CHALOOD NIMSAMER

THE ARTIST'S DAUGHTER, 1985
Ink and watercolor, 13" x 10.5"

This simple but innovative work is one of a series of portraits of the artist's daughter. Chalood describes it as "a Thai Buddhist portrait." The triangular designs above the figures replicate the roof line of the *bod,* or ritual hall, of a temple. Although women cannot become monks, Chalood claims that Buddhist virtues are where you find them, and that his daughter in fact possesses the gentleness and inner peace of the Lord Buddha and of Buddhist monks, his earthly representatives. While some Thai might perceive such a vision as pretentious, it is meant to be loving and respectful.

Loaned by the artist

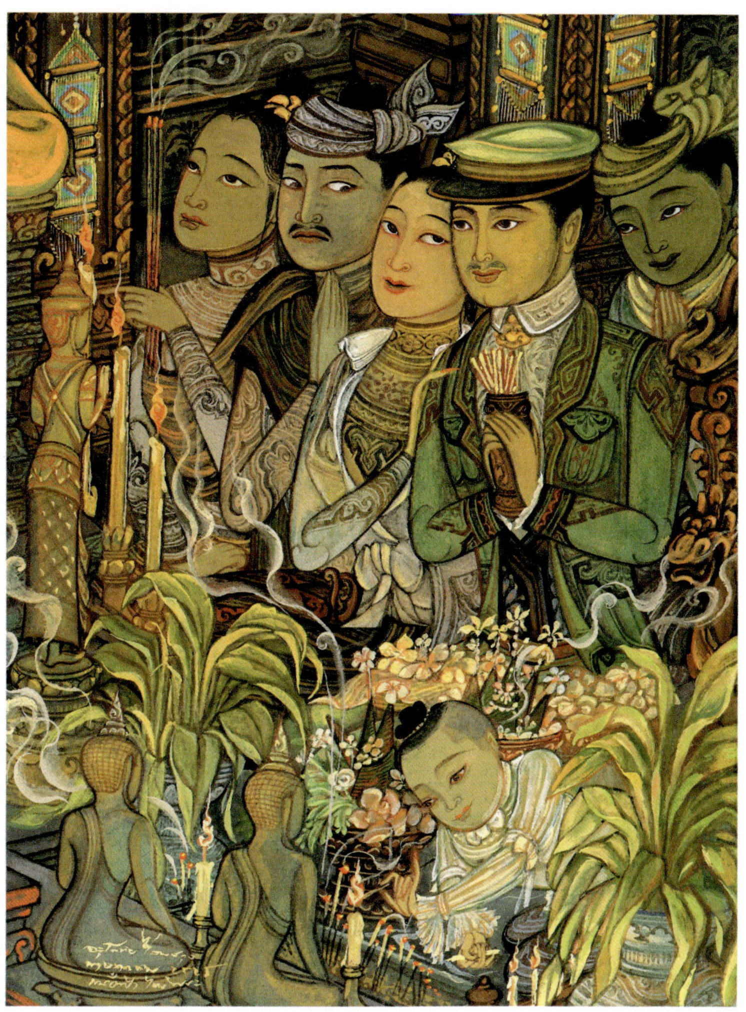

PLATE 25

ARUNOTHAI SOMSAKUL

FORTUNE TELLING, c. 1975

Tempera on paper, 7" x 5"

Most Thai artists shun the portrayal of human frailty or, for that matter, any facial reflection of an individual's emotional state. Arunothai circumvents this convention by removing human beings from the here and now and placing them into fantasies of life during the reign of King Chulalongkorn (1868–1910), a period perceived as Thailand's golden age, toward which there is a profound sense of nostalgia. This miniature depicts human feelings about fortune-telling: the chap with the cannister of sticks is about to discover his own fortune; his lady conveys her support; and the man to her right his anxiety; while the woman to his right is absorbed in her own thoughts. The younger person behind him is a servant beseeching lady luck for the best possible results. The garments of the principals are based on Burmese styles found on temple murals in Northern Thailand, while the composition of the work is meant to suggest a tattoo, and the good luck that it is meant to bring. The child playing with the candle has no clear-cut meaning, other than to evoke the sacred setting.

Loaned by Brian Doberstyn

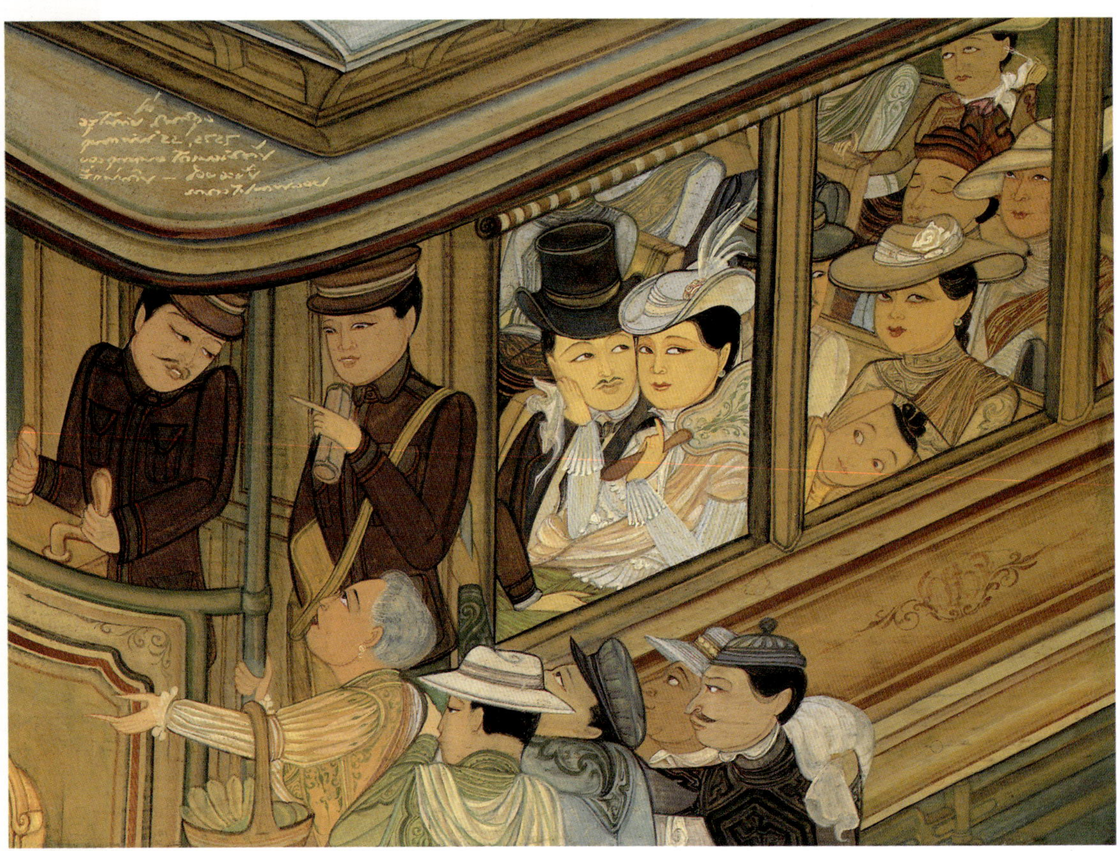

PLATE 26

ARUNOTHAI SOMSAKUL

MOTHER PLOY, C. 1975

Tempera on paper, 5" x 7"

This tram scene depicts a minor event in *Four Reigns* by M.R. Khukrit Pramoj, the most widely read Thai novel of this century. The heroine of the novel is "Mother Ploy," who exemplifies a Thai ideal: she is the perfect spouse, mother, confidante, peacemaker, and homemaker. Here the heroine is portrayed boarding a tram to go shopping, and because she asks directions and is a member of the elite (as revealed by her fine clothes and hands), she suddenly becomes the focus of attention of this Bangkok social scene.

Loaned by Brian Doberstyn

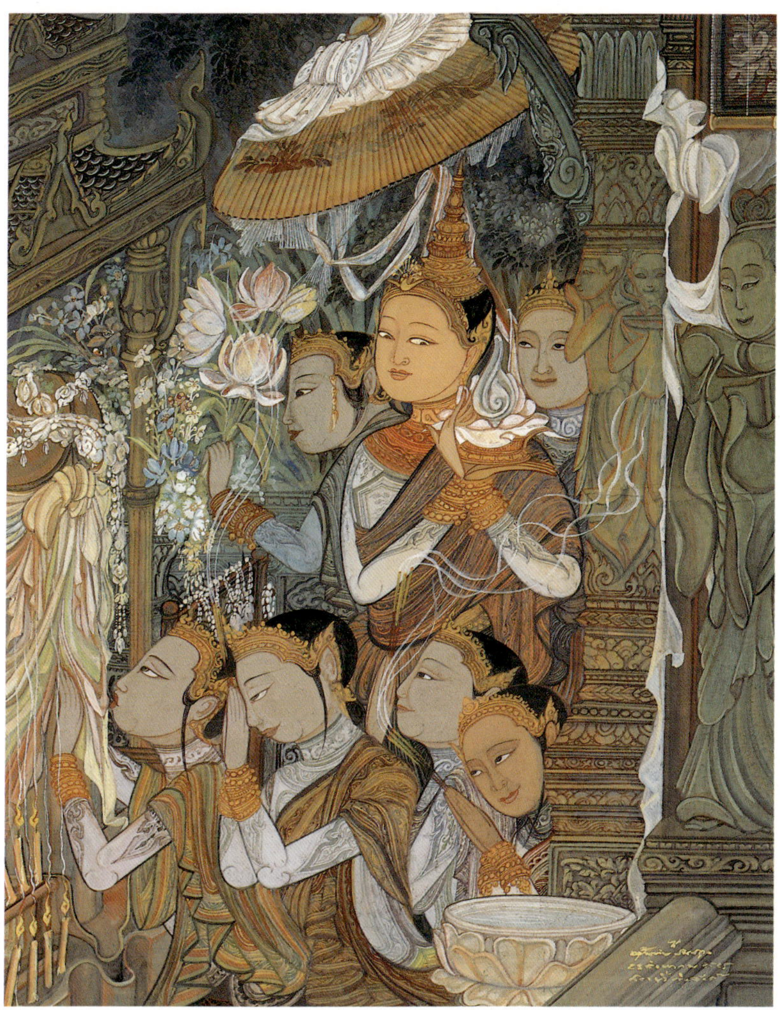

PLATE 27

ARUNOTHAI SOMSAKUL

Homage to Siva Lingam, c. 1975

Tempera on paper, 9" x 7"

Like most of the peoples of world, the Thai have numerous ways for promoting fertility, abundance, and sexual satisfaction. Throughout rural Thailand, boys on the verge of adolescence wear small phallic symbols hanging from their waists to foster their emergent sexuality, and there are numerous shrines throughout the nation where both sexes, but especially women, seek spiritual assistance in dealing with matters of fertility, sexual pleasure, and larger issues of personal happiness. This work is an artistic rendition of such a shrine. The extremely elaborate nature of the scene—the profusion of lingam, flowers, and silks—evokes the actual ambience of these phallic shrines.

Loaned by Marc Bogerd

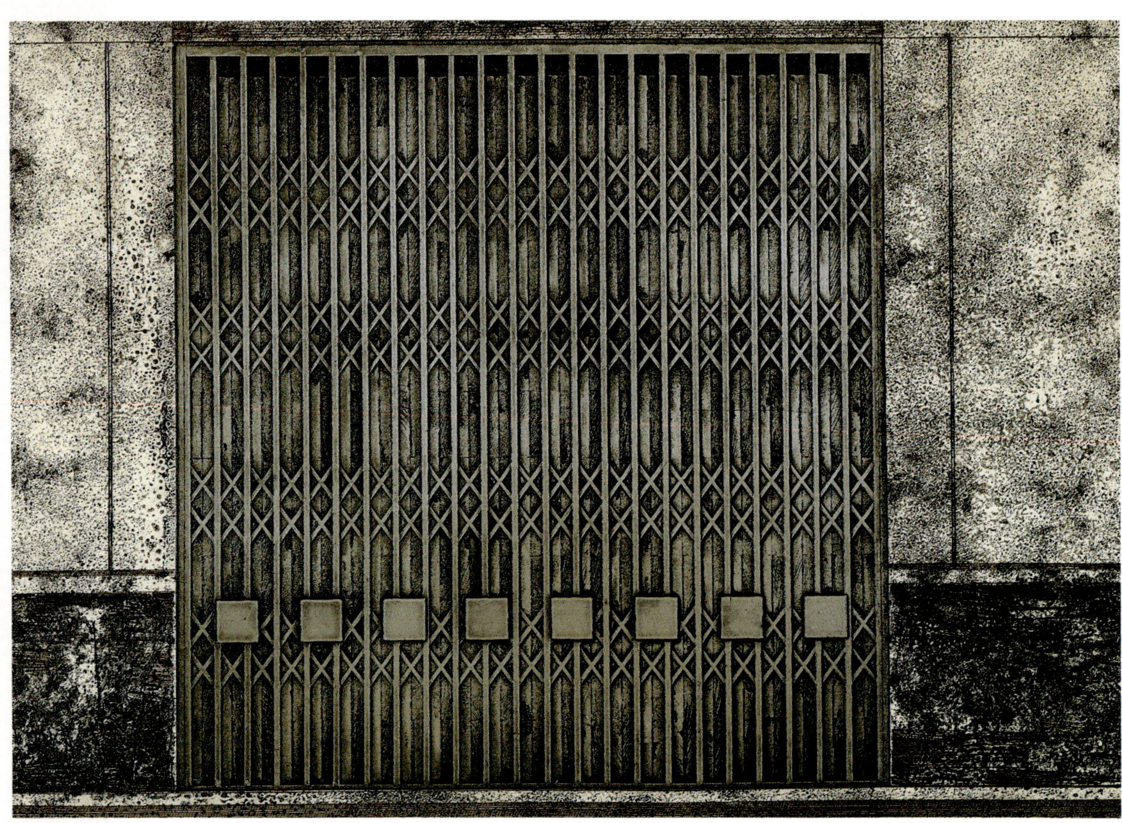

PLATE 28

ITTHIPOL THANGCHALOK

IRON GRATE, 1980
Etching and chine-colle, 22.5" x 29"

While one of the most commonplace sights of Bangkok and of any provincial town in Thailand, a shop front such as this is in fact an unusual subject for a Thai artist to select. Itthipol is one of the few Thai artists to focus on the textures and surfaces of the urban environment.

Loaned by the artist

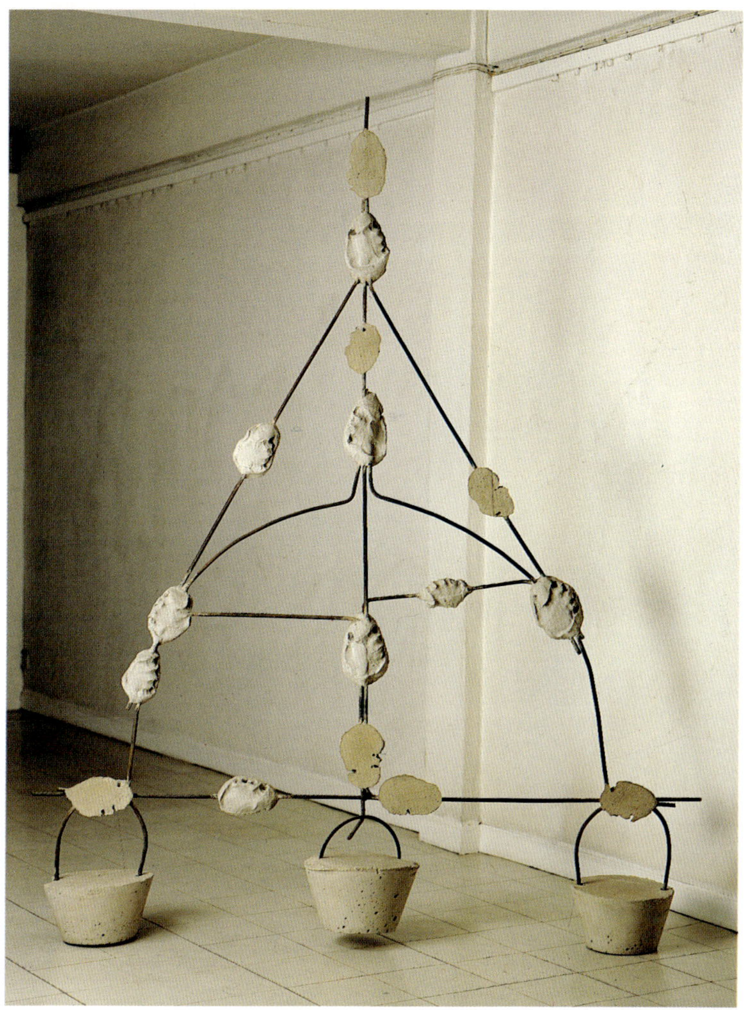

PLATE 29

MONTIEN BOONMA

CONCRETE CONSTRUCTION: HANDS AND STUPA, 1990

Cement, steel rebars, clay, and plastic sockets, 88" x 68.5" x 17"

The basic shape of the Thai stupa is modeled on one of the oldest and most sacred aesthetic forms of Southeast Asia, that of Mount Meru, the center of the universe. Here, the artist has juxtaposed a timeless shape with the architectural materials of contemporary life—concrete and steel rebar. The molded hands represent the unknown construction workers who toil not only on traditional stupas, but on the skyscrapers that have come to dominate the skyline of Bangkok. This celebration of those who build religious structures rather than of those who pay for them or those whose ashes are placed within them is a totally modern Thai conception. Though made of steel and concrete, this sculpture remains upright only because it is delicately balanced—thus illustrating the Buddhist precept that balance and equanimity must be maintained in all things.

Loaned by at the artist, courtesy of Visual Dhamma Gallery

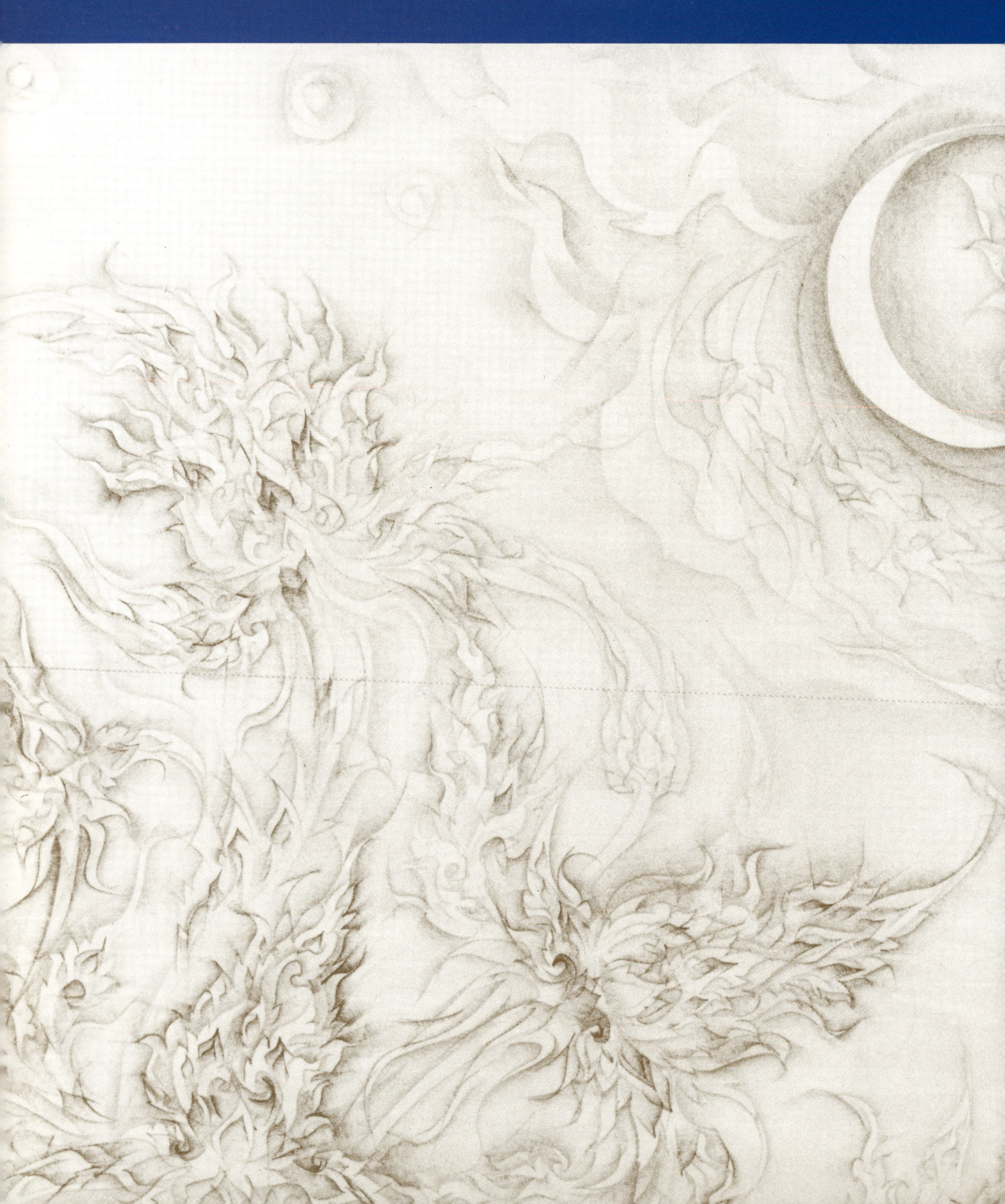

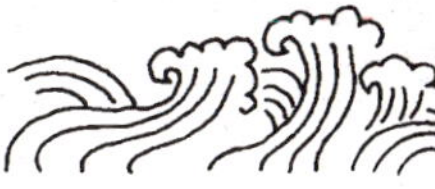

In the water, there is fish. In the fields, there is rice
Whoever wants to trade in elephants, may do so . . .
Whoever wants to trade in silver and in gold, may do so
The faces of the citizens are happy . . .

— from King Ramakhamhang's Inscription, 1292, the historical record marking the rise of the Sukothai kingdom and the founding of the Thai nation

The Thai involvement with the natural universe—their appreciation of it, their sense of security about it, and their celebration of its bounty and beauty—is one of the most recurring themes of Thai art. The Thai conception of "nature" (*thammachaad*) involves a high degree of consciousness and elaboration. Thus, irrespective of their education or sophistication, virtually all Thai know the names of local birds and plants and major stars, and most are fundamentally pantheistic in their readiness to connect humans, plants, animals, gods, and planets into an infinite chain of being. In contrast to many other peoples, they (or nowadays perhaps only a slight majority) still perceive "nature" not as something to be subjugated to human needs or as something to which humans are inherently subjugated, but rather as something with which human beings must always try to be in intimate harmony. This is particularly the case in their attitudes toward their rice fields and water—both of which have been motifs of the Thai way of life since the beginnings of the kingdom. Thus, "nature" is perceived essentially as a source of sustenance and pleasure, providing them with a sense of their place in, and their links to all the other elements of, an infinite universe.

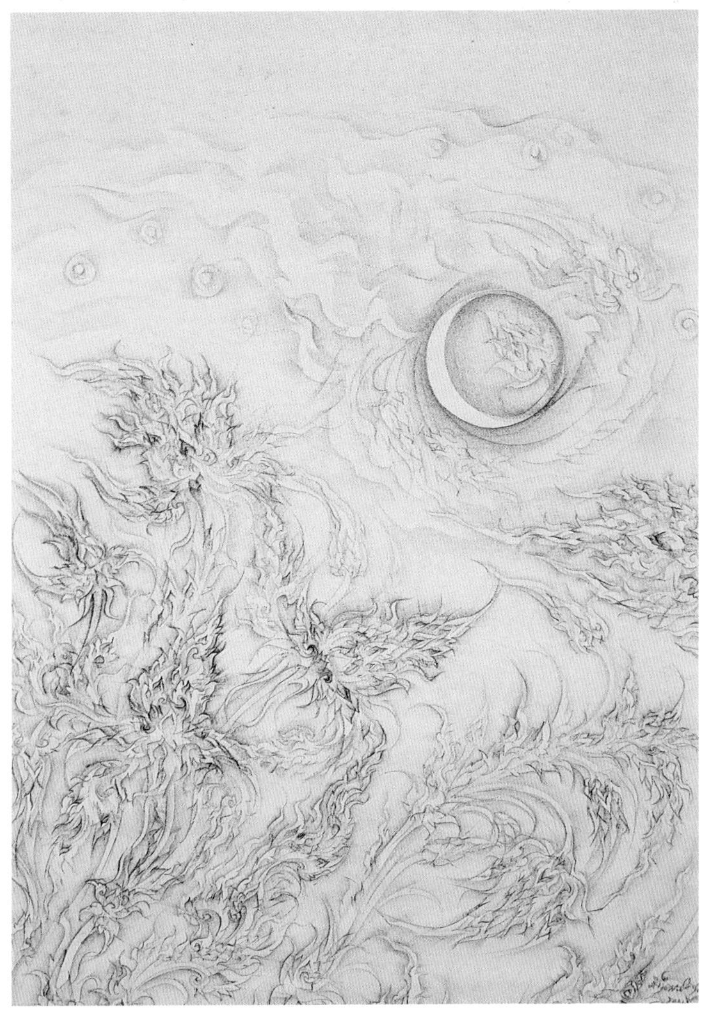

PLATE 30

ANGKARN KALAYAANAPONGSE

MOON OVER RICE FIELDS, 1976
Crayon on paper, 38" x 29"

Among members of the Thai art community there is consensus that no living artist has crystallized the traditional vision of nature as clearly as has Tarn Angkarn ("Master Angkarn") Kalayaanapongse. This assessment of Angkarn may be a product of the Thai belief that artistic and poetic talents are so closely allied as to be found in the same individual, and that Angkarn personifies that truth. Whatever its validity, most educated Thai judge Angkarn to be the kingdom's greatest living poet, perhaps even the greatest of this century. Although Angkarn himself is non-committal about his priorities, his work to date suggests he may give more time to expressing himself in writing than in the visual arts. However, whatever the medium, Angkarn's most abiding concern is to celebrate the pantheistic nature of the universe—a universe comprised of an infinite number of elements, all alive and affecting each other. This work is one modest representation of that vision—rice seedlings dancing in the light of the moon. However, in his inimitable fashion, Angkarn draws the seedlings as *khanok,* the conventional design for flames, thus merging the power of the Earth and the power of Fire—two of the four sources (Earth, Wind, Fire, and Water) of everything. Although Angkarn has made brief visits to neighboring nations of Southeast Asia, he speaks and reads only Thai.

Loaned by Sirichai Narutmitr

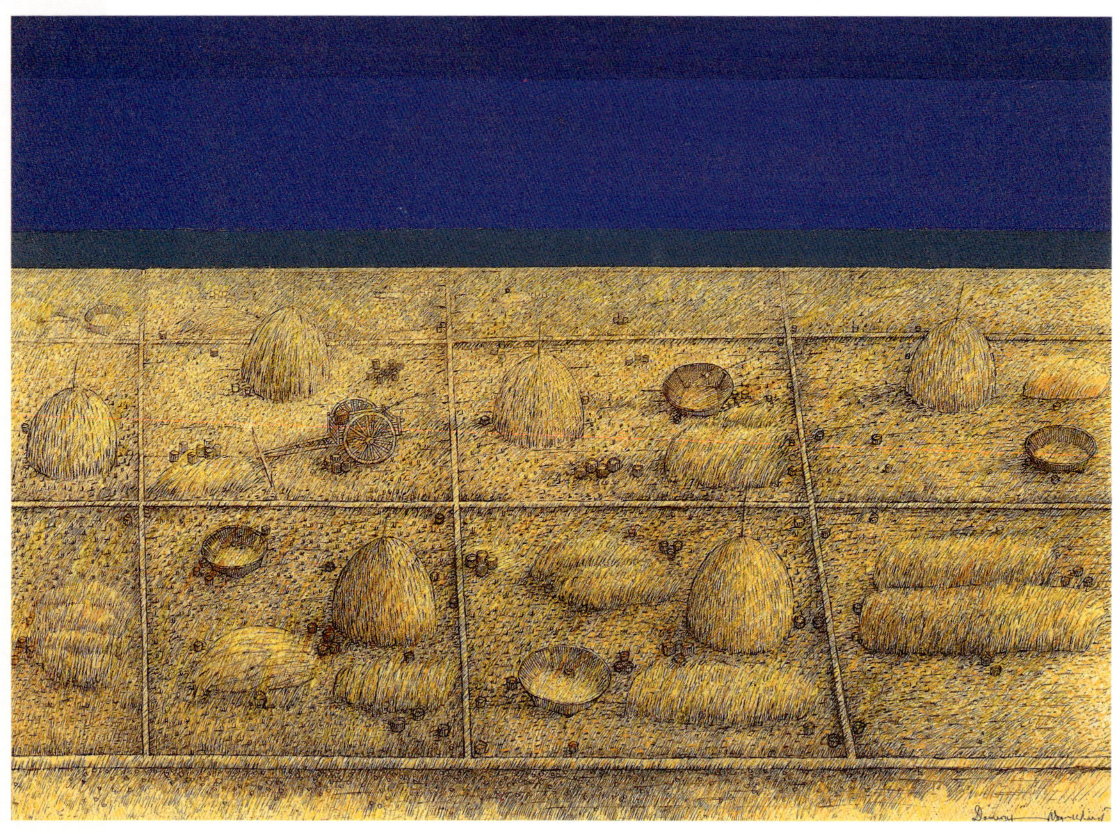

PLATE 31

DAMRONG WONG-UPARAJ

IN THE RICE FIELD, 1971
Acrylic on canvas, 29" x 43"

In its clean lines and uncluttered color fields this semi-abstract interpretation of a rice field reflects Damrong's meditative spirit . This vision of the land after harvest attempts to render the bounty and integrity of nature after it has been properly worked upon by man.

Loaned by Thai Investment and Securities Company Limited

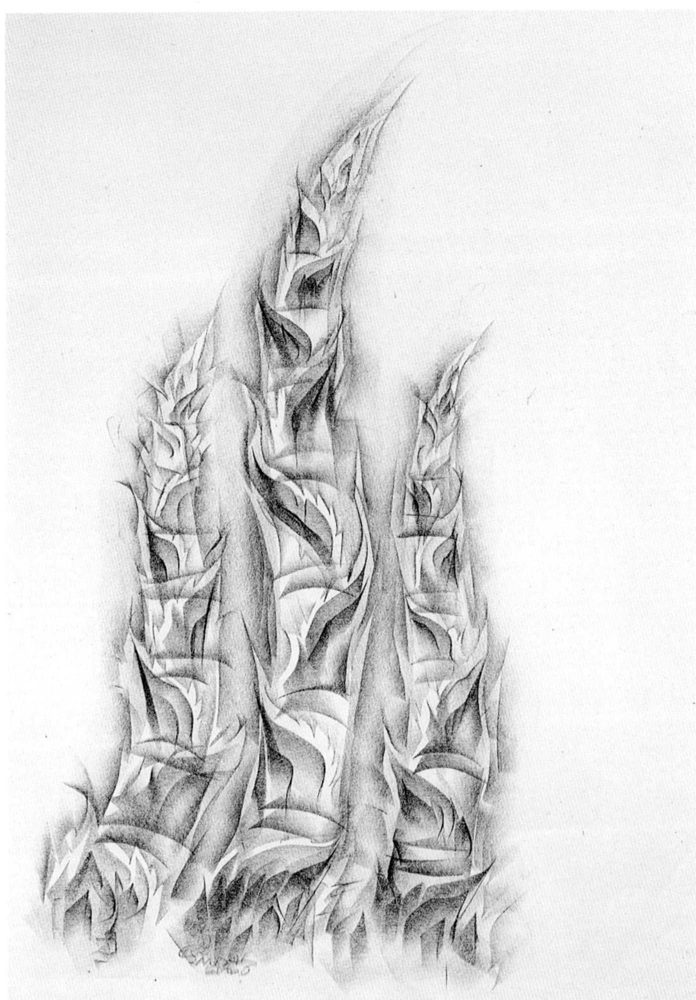

PLATE 32

ANGKARN KALAYAANAPONGSE

THREE BAMBOO SHOOTS, 1979

Crayon on paper, 16" x 12.5"

These simple bamboo shoots are prime symbols of life and fecundity. They are sources of food, shade, and protection against the wind. When cut from their stalks, other shoots will emerge and will multiply indefinitely. The drawing is also a clear example of Angkarn's ability to cut and use the head of a black crayon so that, solely through pressure and control of the crayon's angle, he can inscribe in one stroke both fine lines and heavy shadings.

Loaned by Kanchai Bunphan

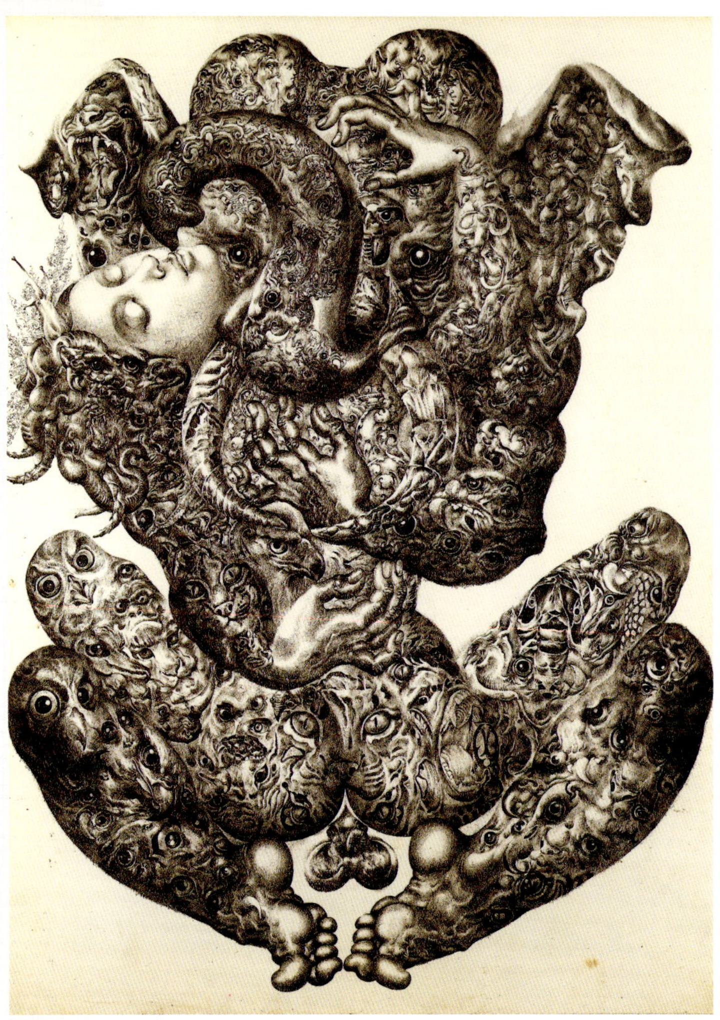

PLATE 33

THAWAN DUCHANEE

"EARTH" FROM THE SERIES "EARTH, WIND, FIRE AND WATER," 1986
Ballpoint pen on paper, 43" x 31"

Thai share the widely-held belief that the universe is comprised of four elements: earth, wind, fire and water. This work is a representation of the first of these elements and portrays the familiar creatures of the Thai jungle—humans, elephants, reptiles, birds, snails, baboons, and jungle cats. At the same time, it is also prototypic of Thawan's enduring interest in merging beasts and humans into inseparable artistic elements—sometimes symbolically, as in this work, and sometimes as expressions of what to him is the reality of their unity in nature.

While enjoying international acclaim, Thawan is considered by many Thai to be the nation's most controversial artist, mainly because of his preoccupation with the darker side of Thai religious practice and belief. Thawan freely melds artistic influences from classical Greece and Botticelli, as in the face of the woman; tantric art from Nepal; Hieronymous Bosch, for his convoluted compositions; and Thai folk beliefs, for his inspirations. Thawan's father was an Army officer and his mother a shaman and healer. It is through her that Thawan developed an intimate knowledge of wild animals.

Loaned by Domnern Garden

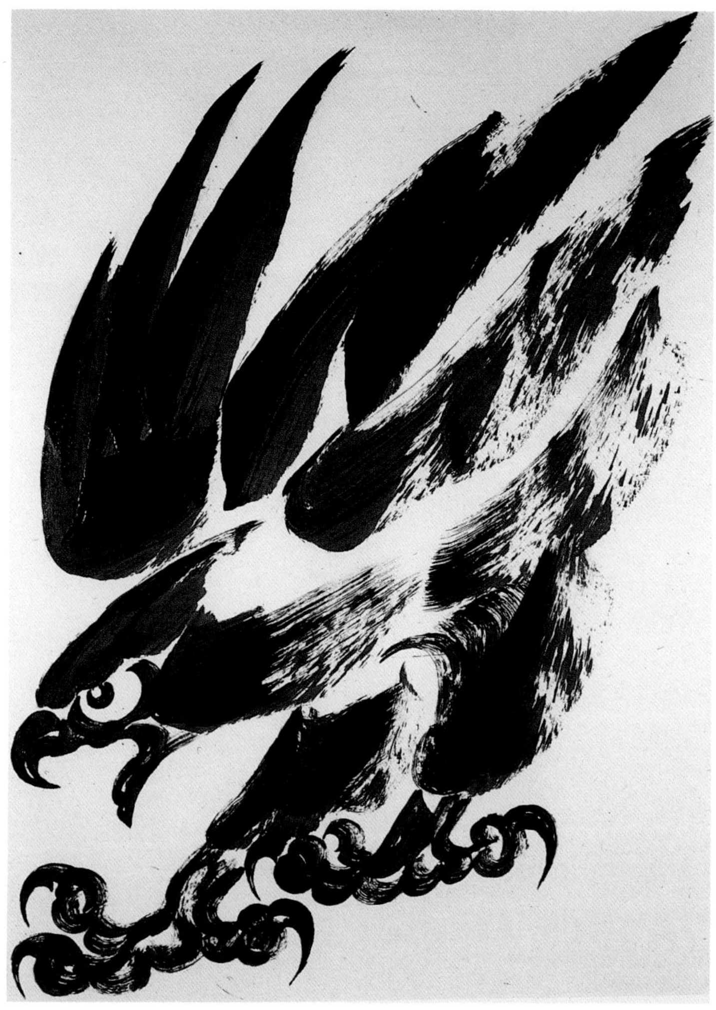

PLATE 34

THAWAN DUCHANEE

WILD BIRD, 1989

Black lacquer on paper, 43.25" x 39"

For all of his dedication to drawing extremely elaborate, fine-lined images of intertwined humans and animals, Thawan occassionally turns his attention to painting large, vibrant gestural works. His typical subjects are tigers, baboons, and birds of prey exploding with instinctual power. This eagle, completed in less than two minutes, is a recent example.

Loaned by the artist

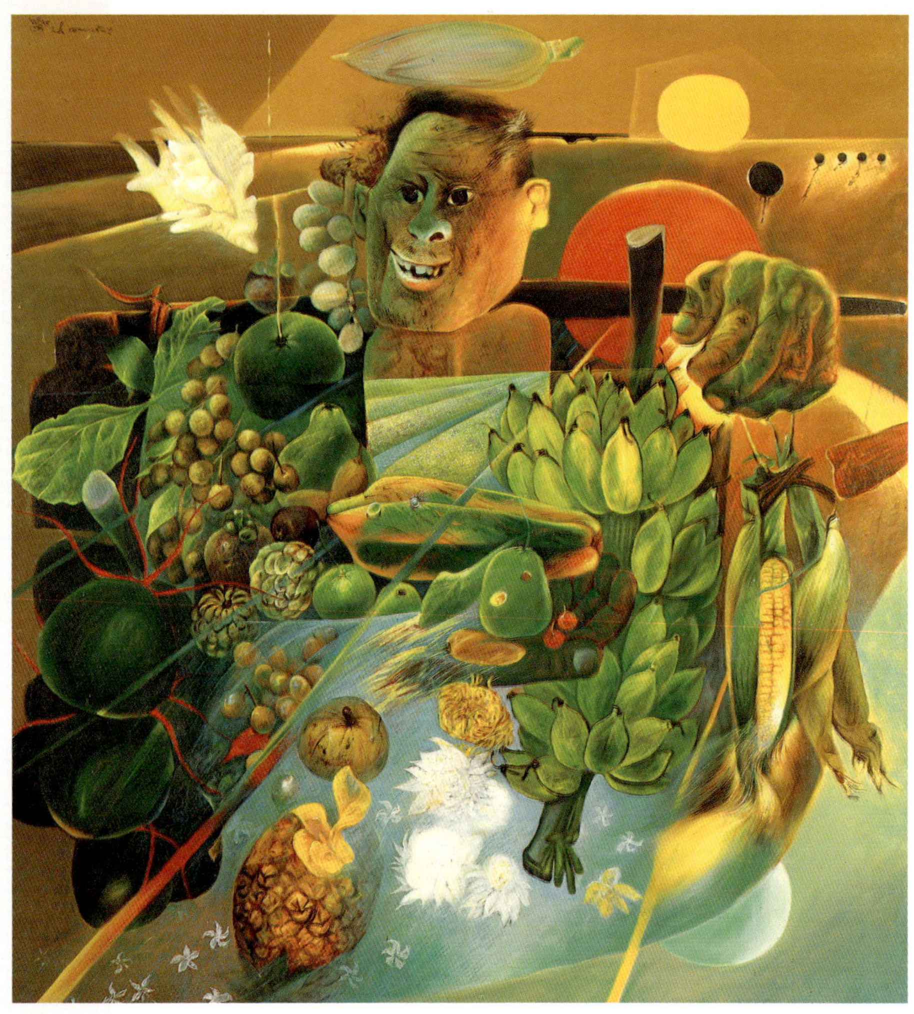

PLATE 35

PRATEUNG EMJAROEN

HAPPY GARDENER, 1973
Oil on canvas, 62.5" x 54.5"

This work is based upon a childhood memory. Born and reared in a gardener's family, Prateung remembers his Uncle Sith: "He was not my real uncle, but our neighbor who had such a kind heart. When you bought one piece of fruit from him, he'd give you two, and when he had nothing more to sell, he'd compliment you. His smile here is the international smile of gardeners. That's the way they all are. Look at that fruit. You work in the shade and you take what you want from the tree. Wouldn't you smile?" Prateung also has some special interpretations of the compositional features of his work. He says that the horizon line and fence rail are expressions of Thailand's peaceful land, although the four holes in the right corner represent bullet holes "to show that even when there is happiness, there is difficulty." The verticals in the banana stalk and fence posts "show the power of gravity, which is a natural force, and that means that everything is as it should be. But the diagonals are the most important, because they show the eternal emanations of the sun. Without the rays of the sun nothing in this painting would exist."

Loaned by the artist

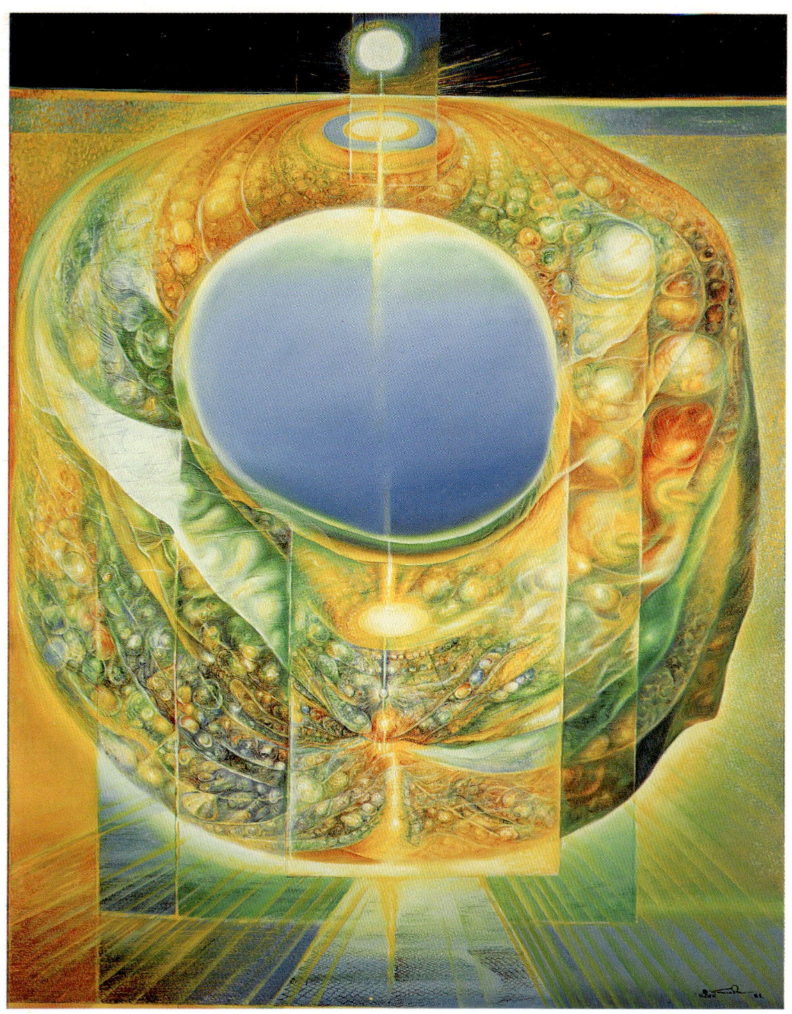

PLATE 36

PRATEUNG EMJAROEN

ENTRY TO THE ETERNAL, 1978
Oil on canvas, 68" x 53.5"

Below the sun and the horizon are the living things of the earth; below that the oceans of the world; and below that, the accumulation of all the fossils that have ever been. In this painting, they are all suspended in space with the rays of the sun dazzling both vertically and diagonally. Thai viewers claim it is a perfect representation of the Buddhist tenet that nature is eternal.

Loaned by the artist

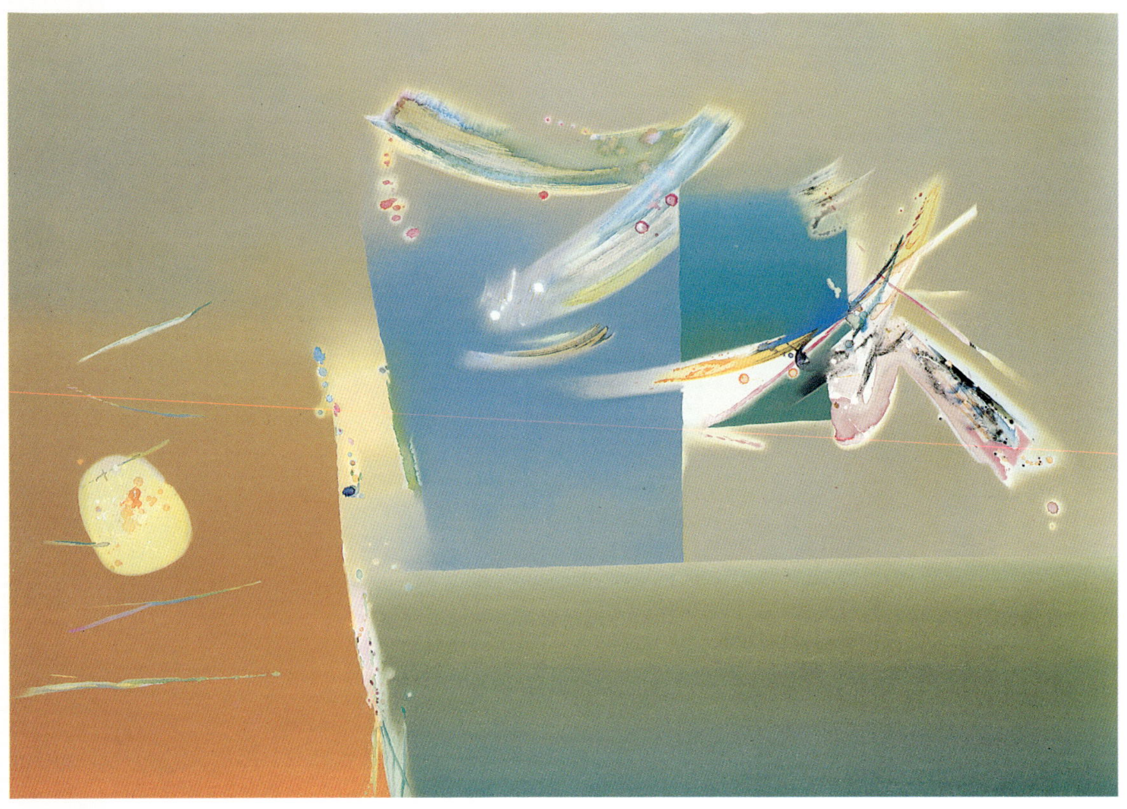

PLATE 37

SOMSAK CHOWTADAPONG

ATMOSPHERIC SPACE, 1981
Oil on canvas, 47.5" x 63"

While the majority of Thai artists have avoided abstract expressionism—partly because it is alien to Thai aesthetic tastes and partly because it sacrifices clarity of meaning for the richness of its colors and forms—a few who have been devoted to it have produced works whose intent is immediately intelligible in the conventional terms of Thai culture. This work, aided by its title, is just such an effort. Here the artist uses strokes of color to structure the inherent open-endedness of space. While this application of color may not seem unusual to Westeners, it has a special poignancy to Thai viewers, most of whom envision the universe in terms of the Buddhist belief in the infinite nature of all life. Here, color and shading provide a way of visualizing infinity.

Loaned by Krit Rattanarak

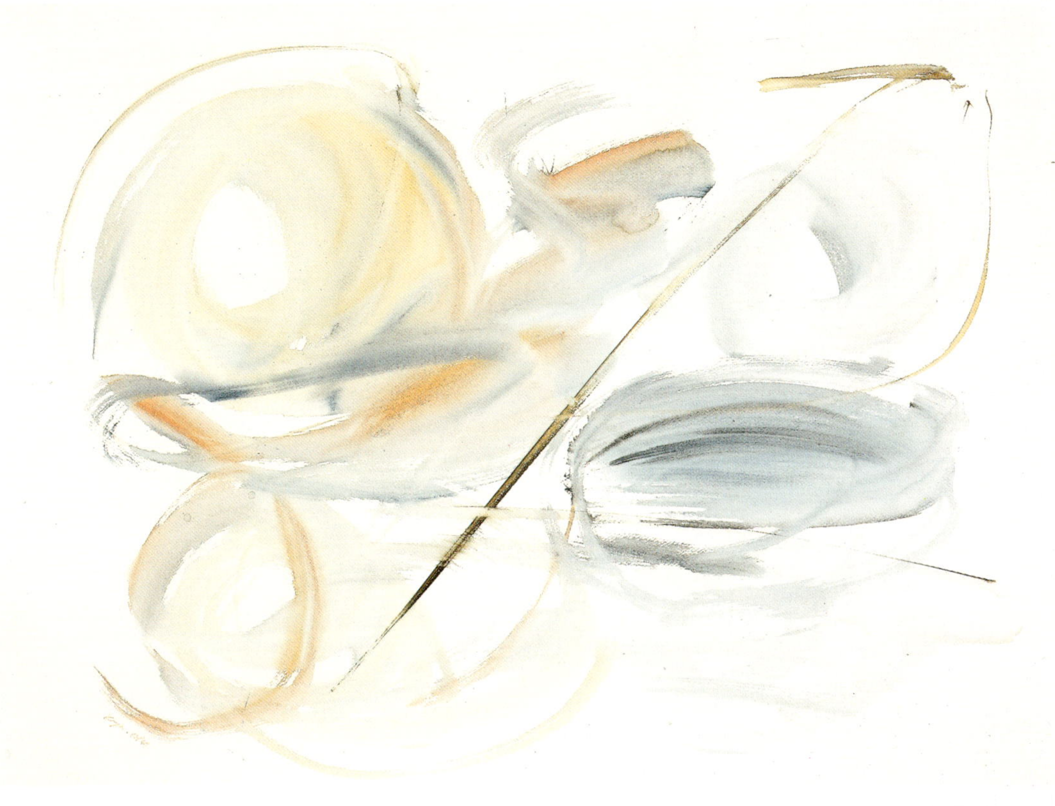

PLATE 38

KANYA CHARONESUPKUL

NIGHT AND DAY, 1991

Watercolor on paper, 29.5" x 41.4"

Many Thai artists are preoccupied with transitions—between life and death, heaven and earth, past and present, and here, between night and day. The artist painted this work in the early morning at the seashore. She was transfixed by the simultaneity of the sun rising and the moon shining, and the problem of how to mark the connections and distinctions between the two diurnal states. The muted colors of the work are a result of the pale reflections of the sandy beach, the dim light of the new day, and the receding light of the moon. The work draws on the Chinese calligraphic tradition in Kanya's family background.

Loaned by the artist

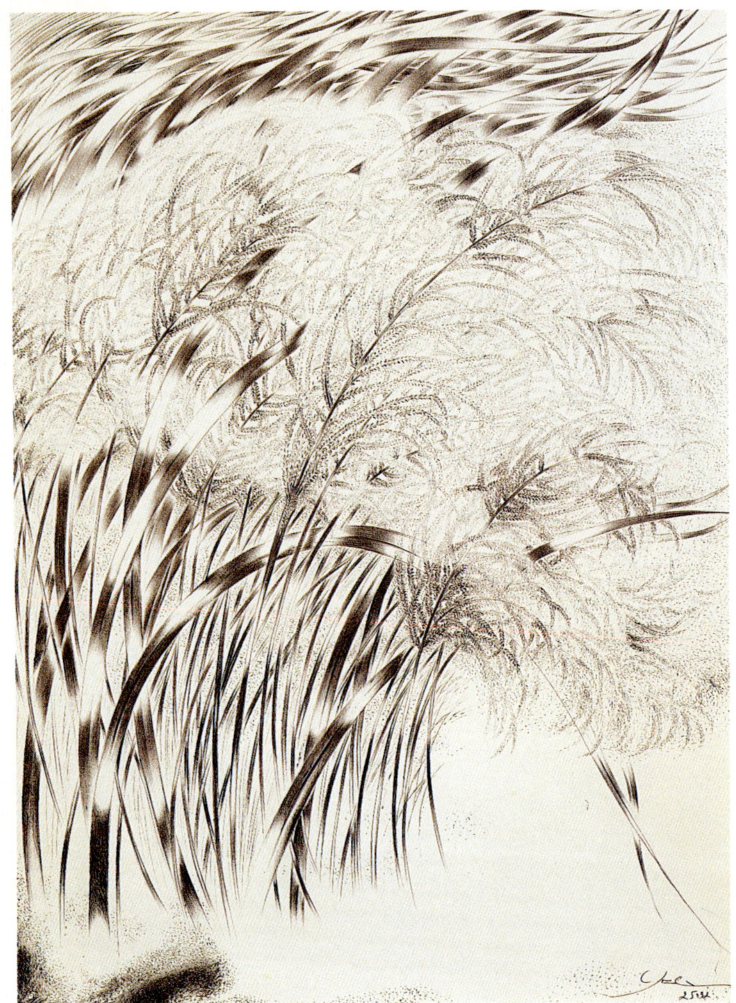

PLATE 39

BOONYING EMJAROEN

FLOWERING GRASS, 1989

Ink on paper, 15" x 11"

The Thai interest in nature can range from the cosmic and metaphoric to the most familiar and elemental. Known mostly for her colorful paintings of blooming flowers, Boonying demonstrates in this work her almost microscopic control of the details of nature. Such fine-lined precision has been a critical feature of the classical and folk art traditions, and is still considered by many Thai as the most important criterion of artistic excellence. Boonying is the spouse of Prateung Emjaroen.

Loaned by the artist

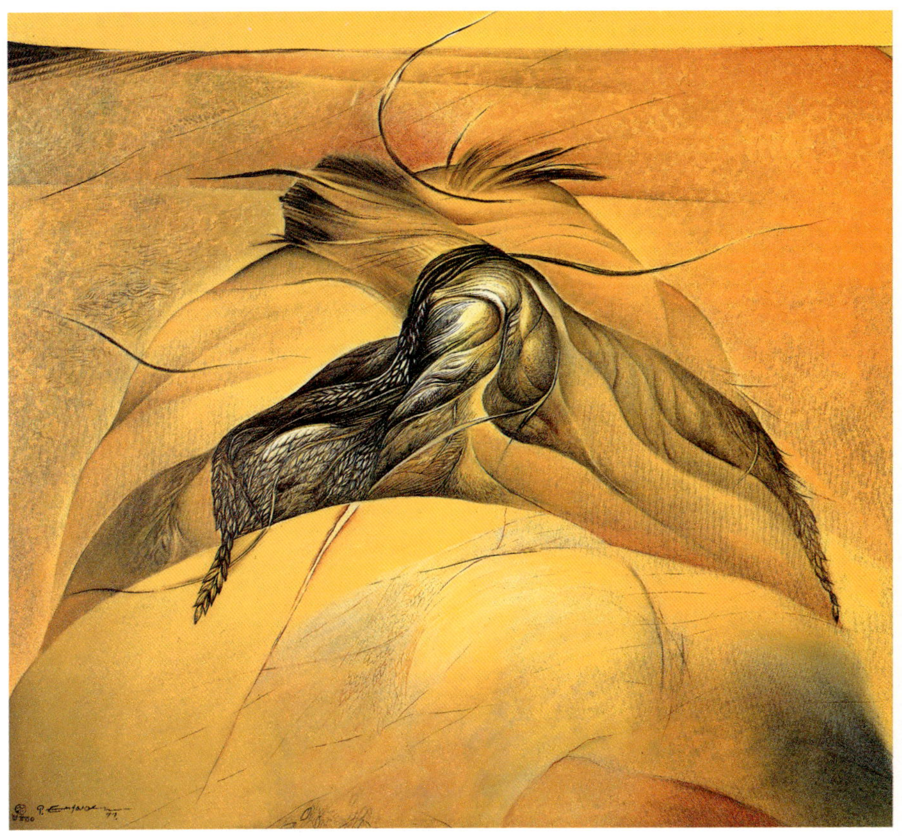

PLATE 40

PRATEUNG EMJAROEN

SHEAVES OF GOLDEN RICE, 1977
Oil on canvas, 39.5" x 35.5"

Rice is one of the great foci of Thai life: it is at once the symbol of all sustenance, fecundity, well-being, and friendship. "To eat" is *"kin khaw,"* or literally "to eat rice." Thai speak of "a meal" as consisting of rice and "with rice" dishes, and when making visits, rice is considered the universal gift. During harvest season people working in the city are expected to return to their villages to bring in the rice, and it is the time of pleasure—of family reunion and closeness, neighborly cooperation, and courting among the young. While Thai artists celebrate rice in all its forms, no vision of rice provides as much joy as does the scene of harvested rice, bursting with promise, and ready for threshing. It is the perfect expression of the munificence of nature.

Loaned by Sivaporn Dardarananda

PLATE 41

THAIWIJIT PUANGKASEMSOMBOON

BENEATH THE BLUE SKY, 1984
Mixed media, 46.5" x 31.5"

This work is meant to convey the joining of the domains of heaven and earth.

Loaned by the Thai Farmers Bank

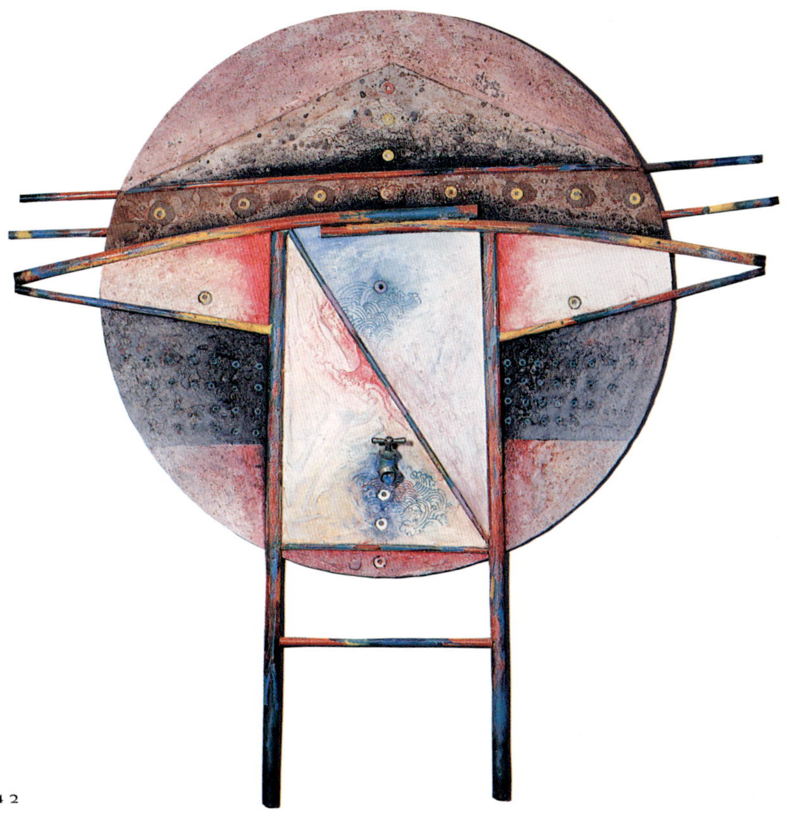

PLATE 42

KAMOL TASSANANCHALEE

WATER *NANGYAI* (5TH SERIES), 1986

Acrylic, stucco, plywood, wood dowels, brass fittings, 50.5" x 48.25"

In a whimsical mixing of American and Thai folk elements, Kamol has created a dripping faucet surrounded by traditional Thai-style waves. This work is one of a series constructed on *nangyai,* or shadow play, frames. The brass washers represent the light-transmitting perforations in a traditional leather *nangyai.* During a performance such a *nangyai,* silhouetted behind a white curtain, would be carried by a man holding the vertical handles.

Private collection

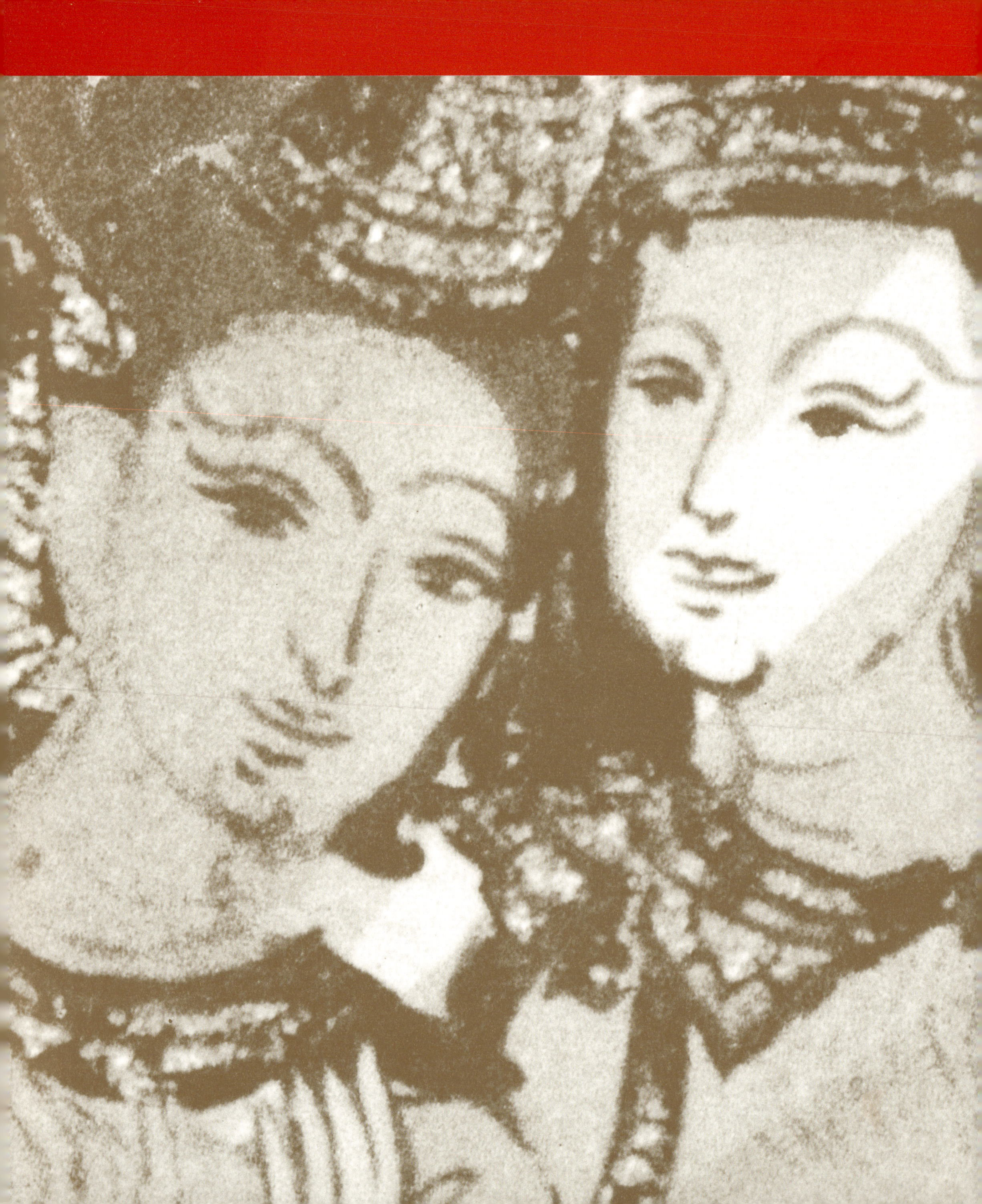

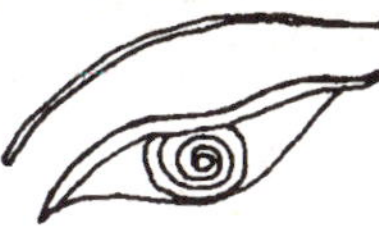

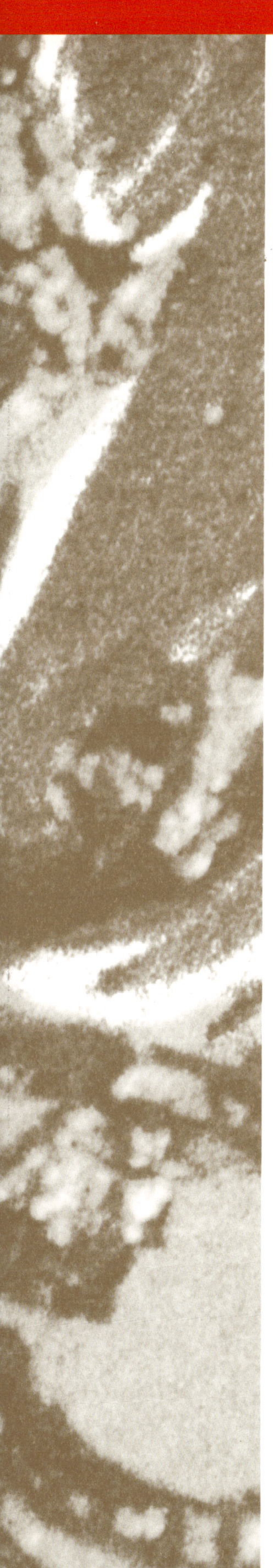

No exhibition of contemporary Thai art would be complete without a section on the Thai exploration of the nature of their own identity in the context of the conflicts and confusions of the modern world. There are a multiplicity of such identity issues—cultural, personal, ethnic, and political.

"Identity" has emerged as a focus of Thai artistic concern as a result of the tumultuous changes that have occurred in the nation during this century, particularly since the end of World War II. Unlike other peoples of Southeast Asia, the politically independent Thai have always had some control over the changes that they have admitted to their lives. But this has not lessened the impact of those changes and their consequences, the ambivalence they feel about them, the breakdown in social consensus that accompanies them, or their profound need to make sense of them. If this exhibit is testimony to the Thai success in dealing with these changes in a stylistically fulfilling way—by developing aesthetic statements that allow them to address many of the conflicting things that are important to them—the works in this section detail the personal and cultural meanings of those conflicts.

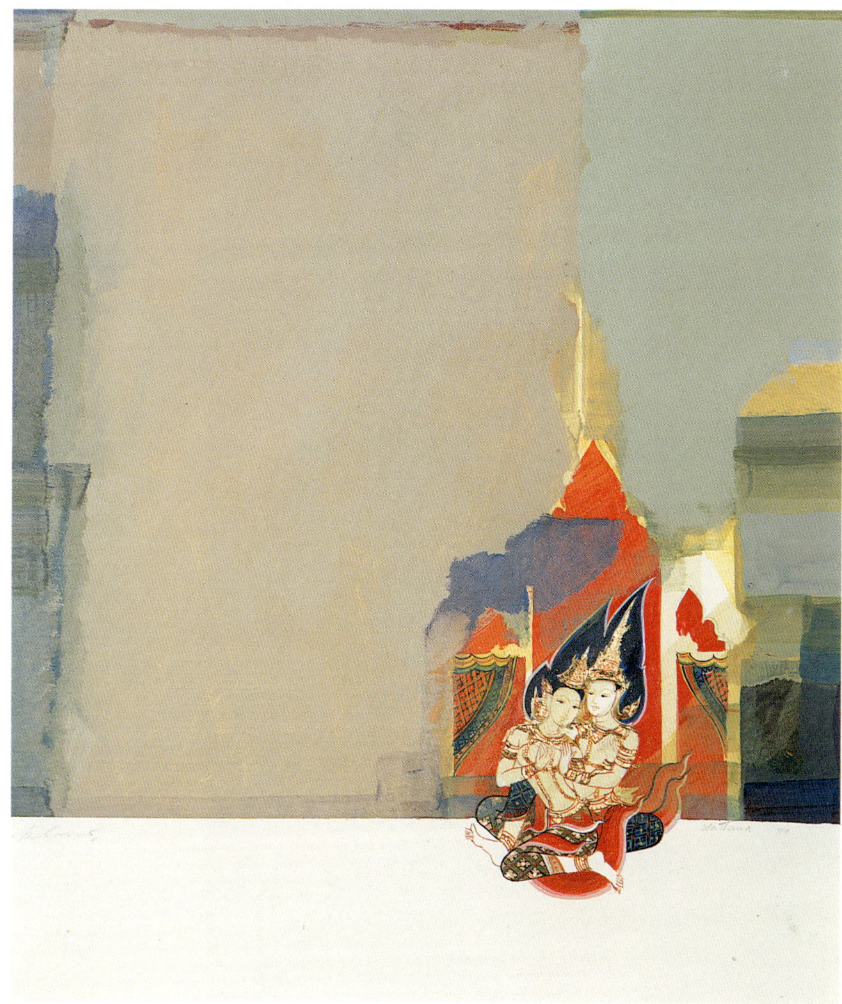

PLATE 43

WATTANA WATTANAPUN

DEWA AND APSARA, 1977
Acrylic on paper, 17" x 14.5"

This work portrays the gods and classical lovers, Dewa and Apsara, embracing one another against the drab and faded background of a disappearing Thai culture. The work shows the intensity of traditional, ideal love as contrasted to the impermanence of things in the modern world. The red of the lovers' immediate environment is meant to convey the nobility and refinement of their status, as well as their sensual involvement. Also, the precisely drawn quality of the lovers is meant to contrast with the empty color fields above them. Wattana is among that small group of Thai artists who has succeeded in both Thai and American art worlds—spending half of his time in Seattle (where he has mostly worked) and half of his time in Chiengmai (where he has mostly rejuvenated himself.) The total circumstances of his life suggest that in the future he will be residing mainly in Thailand.

Loaned by Ashok Gangadean

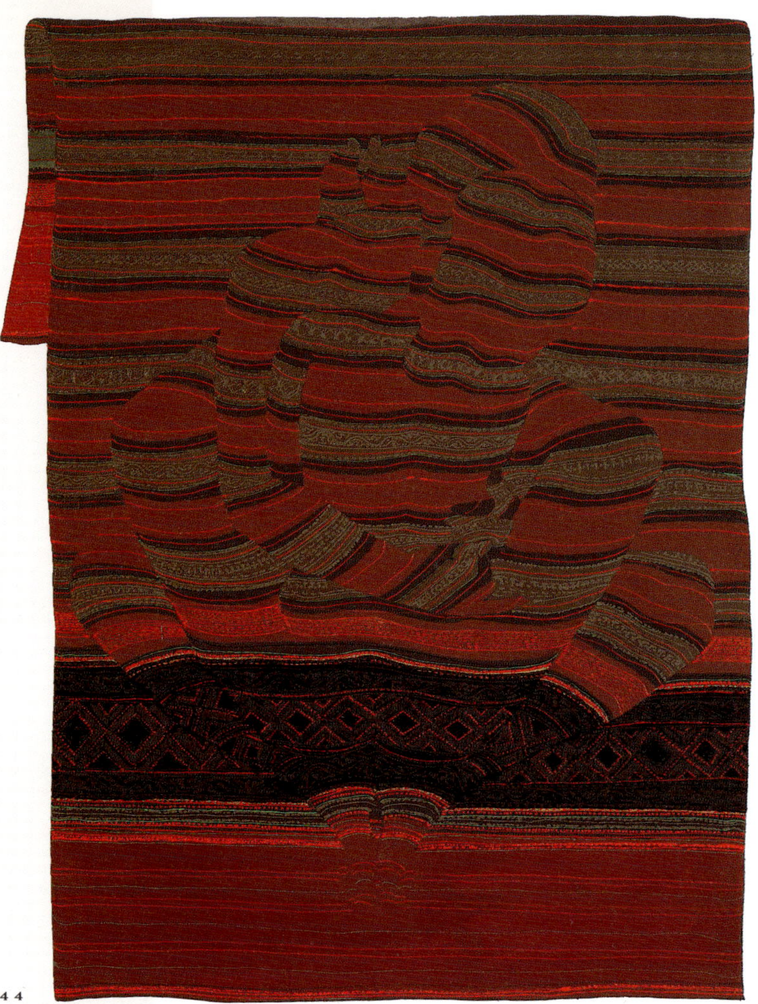

PLATE 44

WATTANA WATTANAPUN

BLACK HEM, 1987
Acrylic on paper, 27" x 26"

From a series entitled "Sun, Sand, Silk, and Sex" this work is intended as a commentary on the Thai tourist industry —which, with more than five million visitors a year, defines Thailand to the external world and represents the kingdom's largest source of foreign exchange. It is the beauty of the colors and patterns shown in this work that indeed have made Thai textiles renowned and valued throughout the world, and one of the major foci of tourist interest. Less obvious, but also significant for both host and tourist, is what occurs underneath the textile. Like most Thai, Wattana's attitude toward such activity is not without equivocation. On the one hand, he says that sex is among the good things in life, to be enjoyed by all. On the other hand, he regrets that in the modern Thai world it is often bought and sold, like any commodity in the international marketplace.

Loaned by Jean McKinnon

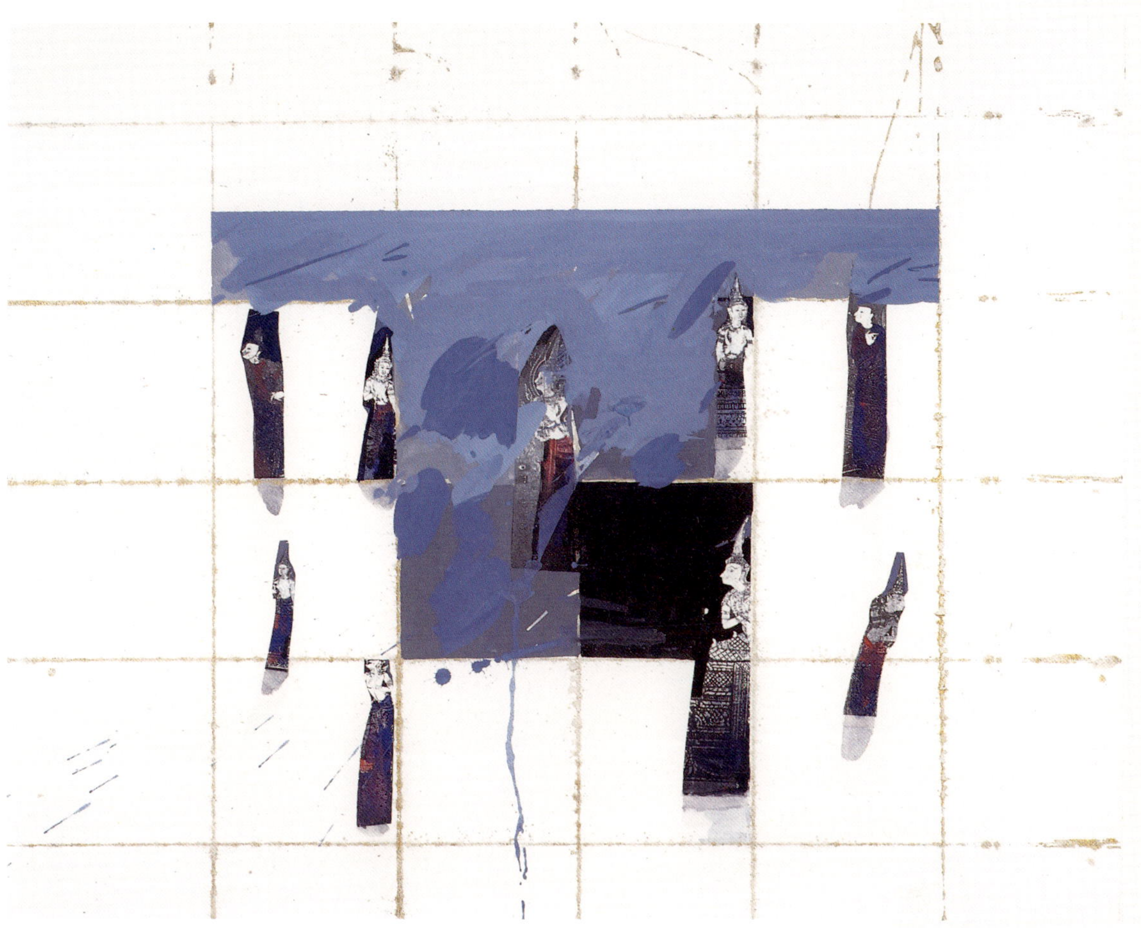

PLATE 45

WATTANA WATTANAPUN

SEARCHING, C. 1979

Tempera, photos, gold leaf dust on paper, 21.5" x 27.5"

This work portrays Thai gods in search of their future. The figures are from photographs of temple murals in the major temple of Ratchaburi Province. The blue color field is the shape and color of a Northern Thai farmer's shirt, which is usually made of indigo cotton. The golden grid—which replicates the grid designs of the Buddha footprints—has for Thai viewers the added meaning that whatever is occurring, it is being done with dedication, focus, and clarity of thought.

Loaned by the artist

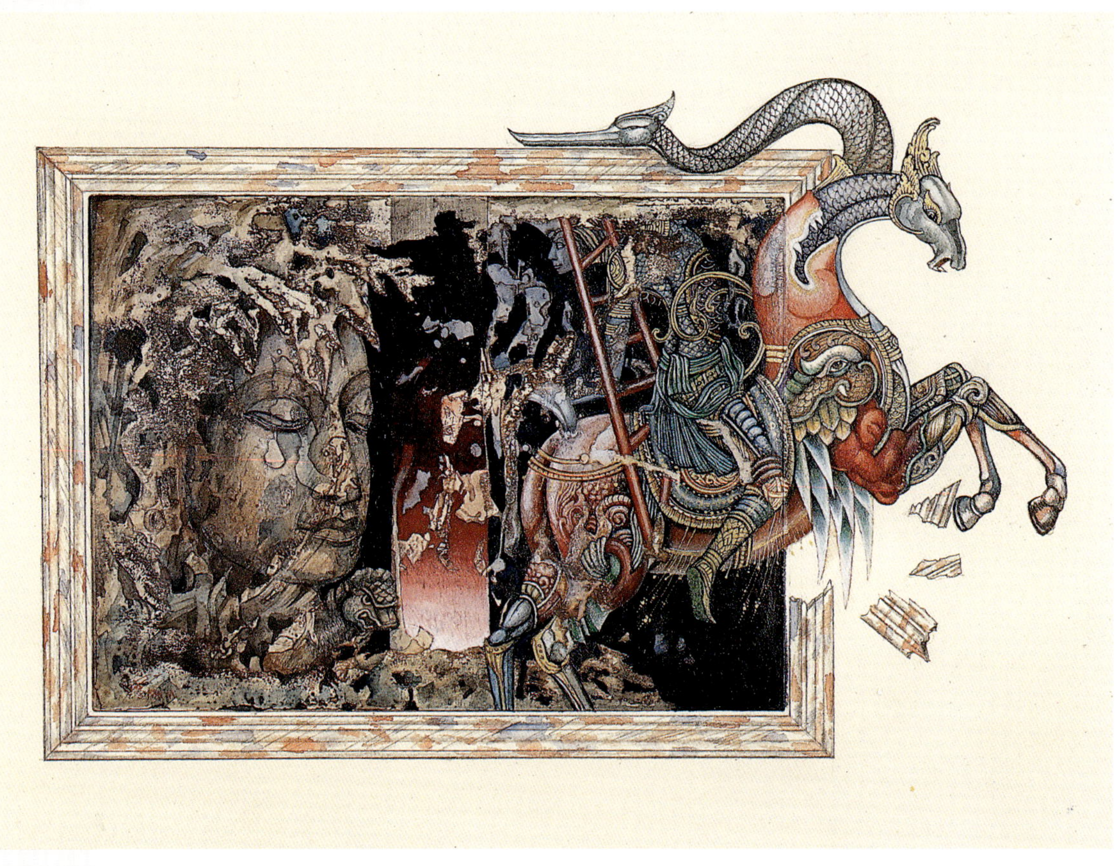

PLATE 46

PANYA VIJINTHANASARN

CONSTRAINT AND DESIRE, 1984

Lithograph with watercolor and gold paint, 7.5" x 11.5"

This work represents one of the central existential conflicts of modern Thai life—between the tenets of Buddhism, the power of tradition, and the stability of nature on the left, and individual desire, animal aggression, and breaking through limits on the right. The artist says that the pink and white color field in the center represents a middle ground of serenity. The figure on horseback is looking back to what he knows is possible, but no longer satisfying. The long-beaked bird stretching back onto the frame is a hamsa, a mythic swan which moves alone in constant search for fulfillment. While the kind of conflict expressed in this work has probably long existed in Thailand, it is particularly acute in the modern world where opportunities are available and where choices can be made, but where there are prices to pay. Trained in Bangkok and London, Panya is perhaps more willing than any other Thai artist to mix Euroamerican styles, colors, and techniques with the moral themes and symbols of the Thai classical tradition. This work reaches back to the conventions of medieval European manuscript painting to convey the essence of a modern Thai experience.

Loaned by Luca Invernizzi Tettoni

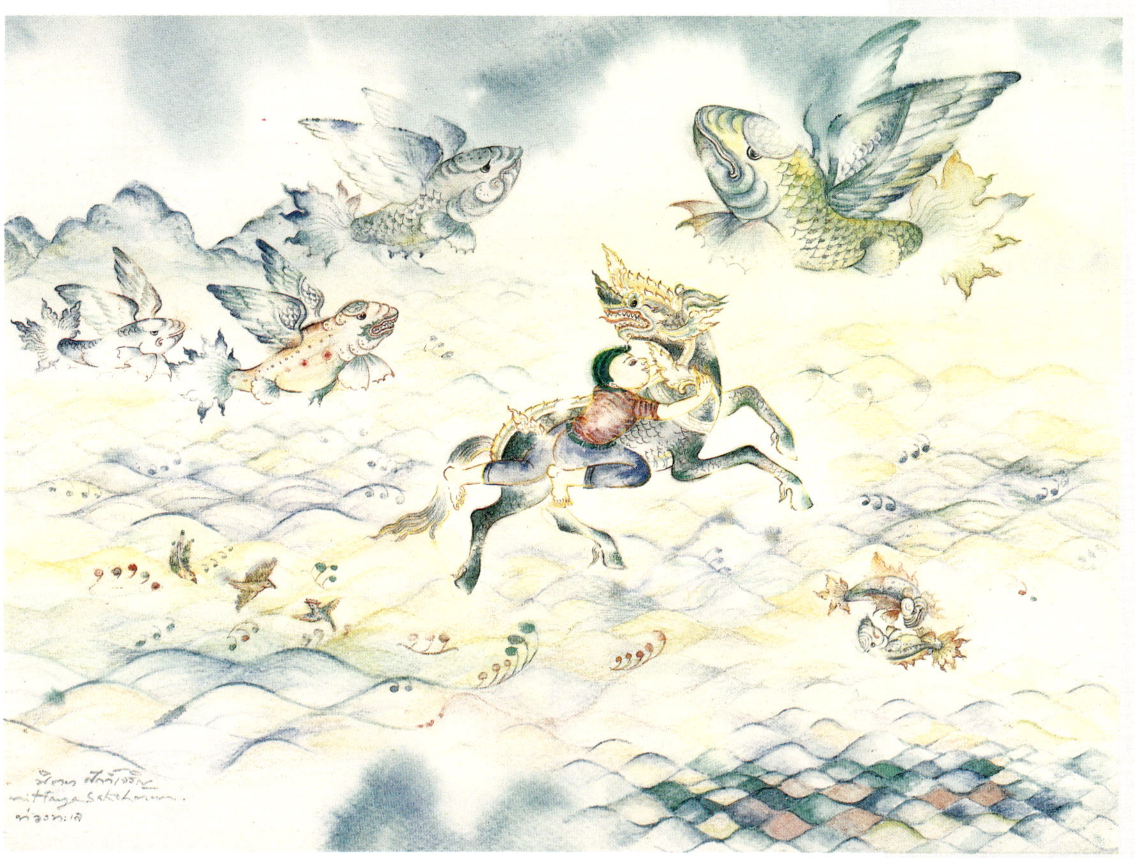

PLATE 47

NITTAYA SAKCHAROEN

THE MANGKORN HORSE, 1985
Watercolor, 16" x 20"

This attempt to link the classical and the modern portrays the miraculous Mangkorn horse with a rider dressed in T-shirt and jeans cavorting through the heavens, slightly above the seas. The Mangkorn horse, a synthesis of the Chinese lion and dragon, was a minor, but favorite, figure in Thailand's classical epic poem, *Phra Aphaimanii*, known to virtually all Thai. The horse could fly through the skies, trot on earth, and swim on and under the sea. He is a symbol of a supernatural helper who is loyal, powerful, and friendly—a creature to be wished for, but not likely to be found, in the modern world.

Working almost exclusively in the classical tradition, Nittaya is one of the few—perhaps the only—known female artist to be awarded commissions to paint Thai temple murals. To escape the tedium of this genre, she produces smaller works placing her classical characters into whimsical modern situations.

Loaned by the artist

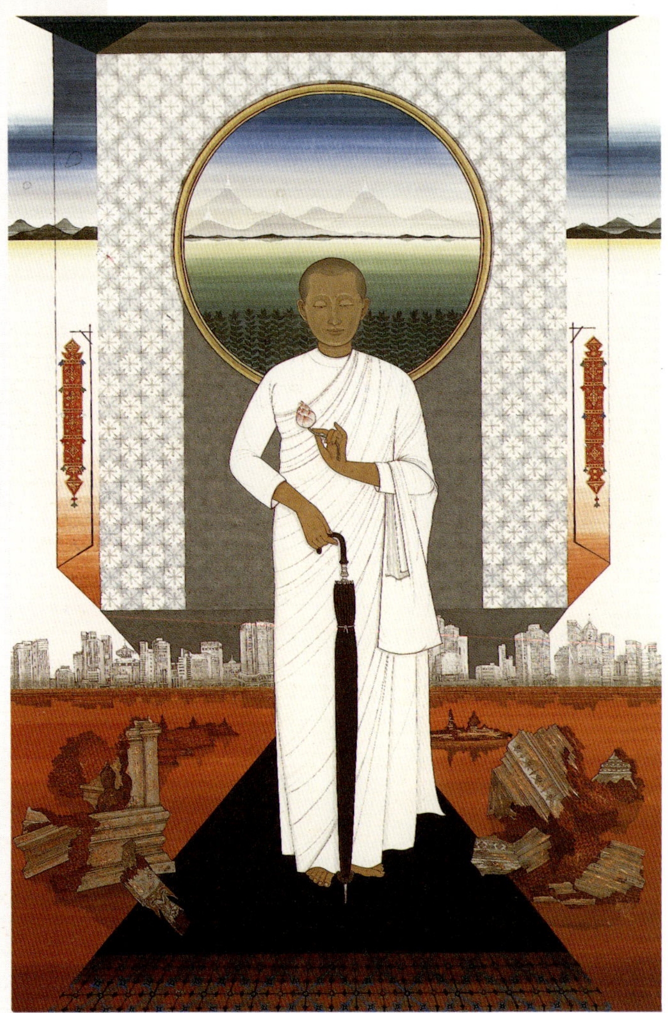

PLATE 48

CHALERMCHAI KOSITPIPAT

THE NUN, 1979

Tempera on canvas, 54" x 37"

The conflict between modern urbanity (the rising city) and the purity of religion (the broken buildings near the nun's feet) is portrayed in this work. Chalermchai feels that nuns, who have no official canonical status, are much purer in their motivation and commitment than are monks, and thus are more perfect symbols of Buddhism. The mountain tops in the background are close to Nirvana. The black umbrella is in part for aesthetic contrast and in part a symbol of one of the more useful features of the modern world.

Loaned by Chulalongkorn University

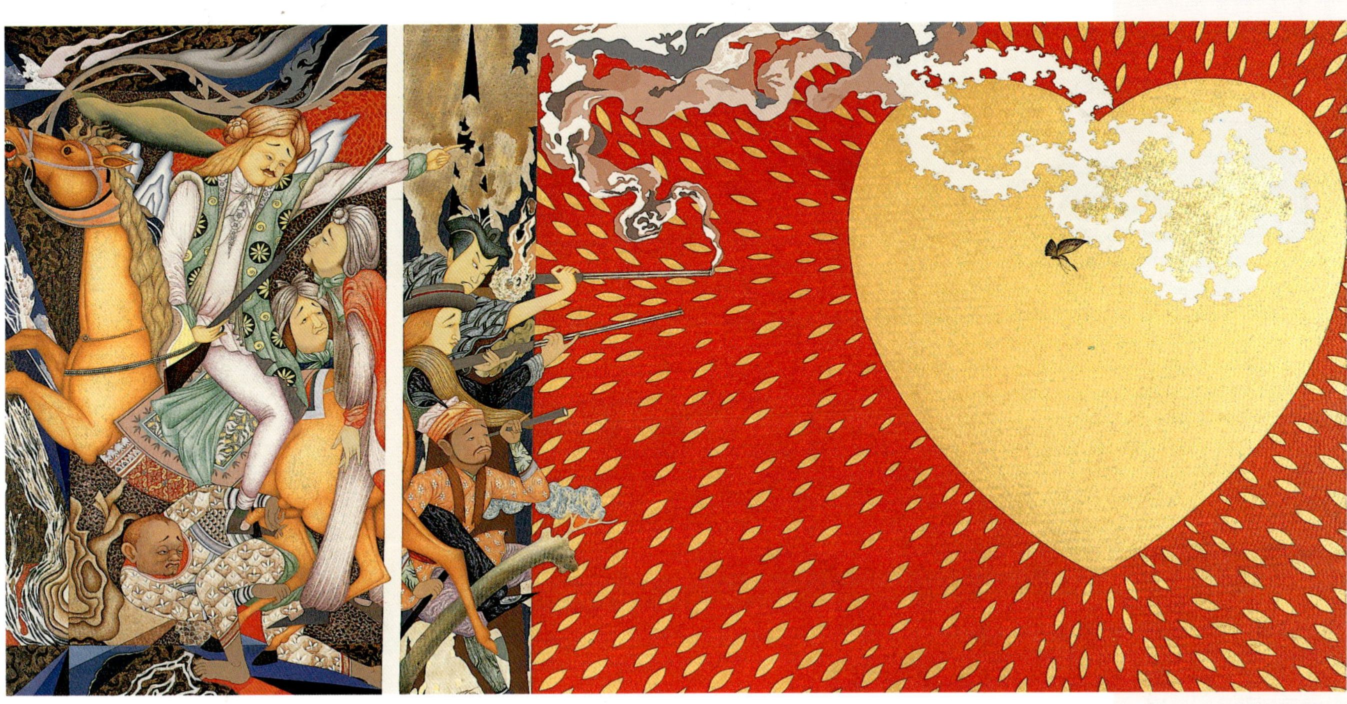

PLATE 49

PANYA VIJINTHANASARN

CRISIS OF CIVILIZATION, II, 1991

Acrylic on canvas, 40.5" x 79.6"

Using the story-telling conventions of traditional temple art, this work is a commentary on both the foreign contribution to the Thai experience and the ecological destruction of Thailand. On the left are some of the foreigners who over the centuries have visited Thailand: a French officer; Arab and Indian merchants; Japanese, English, and Iranian soldiers. Modeled on the figures appearing in the early 19th century wall murals at Wat Suwannarm in Thonburi, the work indicates that the Thai view of foreigners has changed little since that time. Panya says that like their modern counterparts, "these representatives of the civilizations that have come to Thailand stay close to one another, but they really have no relationships with each other. They are interested only in their own power and technology." Panya is equally critical of the Thai response to the foreign presence, here shown in the behavior and posture of a "simple-minded" Thai soldier in the lower left corner of the work. On the right is the spiritual heart of Thai culture. Emanating from the heart are golden rice grains, symbols of energy, set in a red color field, the traditional color of heaven. Weaving its way through the work are organic forms symbolizing nature, and geometric forms symbolizing the products of man. All are being altered or stunted by pollution, a force that is even beginning to affect the great white chain—the symbol of timeless movement and unending change—that weaves its way across the heart. Near the center of the heart is the prey of the foreign soldiers—a lonely butterfly expressing the beauty and fragility of all livings things.

Loaned by the artist

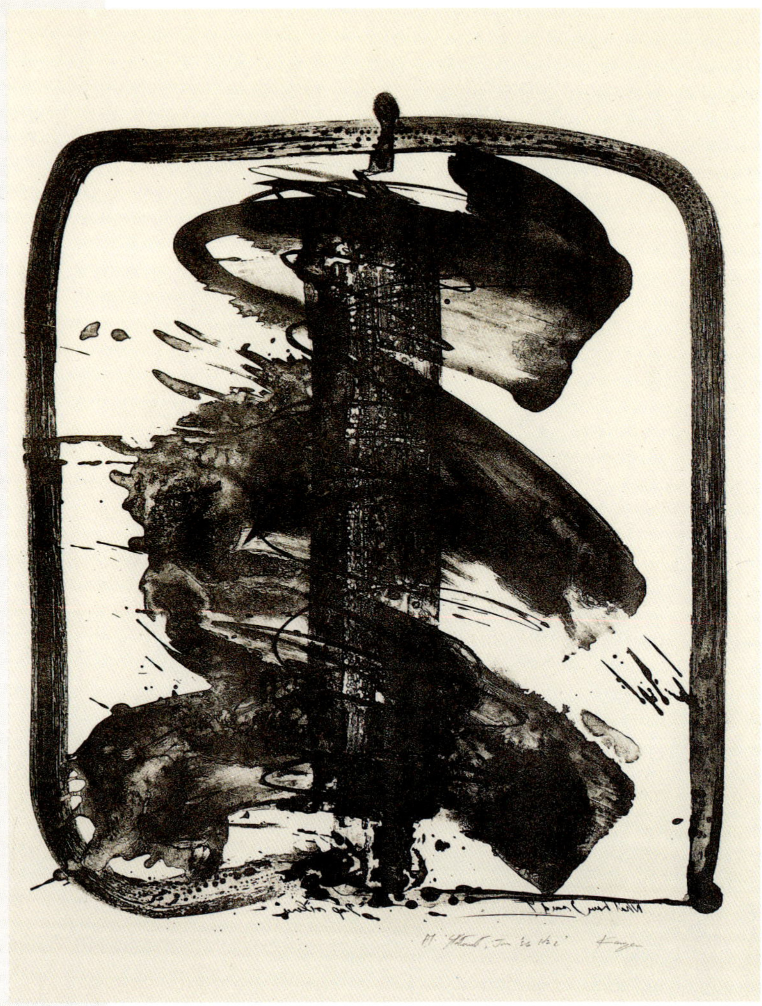

PLATE 50

KANYA CHAROENSUPKUL

STATEMENT, JANUARY 1986, NO. 2, 1986
Lithograph, 28" x 20"

Influenced by Chinese calligraphy, Kanya worked for years primarily in black and white. Unlike most of her Thai compatriots, she used her work to express and reflect her immediate emotional state. Here she focusses on her own anger and the need to limit it. On the lower corner of the lithographic stone she has etched "What have I said?" It is printed here in mirror image.

Loaned by the artist

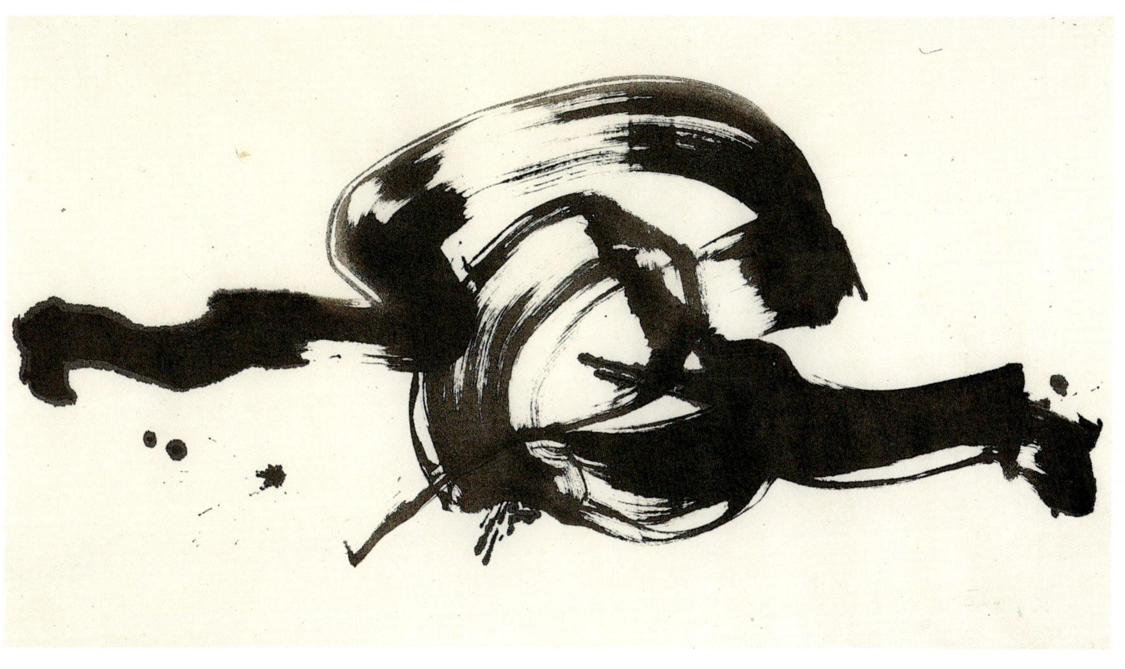

PLATE 51

KANYA CHAROENSUPKUL

INTERPLAY, 1989
Ink on paper, 36" x 72"

Much of Kanya's work focuses on the tension of conflicting forces—between emotions and ideas, the self and others, night and day, or freedom and constraint. This painting is a summary expression of the nature of such opposition. Although never trained in Chinese calligraphy, Kanya has used traditional Chinese brushes and ink since she was introduced to artistic practice.

Loaned by the artist

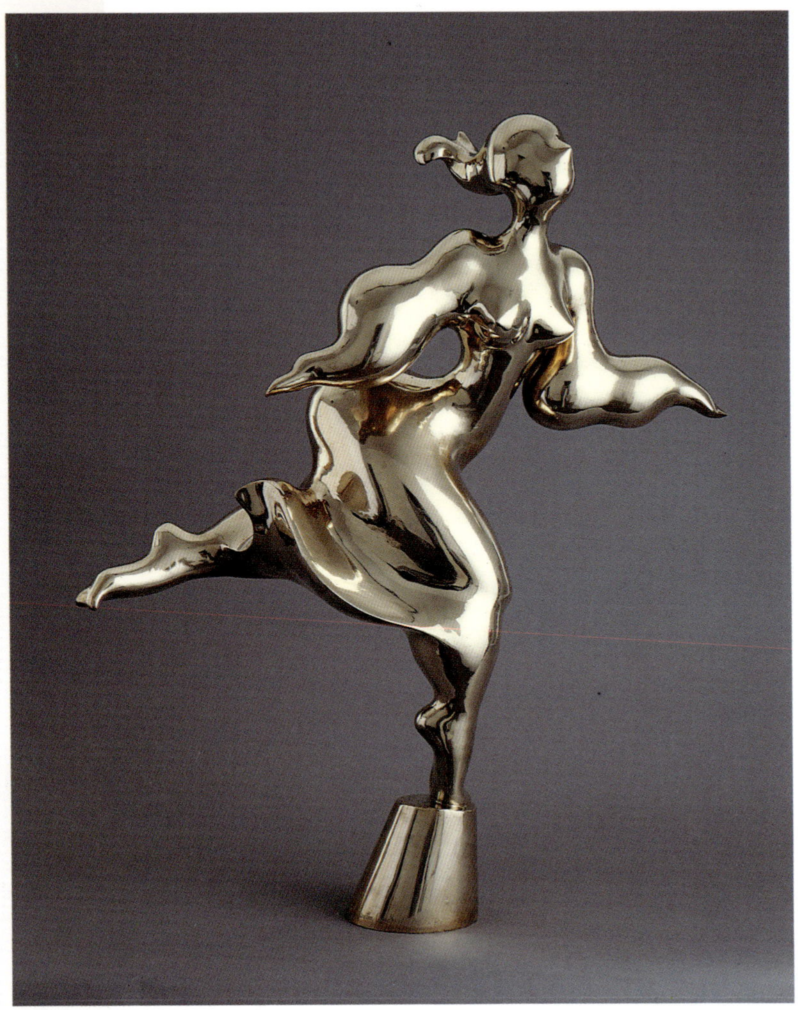

PLATE 52

NONTHIWAT CHANDHANAPHALIN

DESIRE, NUMBER 3, 1985
Brass over chrome, 34.5" x 20" x 16"

The flow and stance of this work strongly suggest the influence of the early 20th century Italian artist and sculptor, Umberto Boccioni, who portrayed figures and forms in motion and the expression of motility, violence, and energy. Nonthiwat, who studied in both Bangkok and Rome, does not deny that he has been inspired by others, but insists that Western expectations notwithstanding, his work is not an expression of the joy of unrestrained physical freedom. Instead, he argues that this "Desire" is a demonstration of the fundamental Buddhist premise that all human beings must struggle with their own desires—the necessity both to fulfill them and to discipline them—as well as with all their other biological and emotional limitations. Thus, simultaneous with the body's flow, there is tension and constraint in the muscles and organs, and what may appear the fulfillment of unmitigated desire is always the result of an inner process of struggle, adaptation, and compromise.

Loaned by the artist

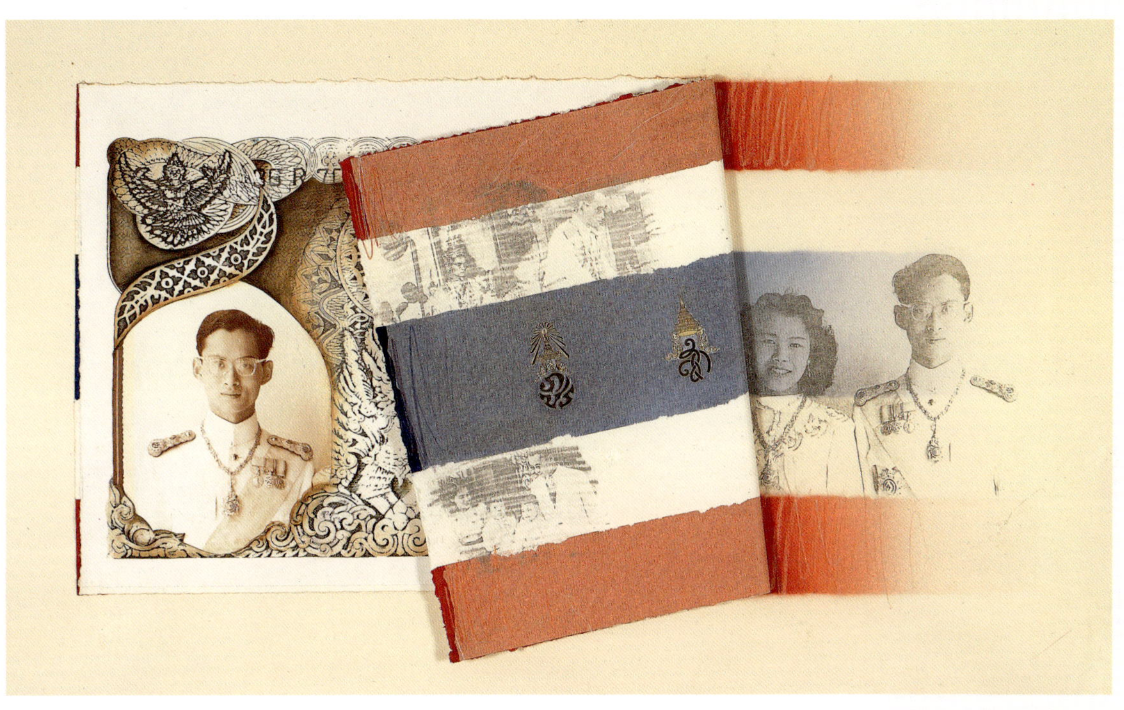

PLATE 53

KAMIN LERTCHAIPRASERT

IN HONOR OF RAMA IX, 1986
Photolithograph, gold leaf, 30" x 68"

Like artists everywhere in the modern world, Thai artists have to make a living and develop a reputation. One of the most obvious ways to do this is to enter the scores of public art competitions that are sponsored annually by banks, government agencies, hotels, and other institutions. While many of these contests focus exclusively on aesthetic matters, some have more complex social or political aims. This work was the prizewinning entry honoring the king on his birthday in a contest sponsored by one of Thailand's major banks. On the right is a famous wedding photo of the king and queen. On the left is a photo of the king superimposed upon an enlargement of Thai currency, and in the center the logos of the royal couple are superimposed upon the red, white, and blue flag of Thailand.

Loaned by the artist

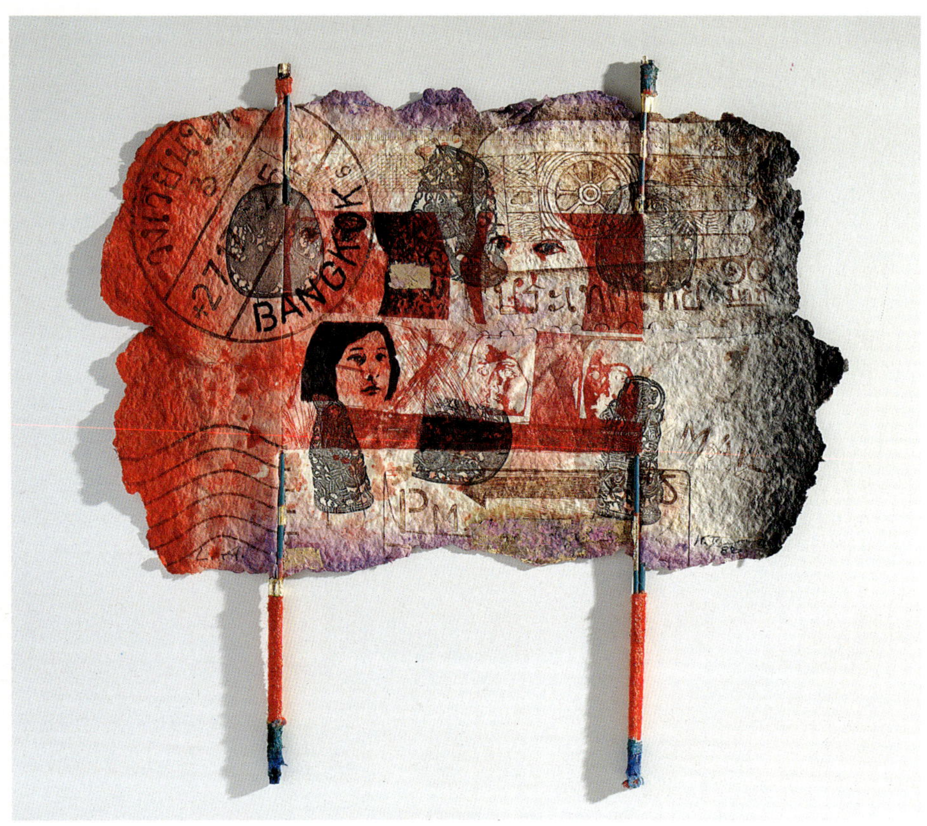

PLATE 54

KAMOL TASSANANCHALEE

"NANGYAI," FIRST SERIES, 1982

Acrylic, gold leaf, handmade paper, wood dowels, and photo etchings, 21" x 24"

During his early years in the United States, the artist maintained contact with home through letters, and soon the letters themselves—their paper, postmarks, cancellation marks, place names, and Thai printing—became symbols of what he left behind. This work represents the artist's memories of his homesickness and the search for his own identity in a foreign land. The *nangyai* frame and design, and the handmade paper, provide the basic terms of his search. In addition, he locates his self-portraits near images of a Buddha footprint and real *nangyai*.

Private collection

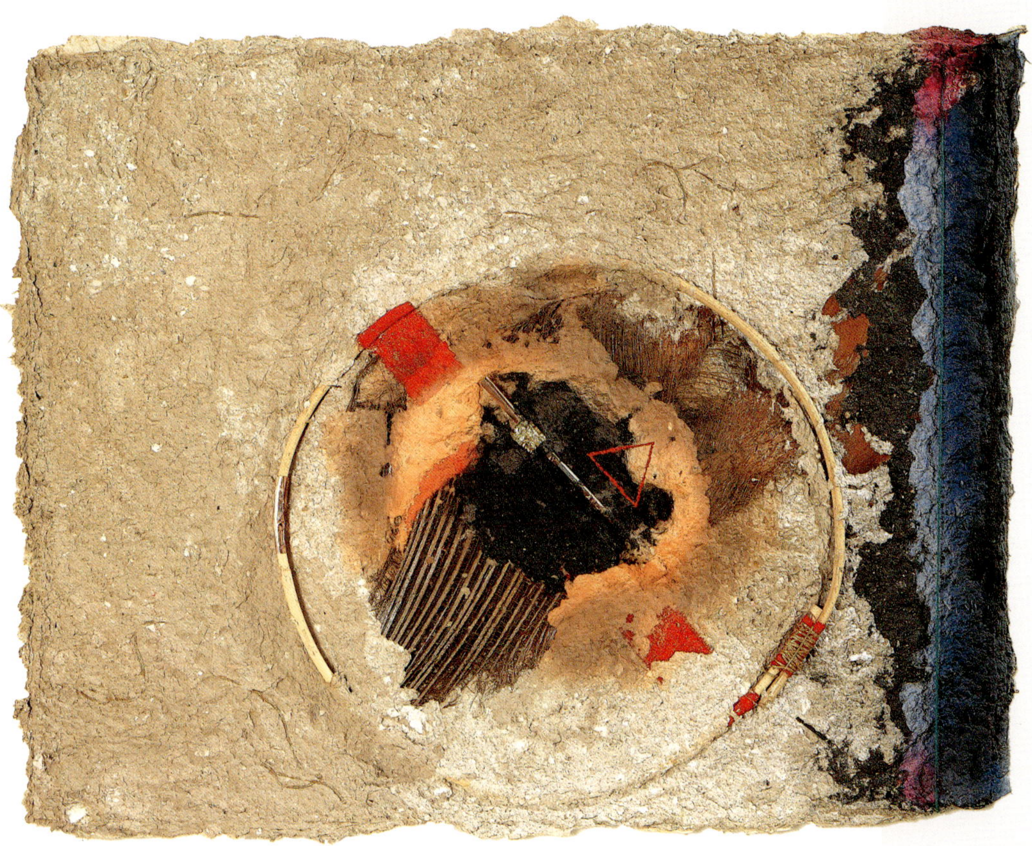

PLATE 55

THAVORN KO-UDOMVIT

Circle of Death, 1986

Handmade paper, bamboo, gold and red paper, palm leaf bark, and embers, 24" x 30"

Chinese have been immigrating into Thailand for at least half a millennium, but during the past century the nation's Chinese minority has become increasingly integrated into the national culture. Some scholars have indicated that as much as half the population of Bangkok may be Chinese in origin or descent, although nowadays most of these persons consider themselves to be "Sino-Thai."

In the contemporary art scene, the ethnic concerns of individual artists are viewed as one of the principal fonts of aesthetic enrichment, and certain artists continually experiment with ethnic themes and styles. Thavorn is one such artist. Virtually everything he does relates to his search for his Chinese identity. This work is a celebration of his links to his family. Its elements are the paraphernalia—gold and orange paper symbolizing wealth; red paper symbolizing life and regeneration—that are put to the torch during an annual rite honoring parents, grandparents, and other ancestors. The bamboo ring encloses and delimits the fire. However, because all the material of the work rests upon a base of handmade Thai paper, it is also a metaphor for the status of the Chinese in Thailand.

Loaned by the artist

KAMIN LERTCHAIPRASERT

LIVING LETTERS, 1991

Acrylic on paper, nine panels, 22" x 22" each

Like many people, the Thai have a love for their language—its sounds, rhythms, its amenability to puns and other word games, and its emotional expressiveness. This love affair extends to the Thai writing system which since the 13th century has been a primary symbol of the unity and continuity of Thai culture. Unlike English, every consonant of the Thai alphabet is associated with a particular noun. Thai learn their alphabet in terms of these nouns, and the association between a letter and the object which signifies it is a permanent feature of the verbal world of most Thai.

Kamin's montage takes this association further by providing a visual rendition of the object to which a particular letter refers. The result is a paean to the pleasures of using the Thai writing system. From left to right, the letters read:

K for "kai" meaning chicken, which is revealed in the fury and blood of a cockfight.
N for "naeaen" meaning a Buddhist novice, represented by the saffron color of his robes.
T for "taahaan" meaning soldier, who is dark and fearsome and whose actions are hard to define.
T is for "thau thong" meaning flag, which is of course a rendition of the Thai flag.
N is for "nuu" meaning mouse, represented by the soil of the rice fields through which mice roam.
P is for "phyng" meaning bee, represented by the color of their hives and of the honey they produce.
L is for "lau chalaa" meaning a large kite soaring through the sky.
H is for "hau nok-khuu" meaning an owl whose hoot is often a harbinger of trouble. This work represents the artist's image of "trouble."
Y is for "Yau Yuk" meaning the giant that protects Bangkok—the center of color and dazzle.

Loaned by the artist

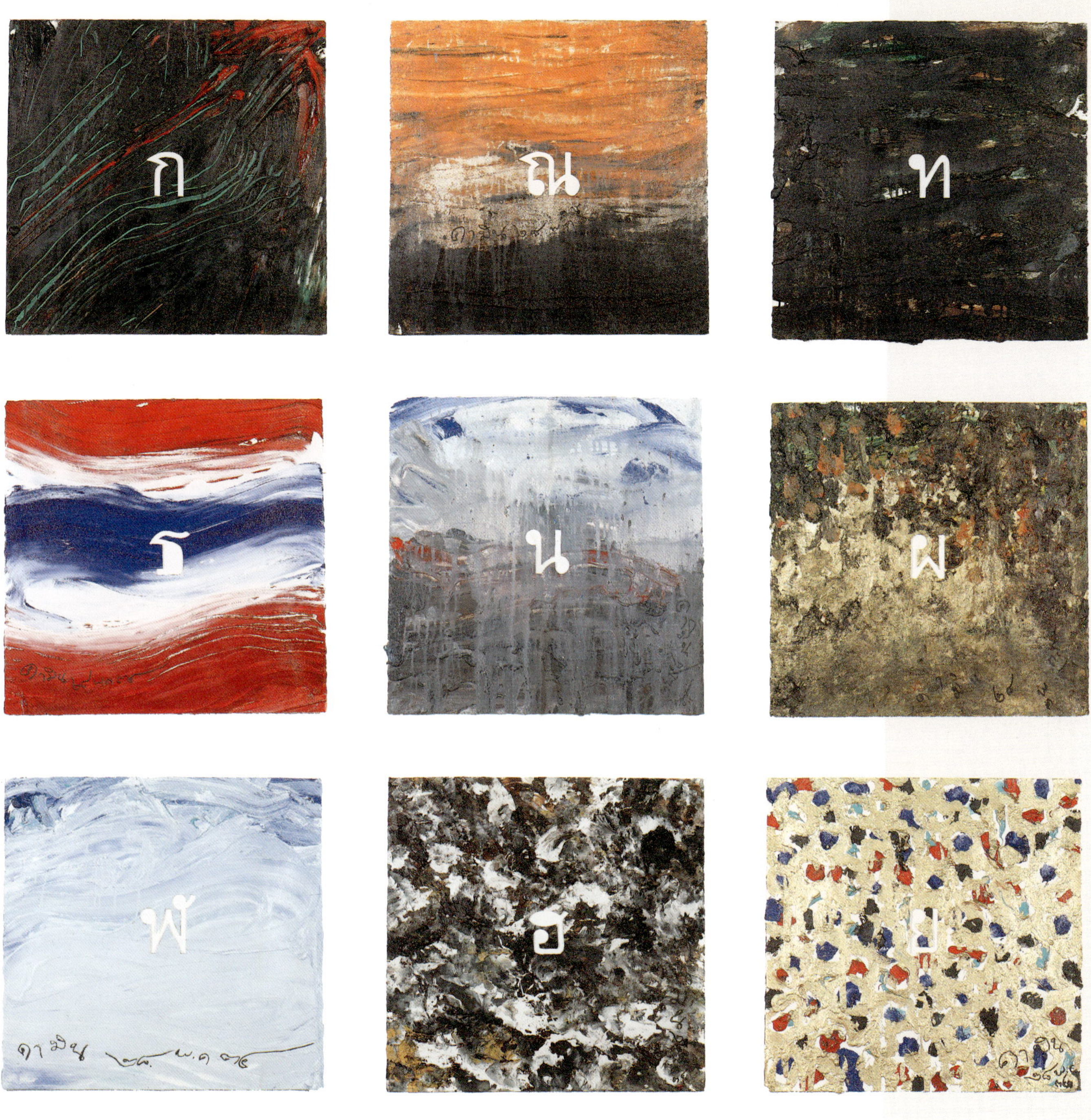

ANGKARN KALAYAANAPONGSE

born 1926

Officially recognized by the Thai government as one of four living "National Artists" and considered one of the greatest Thai poets of this century, Angkarn is the most honored artist in Thailand—mainly because of the subtlety with which he has energized some of the central symbols of the Thai religious tradition. Angkarn works most comfortably in crayon on paper, but his wall murals and large acrylics on canvas are his most acclaimed contributions. Born and reared in Southern Thailand, he is the descendant of a family of wood carvers and goldsmiths.

ARUNOTHAI SOMSAKUL

born c. 1948

The son of a physician, Arunothai studied at Silpakorn University and at the San Francisco Art Institute. Arunothai is unique in Thailand for his almost exclusive interest in miniatures and in his attention to the ironies and contradictions of the human condition.

BOONYING EMJAROEN

born 1946

A student of Prateung Emjaroen as well as his wife, Boonying is best known for her color-saturated paintings of profusions of flowers. However, her most serious work is in pen and ink drawings in which she reduces the forms of nature into their most precise, elemental constituents.

CHALERMCHAI KOSITPIPAT

born 1954

Born and reared in a middle-class merchant family in Chiengrai in Northern Thailand, Chalermchai studied at Poh Chang, Silpakorn, and the Slade School in London. Because of his melding of moral subject matter and modern situations, his detailed and precise draftsmanship, and the accessibility of the meaning of his art to most viewers, he is one of the most sought after artists in Thailand. Together with Panya, Chalermchai created the wall murals at the Thai temple at Wimbledon, England—the most innovative Thai religious paintings of the 20th century.

CHALOOD NIMSAMER

born 1929

Recognized as one of the principal heirs of Silpa Bhirsari, Chalood studied at Silpakorn University and in Rome and New York, and has consistently been one of the most "integrative" of Thailand's artists. He is accomplished in sculpture, drawing, and printmaking as well as in painting, and is widely acclaimed for having been a three-time winner of the kingdom's National Art Exhibition. Among his own students are artists such as Chalermchai, Panya, Itthipol, Kanya, Somsak, and Thavorn.

CHAMREUNG VICHIENKET

born 1931

Thailand's most senior sculptor and the senior member of a family of sculptors, Chamreung learned his craft directly from Silpa Bhirasri. Almost all of his work involves a synthesis of both contemporary Euroamerican and classical Thai elements. During most of his career he has taught at Silpakorn University.

DAMRONG WONG-UPARAJ

born 1936

The son of a Northern village silver craftsman, Damrong studied at Poh Chang, Silpakorn, and later in London, Philadelphia, and Kyoto. While most of his paintings depict landscapes and village scenes, he works almost exclusively from memory in the privacy of his studio focussing on the aesthetics of line and perspective. A professor at the Nakorn Pathom campus of Silpakorn University, Damrong serves as a critical liaison between the community of artists and museums, galleries, and collectors.

ITTHIPOL THANGCHALOK

born 1946

A graduate of Silpakorn University and the University of Washington at Seattle, Itthipol is one of Thailand's premier specialists in mixed media and graphics. He is particularly well-known for his artistic transformations—in part representational, in part decorative—of the textures and colors of urban surfaces and shapes. He is a faculty member at Silpakorn.

JIRAPAT PITPREECHA

born 1956

The son of a provincial merchant from Southern Thailand, Jirapat attended Chulalongkorn University and Long Island University. Recognized as one of Thailand's most brilliant colorists, his work has been mostly in abstract expressionism and has focussed on the qualities of the urban environment. Jirapat is a member of the Fine Arts faculty at Chulalongkorn.

KAMIN LERTCHAIPRASERT

born 1964

Kamin studied at Silpakorn University and has spent a year in New York City as a freelance art student. Acknowledged as one of Thailand's most versatile and experimental younger artists, Kamin works in different media on subjects as varied as human suffering, patriotism, and the nature of personal and cultural identity. He is the youngest son of a Bangkok biscuit manufacturer.

KAMOL TASSANANCHALEE

born 1944

The son of a gardener and grandson of a temple mural painter, Kamol was born and reared in Thonburi and attended Poh Chang Art College. At the age of 25, he came to the United States, studied at Otis Art Institute, and developed into a major California artist, but has always retained his artistic links to Thailand. In addition to integrating Thai themes and materials with influences from Rauschenberg and American Indian motifs, he has become the principal liaison figure between the Thai and Euroamerican art worlds.

KANYA CHAROENSUPKUL

born 1947

The daughter of a provincial Chinese merchant and Thai mother, Kanya studied at Silpakorn and the Chicago Art Institute, and created the first lithography studio in Thailand. As her career has progressed she has gone increasingly from abstract, black and white gestural work to the use of color and the detailed rendition of the internal structure of stone and flowers. Kanya is unique in the Thai art world in affirming the propriety of using one's art to work through important personal issues.

MISIEM YIPINTSOI

born 1906, died 1988

Born in Thailand to an elite Indonesian Chinese merchant family, Misiem took up art in mid-life after an extended trip to Europe. Working first as a painter and then as a sculptor, she became one of Thailand's most innovative and productive artists. Silpakorn University —which she never attended—has honored her posthumously with the establishment of a sculpture garden of her own work. Like Chalood, Misiem was also a three-time gold medalist at the kingdom's National Art Exhibition.

MONTIEN BOONMA

born 1953

The son of a school teacher, Montien studied at Poh Chang, Silpakorn, and the University of Paris. He says he did not develop his sense of being a Thai artist until he returned from France and rediscovered Thai materials—looking not only to their forms, colors, and textures, but to their odor, internal composition, and function in society. As a serious Buddhist, he also became profoundly interested in the potentiality of these materials—how they might change, or be changed.

NITTAYA SAKCHAROEN

born 1949

Primarily a classical artist, Nittaya is the only living woman known to be given the responsibility for designing and painting the wall murals of a major national temple. To amuse herself, she often does playful works which merge her classical style with contemporary situations and sentiments. A graduate of Poh Chang Arts College, and apprentice to Tarn Kudt, Thailand's pre-eminent classical artist, she has also been a poet and songwriter.

NONTHIWAT CHANDHANAPHALIN

born 1946

A graduate of Silpakorn University, Nonthiwat also studied sculpture in Carrara, Italy. While he has done numerous works of public statuary, his principal artistic preoccupation has been the inherent conflict between Buddhist ideals of discipline and restraint and Western ideals of freedom and spontaneity. Nonthiwat is a faculty member at Silpakorn University

PANYA VIJINTHANASARN

born 1956

The son of a pineapple farmer from peninsular Thailand, Panya was apprenticed to Tarn Kudt, and also studied at Poh Chang, Silpakorn, and the Slade School in London—where he says he was deeply influenced by the illuminated works of William Blake. Imbued with the spirit of integrating Thai and Western artistic traditions, Panya, together with Chalermchai, designed and painted the wall murals at the Thai Buddhist temple in London—the most acclaimed Thai religious paintings of this era.

PICHAI NIRAND

born 1936

Grandson of a wood carver, and son of a deep-sea diver who also does flower designs and vegetable carving, Pichai attended the College of Fine Arts and Silpakorn. Like Angkarn, with whom he has collaborated over the years, he does highly original contemporary works on classical themes. Pichai paints virtually every day, but for 25 years also been an official in the Department of Fine Arts, where he recently designed the largest stone *thammachak* (the wheel symbolizing the Buddhist "Law of Perpetual Change") ever created. It is installed at the Buddhist Park at Buddha Monthorn, southwest of Bangkok.

PRATEUNG EMJAROEN

born 1935

The son of a fruit gardener, Prateung lived a comfortable family life until he was 12, when his father died, leaving the family in financial distress. After a series of jobs, he was apprenticed to a movie poster company, and in time developed into one of the nation's premier poster painters. After seeing a Hollywood film on the life of Van Gogh, he suddenly gave up his job to become a creative artist. He struggled for many years as a self-taught painter, until he developed his own distinctive style and a large coterie of clients, colleagues, and students. He is now recognized as Thailand's most accomplished interpreter of the beauty and visual complexity of nature.

SAOWAPHA VICHIENKET

born 1932

The spouse of a sculptor and the mother of a painter and a sculptor, Saowapha was trained by Silpa Bhirasri at Silpakorn University. Like her husband, she constantly works towards the synthesis of Thai classical and contemporary Euroamerican artistic conventions, but unlike him, she focusses on the workaday movements and postures of women—the form of the body when negotiating a flooded street, playing with an infant, or in the act of meditation. Saowapha teaches sculpture at Silpakorn University.

SAWAT TANTISUK

born 1925

Trained at Poh Chang and Silpakorn, Sawat also studied for four years in Italy, and became one of Silpa Bhirsari's most acclaimed students. For several years he stayed close to European subjects and styles, but in his prime he turned increasingly toward the development of a distinctively Thai form of abstract expressionism—focussing on birds in flight, the angles and lines of Buddhist temples, and the play of light and darkness on the sea. Sawat is a professor emeritus at the College of Fine Arts and was recently recognized as one of Thailand's "National Artists."

SOMPOP BUDTARAD

born 1957

The son of provincial school teachers from the Northeast of Thailand, Sompop studied at Poh Chang and Silpakorn University. He later worked as an apprentice to Panya and Chalermchai on the murals at the Thai temple in Wimbledon, and after their return to Bangkok, stayed on to design and complete several unfinished sections of the temple. Sompop is recognized as the most radically experimental and contemporary of the Wimbledon group.

SOMSAK CHOWTADAPONG

born 1949

The son of a sugar mill worker and hairdresser, Somsak discovered his talent when as a child he repeatedly won art contests sponsored by a children's TV program. He later studied at Silpakorn and in Italy and Japan. Recognized as one of Thailand's most subtle colorists, Somsak's works have been concerned with the exploration of space—from the open-endedness of the stratosphere to the confined space of fanciful gardens with well-defined borders and contrasting textures. He is currently a faculty member at the College of Fine Arts.

THAIWIJIT PUANGKASEMSOMBOON

born 1959

Born and brought up in Southern Thailand, Thaiwijit studied at Silpakorn and in Cracow, Poland. He has also spent time with various art groups in Canada and the United States. Widely acclaimed for his use of color, he has recently shifted his attention from his precisely crafted representations of nature to very free and dynamic abstractions expressing body movements and emotional states.

THAVORN KO-UDOMWIT

born 1956

Born into an urban Sino-Thai merchant family, Thavorn studied at Silpakorn and also spent a year in New York and Baltimore. While he has worked in a variety of media, his subject matter has almost always been his search for his Chinese identity within the context of Thai culture. A subtle and delicate craftsman, Thavorn's most recent work has focussed on contrasting applications of color, line, and the texture of natural materials against a background of handmade Thai paper.

THAWAN DUCHANEE

born 1939

The youngest son of an army officer and a mother who worked as a traditional healer, Thawan is Thailand's internationally best-known artist. Born and brought up in Chiengrai in Northern Thailand, he studied at Poh Chang, under Bhirasri at Silpakorn, and in Holland for five years. A true polyglot and rhetorician, Thawan is his nation's most complete postmodernist—freely merging influences from Western classical and renaissance sources, Thai folk beliefs, Hieronymous Bosch, and tantric art. While Thai intellectuals and connoisseurs are fascinated with his work, he sells mostly to Europeans, although some of his work is also in museums in Japan and the U.S. Thawan has travelled and worked in numerous countries, but always returns to his permanent home in Thailand.

VIBOON LEESUWAN

born 1947

Trained at the College of Fine Arts and Silpakorn, Viboon is one of Thailand's most accomplished printmakers. He has been a guiding force in the development of abstraction in printing, and in painting prints with color and texture. In addition to his creative visual work, Viboon is one of the kingdom's foremost scholars on the history and forms of Thai folk art. He is currently a faculty member at Silpakorn's Nakorn Pathom campus.

WATTANA WATTANAPUN

born 1941

Born and brought up in Petchaburi near Bangkok, Wattana was trained at Silpakorn and at the Rhode Island School of Design. Like Kamol, he has spent a significant part of his professional life in the United States—having taught art at Haverford, Oberlin, and the Rhode Island School of Design, and also having worked and taught for an extended period in Seattle. However, his permanent home has been in Chiengmai, and he has repeatedly returned to Thailand to rejuvenate himself. Wattana's art has also been divided—between his abstract expressionist work that met the decorative needs of American clients and his powerful social commentaries that addressed the cultural needs of those who know and love Thailand. As the years have passed, his social commentaries have become less polarized and aesthetically more subtle.

Amnaad Yensabaaj, *Prawadsaad Silpakam Ruam Samaj Khong Rattanakosin.* (The History of Contemporary Art During the Rattanakosin Era) (In Thai) Bangkok: Teacher Training, Ministry of Education, 1981.

Boisselier, Jean, *The Heritage of Thai Sculpture.* New York: Weatherhill, 1975.

——, *Thai Painting.* Tokyo: Kodansha International, 1976.

Buchloh, Benjamin H.D., "The Whole Earth Show: An Interview With Jean-Hubert Martin," *Art in America,* 77 (6): 150–213, May 1989.

Centre Georges Pompidou, *Magiciens de la terre.* Paris, Centre Georges Pompidou (Musée national d'art moderne), 1989.

Clifford, James, "Histories of the Tribal and the Modern" and "On Collecting Art and Culture," *The Predicament of Culture.* Cambridge, Harvard University Press, 1988.

——, Interview conducted by Brian Wallace, "The Global Issue: A Symposium," *Art in America,* 77 (7): 86–87 and 152–153, July 1989.

Damrong Wong-Uparaj, *Professor Silpa Bhirasri.* (In Thai and English) Bangkok: Pananya Publishers, 1978.

——, *Thai Art: Past and Present.* Bangkok: National Culture Commission, 1985.

Fischer, Joseph, editor, *Modern Indonesian Art: Three Generations of Tradition and Change, 1945–1990.* Jakarta and New York: Panitia Pameran KIAS (1990–91) and Festival of Indonesia, 1990.

Geertz, Clifford, "Art As A Cultural System," *Modern Language Notes,* 91:1473–1499, 1976.

Graburn, Nelson, editor. *Ethnic and Tourist Arts: Cultural Expressions from the Fourth World.* Berkeley, University of California Press, 1976.

Griswold, Alexander B., *Towards a History of Sukhodaya Art.* Bangkok: Fine Arts Department, 1967.

Holt, Claire, *Art in Indonesia.* Ithaca: Cornell University Press, 1967.

Hoskins, John, *Ten Contemporary Thai Artists.* Bangkok: Graphis Company, 1984.

Joti Kalyanamitra, *Six Hundred Years of Work by Thai Artists and Architects.* Bangkok: Fine Arts Commission of the Association of Siamese Architects, 1977.

Marcus, Russel, *Forms of Man: The Buddhist Vision of Thawan Duchanee.* Ojai: Books Marcus, 1974.

Miyagawa, Torao, *Modern Japanese Painting.* Tokyo, Kodansha International Limited, 1967.

Myers-Moro, Pamela, "Ecleticism and the Appropriation of Diversity in Thai Music." Paper delivered at California Folklore Society Annual Meeting, April 1990. Available through Department of Sociology and Anthropology, Illinois Wesleyan University.

Palwin, Alfred, *Dhamma Vision.* Bangkok: Visual Dhamma, 1984.

Paothong Thongchua, Piriya Krairiksh, Pisanu Supanimit, *Art in Thailand Since 1932.* (In Thai and English) Bangkok: Thai Khadi Research Institute, Thammasat University, 1982.

Phillips, Herbert P., *Thai Peasant Personality.* Berkeley: University of California Press, 1965.

——, *Modern Thai Literature.* Honolulu: University of Hawaii Press, 1987.

Piriya Krairiksh, *Art Styles in Thailand: A Selection from National Provincial Museums and an Essay in Conceptualization.* Bangkok: Department of Fine Arts, Ministry of Education, 1977.

Rattanakosin (The working group for Sculptures of Rattanakosin), *Sculptures of Rattanakosin.* Bangkok: Fine Arts Department, 1982.

——, *Rattanakosin Painting.* Bangkok: Fine Arts Department, 1982.

Said, Edward, *Orientalism.* New York: Random House, 1978.

Shively, Donald, H., editor, *Tradition and Modernization in Japanese Culture.* Princeton, Princeton University Press, 1971.

Silpa Bhirasri, "Contemporary Thai Art," *Modern Art of Asia: New Movements and Old Traditions,* edited by Japan Cultural Forum. Tokyo, Toto Shuppan Co., 1961.

Smithies, Michael, "The Bangkok Art Scene in the Early 1960's: A Personal Souvenir," *Journal of the Siam Society.* Bangkok, 1975.

Spiro, Melford E., *Burmese Supernaturalism.* Englewood Cliffs, New Jersey: Prentice-Hall, 1967.

Subhadradis, Diskul, M.C., *Art in Thailand: A Brief History.* Bangkok: Krung Siam Press, 1972.

——, *Sukothai Art.* Bangkok: Cultural Committee of the Thailand National Commission for UNESCO, 1979.

Sullivan, Michael, *The Meeting of Eastern and Western Art.* Berkeley, University of California Press, 1989.

Takashima, Shuji, J. Thomas Riner with Gerald D. Bolas, *Paris in Japan: The Japanese Encounter With European Painting.* Tokyo, The Japan Foundation, 1987.

Tambiah, Stanley J. *Buddhism and the Spirit Cults in North-east Thailand.* Cambridge: Cambridge University Press, 1970.

Van Beek, Steve, *The Arts of Thailand.* Hong Kong: Travel Publishing Asia, 1985.

Wenk, Klaus, *The Buddhist Art of Thawan Datchani: The Ten Last Lives of Buddha, Twelve Drawings by Thawan Datchani.* Zurich: Inigo Von Oppersdorff, 1981.

Wiyada Thongmitr, *Khrua In Khong's Westernized School of Thai Painting.* Bangkok: Thai Cultural Data Centre, 1979.

Yamada, Chisaburoh F., *Dialogue in Art: Japan and the West.* Tokyo, Kodansha International Limited, 1976.

Zagorski, Ulrich, *Dhamma: Twenty-five Drawings by Chalermchai Kositpipat.* Bangkok: Asia Books, 1982.

ABOUT THE AUTHOR

Herbert P. Phillips is Professor of Anthropology at the University of California at Berkeley and director of "The Integrative Art of Modern Thailand" project. A graduate of Harvard College and Cornell University (Ph.D.), he has also taught at Michigan State University and Thammasat University in Bangkok. He is the author of *Thai Peasant Personality, Modern Thai Literature,* and numerous other essays on Thai culture and society.